CORRECTION SYMBOLS IN ALPHABETICAL ORDER

Boldface numbers refer to chapters or sections of the workbo

ab	Faulty abbreviation, **28**	*p*	Error in punctuation, **20–25**	
ad	Misuse of adjective or adverb, **9**	. ? !	Period, question mark, exclamation point, **20**	
agr	Error in agreement, **8**	⌃	Comma, **21**	
appr	Inappropriate diction, **31a**	;	Semicolon, **22**	
awk	Awkward construction	⌄	Apostrophe, **23**	
ca	Error in case form, **6**	" "	Quotation marks, **24**	
cap	Use capital letter, **26**	: — ( ) [ ] . . . /	Colon, dash, parentheses, brackets, ellipsis mark, slash, **25**	
con	Be concise, **31c**			
coord	Faulty coordination, **16a**			
cs	Comma splice, **11a–b**			
d	Error in diction, **31**	*par,* ¶	Start new paragraph, **3**	
dev	Inadequate essay development, **1**	¶ *coh*	Paragraph not coherent, **3b**	
		¶ *dev*	Paragraph not developed, **3c**	
div	Incorrect word division, **30**	¶ *un*	Paragraph not unified, **3a**	
dm	Dangling modifier, **14g**	*pass*	Ineffective passive voice, **18d**	
emph	Emphasis lacking or faulty, **18**	*ref*	Error in pronoun reference, **12**	
exact	Inexact word, **31b**	*rep*	Unnecessary repetition, **31c–2**	
frag	Sentence fragment, **10**	*rev*	Proofread or revise, **2**	
fs	Fused (run-on) sentence, **11c**	*run-on*	Run-on sentence, **11c**	
gr	Error in grammar, **5–9**	*shift*	Inconsistency, **13**	
hyph	Error in use of hyphen, **34d**	*sp*	Misspelled word, **34**	
inc	Incomplete construction, **15c–e**	*spec*	Be more specific, **3c, 4c**	
ital	Italicize (underline), **27**	*sub*	Faulty subordination, **16b–c**	
k	Awkward construction	*t*	Error in verb tense, **7**, *pp. 129–30*	
lc	Use lowercase letter, **26f**			
log	Faulty logic, **4**	*trans*	Better transition needed, **3**	
mixed	Mixed construction, **15a–b**	*var*	Vary sentence structure, **19**	
mm	Misplaced modifier, **14a–f**	*vb*	Error in verb form, **7**, *pp. 121–24*	
mng	Meaning unclear			
no cap	Unnecessary capital letter, **26f**	*w*	Wordy, **31c**	
no ⌃	Comma not needed, **21j**	*ww*	Wrong word, **31b**	
no ¶	No new paragraph needed, **3**	//	Faulty parallelism, **17**	
		x	Obvious error	
num	Error in use of numbers, **29**	⋀	Something missing, **15e**	

THE LITTLE, BROWN WORKBOOK

SECOND EDITION

Quentin L. Gehle
With the Editors of Little, Brown

Little, Brown and Company
BOSTON   TORONTO

Copyright © 1983 by Little, Brown and Company (Inc.)

All rights reserved. No part of this book may be reproduced
in any form or by any electronic or mechanical means including
information storage and retrieval systems without permission
in writing from the publisher, except by a reviewer who may
quote brief passages in a review.

ISBN 0-316-28979-5

9 8 7 6 5 4 3 2 1

HAL

Published simultaneously in Canada
by Little, Brown & Company (Canada) Limited

Printed in the United States of America

Preface

Like its predecessor, the second edition of *The Little, Brown Workbook* is a complete composition text that provides concise guidance and ample exercises on all elements of writing. It moves from the largest to the smallest elements, beginning with the whole paper and paragraphs and then becoming increasingly focused on sentence grammar and style, punctuation, mechanics, and words. Its exercises give students considerable practice in identifying and revising errors and in producing effective writing of their own. Its usage recommendations are generally conservative, stressing the conventions of standard, written English that students will be expected to observe throughout college and beyond.

The workbook can serve independently as the primary text in a course; the exercises are set on separate pages so that they can be removed without destroying the textual material. Or the workbook can supplement another text such as *The Little, Brown Handbook*, Second Edition. The workbook and handbook complement each other: They share a common vocabulary and approach to writing, their organizations are parallel, and their rules, correction codes, and correction symbols are identical. But the workbook's explanations are simpler than those in the handbook, dealing less often with exceptions and fine points of usage, and the workbook's exercises are more basic and more plentiful in areas that give inexperienced writers the greatest difficulty.

This edition of the workbook is substantially improved in response to suggestions from dozens of first-edition users. A full index now appears at the back of the book. The text itself has been expanded in places and clarified throughout. The models for writing, especially in the chapter on paragraphs, are now all student written. The first-edition exercises have been extensively revised, partly for the sake of change, but mainly to provide more opportunities for rewriting and sentence combining. The exercises on persistent problems such as case, verbs, agreement, fragments, and commas have been expanded to provide additional practice. New review exercises, ending most chapters on sentences and punctuation, require students to recognize and revise errors within paragraphs. And new self-tests, beginning the chapters on sentences, punctuation, and mechanics, allow students to gauge their knowledge of forthcoming material and to identify their specific weaknesses. The answers to these self-tests, keyed to sections of the workbook, appear at the back of the book. Answers to all the other exercises appear in the complimentary instructor's manual that accompanies the workbook and in a separate booklet that is available free to students at the instructor's option.

The instructor's manual, written by Judith Stanford of Merrimack College and new to this edition, offers helpful suggestions for using the workbook in both developmental and standard courses in composition. It includes useful sections on motivating students and essay revision, and both sections are augmented by many class-tested exercises.

Many people have contributed to this revision, either in responses to a survey or in reviews of the manuscript. Special thanks for detailed and constructive analyses are due Carol Abate, West Valley College; Alicia Butler, University of Oregon; Robert Dees, Orange Coast College; Eleanor R. Garner, George Washington University; Clement Howton, John C. Calhoun State Community College; Peggy Jolly, University of Alabama at Birmingham; Martin L. Kornbluth, Eastern Michigan University; Delores Lipscomb, Chicago State University; Natalie Maynor, University of Mississippi; David Merrill, Abilene Christian University; Loraine Murphy, University of Dayton; Donna Reid, Chemeketa Community College; Fred Rodgers, Chemeketa Community College; Donna Schouman, Macomb County Community College; Judith Stanford, Merrimack College; William B. Watterson, Lees-McCrae College; and James H. Weidner, Burlington Community College. Finally, thanks to the many people at Little, Brown who have contributed time, energy, and encouragement for this revision, particularly Janet Beatty, Developmental Editor; Sue Warne, Book Editor; and Donna McCormick, Editorial Assistant.

Contents

I The Whole Paper and Paragraphs

1 *Developing an Essay*

An **essay** is a nonfiction composition in which you discuss or interpret a topic, offering your view of it. Effective essay development involves four main steps: (1) discovering a subject and limiting it to manageable size, (2) generating ideas about the subject, (3) developing a statement of your purpose in writing the essay, and (4) organizing ideas clearly.

1a | Discovering and limiting a subject

You may be assigned a subject for an essay, or you may be required to invent one from your own store of experiences and interests. Once you have a subject, you will almost certainly have to narrow it to a topic that suits your purpose and for which you can provide specific information to interest readers. Each of the broad subjects below can be subdivided into several specific topics that would be suitable for a brief essay.

BROAD	SPECIFIC
music	the unique sound of Stan Kenton's band the appeal of Kenny Rogers why I enjoy Bach
family relationships	what I've learned from my older brother why grandparents are often indulgent the problems of being a househusband
transportation	why I hate to fly teaching my sister to drive how to bargain with a used-car dealer

1b | Developing the topic

When you have a specific topic that interests you, begin thinking of the particular information that will convey your interest convincingly to your readers. Write down the ideas that occur to you; or if ideas are slow in coming, try one of the following strategies.

1 | Generating ideas by writing

As you think about your topic over a couple of hours or a few minutes, jot down ideas, trying to capture in notes all the associations your topic brings to mind. Don't stop the flow of ideas by rejecting any that seem uninteresting or repetitious. Those same ideas may later prove useful.

Another way to develop a topic is to take a blank piece of paper, bring your topic into mind, and write without stopping until you have filled the entire page. Focus attention on keeping your pen or pencil moving, and pay no attention to the organization of ideas or to correct grammar or spelling. (You will work on these aspects later.)

2 | Generating ideas by asking questions

Asking a series of journalist's questions may lead you to useful information for developing ideas. For example, *who* is involved? *What* happened? *When? Where? Why? How?* Also helpful are exploratory questions such as the following: How can my point be illustrated? What does my topic include and exclude? What are its components and characteristics? Can it be categorized? How does it compare or contrast with similar subjects? What are its causes and effects? Is a process involved? (See 3c, where these questions are also used to develop paragraphs.)

Following these and other steps in developing your essay will help you get it started and generate thorough content for your treatment.

1c | Grouping ideas

Once you have ideas about your topic, you need to arrange them into a pattern that shows their relations and reflects your purpose. This step will also help you eliminate ideas that are irrelevant or repetitious and identify which of the remaining ideas need more development. Group your ideas into several general categories, each treating a main division of the topic. The rough groups of ideas below are for a paper on coping with fear of air travel.

Relaxing before a flight
  Getting to sleep
    reading books
    looking at pictures
  Distracting myself on the way to the airport

Relaxing during a flight
  Choosing a seat
  Eating
  Reading
  Listening to music

Discovering and limiting a subject

Limit each of the ten subjects to two specific topics suitable for a brief essay.

Example: Subject: student government
Topics: a. *why students should be elected to the college governing board*
b. *why students do not care about campus government*

1. Subject: student housing
   Topics: a.

   b.

2. Subject: hobbies
   Topics: a.

   b.

3. Subject: athletic equipment
   Topics: a.

   b.

4. Subject: class schedules
   Topics: a.

   b.

5. Subject: marriage
   Topics: a.

            b.

6. Subject: cooking
   Topics: a.

            b.

7. Subject: vacations
   Topics: a.

            b.

8. Subject: comedy
   Topics: a.

            b.

9. Subject: pets
   Topics: a.

            b.

10. Subject: careers
    Topics: a.

             b.

| *Generating ideas
and grouping them* | EXERCISE **1-2** |

Choose one of the specific topics you came up with in Exercise 1-1 or a different specific topic. Develop ideas for a brief essay using one of the methods discussed on pages 1–2. Then, on the next page, weed out the repetitions or irrelevant ideas and group the remaining ones under two to four main points.

1. Topic: _____

   Ideas: _____

   _____

   _____

   _____

   _____

   _____

   _____

   _____

   _____

   _____

   _____

   _____

   _____

   _____

   _____

   _____

_____

_____

_____

2. Groups of ideas: _____

_____

_____

_____

_____

_____

_____

_____

_____

_____

_____

_____

_____

_____

_____

_____

_____

_____

1d | Developing the thesis

To be effective, your essay must be controlled by a single idea, its chief points and specific information relating clearly to your purpose. This idea is the essay's **thesis**.

1 | Conceiving the thesis sentence

The thesis of an essay often appears in a single sentence (the **thesis sentence**) near the essay's beginning. The thesis sentence has three primary functions:

1. It narrows the topic to a single dominant idea.
2. It asserts something about the topic, conveying your approach.
3. It may provide a preview of your ideas and how you will arrange them.

The following thesis sentence fulfills these functions.

TOPIC	THESIS
Teaching my sister to drive	Teaching my sister to drive was really frustrating: The lessons required too much patience and courage.

2 | Writing and revising the thesis sentence

Developing an effective thesis sentence that conveys your purpose completely and concisely may require several attempts. For instance, from the group of ideas on page 2 about fear of air travel, the student wrote the following thesis sentence:

Flying can frighten a person sometimes.

But this thesis does not convey much information about the topic, nor does it reveal the writer's special perspective. Revised as shown below, the sentence is more effective because it narrows the topic for unity to convey a single dominant idea, it asserts something that indicates the writer's approach to the idea, and it provides a preview of the two-part development that will follow the thesis.

Because flying terrifies me, I have developed several techniques to help me cope with that fear both before and during a flight.

Several common errors in thesis sentences are illustrated below, along with revisions.

ORIGINAL	REVISED
Many popular television programs are criticized for catering to the lowest common denominator of the audience. [A statement of fact, providing no assertion or personal viewpoint.]	The widespread criticism of popular television programs is not severe enough; the programs not only fail to enlighten us but also can prevent us from dealing effectively with our own lives.

ORIGINAL

I started reading science fiction long before I discovered the classics, and I have to agree with those who say that science fiction is less than it could be. [Sentence is disunified and unspecific: What do the classics have to do with the assertion in the second half? And what precisely does the second half mean?]

REVISED

Though I am a long-time fan of science fiction, I do not believe that its writers have been successful at imagining experiences and forms of life that are totally different from our own.

1e | Considering an audience

To communicate effectively to your readers — your audience — you must consider their interests and needs as you select a topic, develop an attitude toward it, and decide what specific information to use to express your view.

1 | Using specific information

The student writing about fear of flying is presumably addressing an audience of other fearful flyers and will thus provide specific ways of coping with fear. If he were addressing flight attendants instead, he might discuss the ways they can assist reluctant air travelers. In sum, considering audience needs and interests can help you shape and develop your topic.

2 | Adopting a suitable tone

The tone of your writing comes from the use you make of ideas, words, and sentence structures, and it will influence how your readers react to what you say (see also 4a). If you want to be seen as serious and thoughtful, you will be aided by formal sentence structure and words, as well as by sensible, well-supported assertions. If, in contrast, you want to adopt a light attitude toward your subject — if you are writing to fellow students, say, about how to choose an easy course — you may want to employ an informal sentence structure, a conversational vocabulary, and a humorous approach.

3 | Writing to a general audience

Most writing done for college courses is directed at a general, college-level audience. Even if your only readers are your instructors, you can assume that they are alert and thoughtful, open to what you have to say, but nonetheless insistent on writing that is fresh and clear with strong, well-supported assertions.

Developing the thesis sentence

Write thesis sentences for the five topics given below and for five additional topics of your own, including the one for which you generated and grouped ideas in Exercise 1-2. Be sure that the theses are specific, limited, and unified and that they clearly state your viewpoint and purpose.

Example: Topic: the disadvantages of solar energy
Thesis sentence:

The advantages of solar energy are outweighed by the disadvantages: prohibitive cost, inefficiency, and, for large areas of the country, impracticality.

1. Topic: the advantages (or disadvantages) of choosing a major early
Thesis sentence:

2. Topic: why I dislike (or like) camping
Thesis sentence:

3. Topic: why computer science should (or should not) be required in college
Thesis sentence:

4. Topic: why the telephone company's commercials offend (or delight) me
   Thesis sentence:

5. Topic: why films should (or should not) be censored
   Thesis sentence:

6. Topic (from Exercise 1-2):
   Thesis sentence:

7. Topic:
   Thesis sentence:

8. Topic:
   Thesis sentence:

9. Topic:
   Thesis sentence:

10. Topic:
    Thesis sentence:

| Revising the
| thesis sentence

EXERCISE **1-4**

Rewrite the ten thesis sentences below to make them limited, specific, unified, and assertive.

Example: Legislators do not communicate enough with their constituents.

State legislators should improve communication with voters by scheduling local meetings regularly and by mailing newsletters before and after assembly sessions.

1. Many people believe that handguns cause unnecessary deaths.

2. Religious cults serve a valid purpose.

3. Some teachers do not know how to lead a class discussion.

4. The government owes a college education to every citizen who wants one.

5. Sometimes use of slang can be very effective.

6. Hunting wild animals, as long as they are not in danger of extinction, can actually help nature.

7. Travel to foreign countries is educational.

8. The energy shortage will change our lives.

9. Silence is often the best response to anger.

10. Coughing can have an important role in communication.

1f | Organizing an essay

The final step in developing an effective essay is to arrange main points and supporting information in a clear, logical sequence.

1 | Arranging and outlining the parts of an essay

There are several common ways to organize an essay that correspond to readers' habitual ways of thinking. One pattern is **spatial,** examining a topic (such as a place or a person) by moving in space from one location to another, as when we survey a scene from the farthest point to the nearest, or vice versa. Another common organizing scheme is **chronological,** reporting events as they occur over time, earliest first. (For examples, see the paragraph on p. 29.)

Two other organizing patterns are **general to specific** and **specific to general.** In the first pattern the main ideas come before the details that support them, as in an essay that makes initial strong claims about, say, gun control and then presents the evidence for the claims. In the specific-to-general pattern the details come first and build to the more general ideas, as might occur in an essay that describes the styles of specific big bands before generalizing about the sound they have in common (see also the paragraph about Harvey on p. 30). A similar pattern is the *climactic* one, which is the arrangement of material in order of importance. You may also arrange items by the principles of *most familiar to least familiar* or *simple to complex.*

The organizing plan you select will depend on your topic and what you want to say about it. No matter what the plan, however, you will want to develop an outline of your main ideas and supporting information before you begin writing. Remember that an outline is an aid to you, the writer. Thus a brief, vague outline will be useless. A highly detailed outline may inhibit you from exercising flexibility as you think and write about your idea. Two useful work plans are the informal and the formal outlines.

An **informal outline** arranges the general and specific points of the essay in the order in which they will appear in the essay. It resembles the preliminary groups of ideas on page 2, but the organization should be smoother and the outline should not contain repeated or irrelevant ideas. The informal outline will probably also use at least two and probably more levels of subordination — for example, specific facts subordinated to more general ideas subordinated to main points.

A **formal outline** takes the informal outline one step further. Its more rigid form can help you place elements in careful relation to each other, with levels of subordination (perhaps three or more) clearly indicated. It can also help you fill in gaps, eliminate redundancies, and make wording more precise. The formal outline follows a typical pattern: Main points, often corresponding to the topic of an entire paragraph, are preceded by capital Roman numerals (*I, II,* and so on); chief subpoints, the support for the main points, are preceded by capital letters (*A, B,* and so on); and specific supporting details, examples, and reasons are preceded by Arabic numerals (*1, 2,* and so on). (A fourth level of subordination may be indicated by small letters, *a, b,* and so on.) You may write the outline in complete sentences or in phrases, but whichever manner of expression you choose, use it consistently throughout the outline. Ideas at the same numbered or lettered level should be parallel in wording, importance, and specificity. Ideas at the same level or at different levels should not overlap, and sublevels should fit logically under the levels above them. Be sure that all headings are matched by at least one other heading at the same level. An *A* without a *B* or a *1* without a *2* implies, illogically, that the preceding level is divided into only one part.

The following detailed topic outline, for the paper on fear of air travel, illustrates a formal outline.

THESIS SENTENCE Because flying terrifies me, I have developed several techniques to help me cope with that fear both before and during a flight.

FORMAL OUTLINE
I. Relaxation methods before a flight
  A. Trying to sleep the night before
    1. Reading an architecture book
    2. Contemplating pictures
  B. Riding to the airport
    1. Talking to the cab driver
    2. Looking out the window
  C. Reading in the airport lounge

II. Relaxation methods during a flight
  A. Taking a seat
    1. Choosing a location
    2. Choosing a travel companion
  B. Eating
  C. Reading
  D. Listening to music
  E. Staying in my seat
  F. Refraining from looking out the window

2 | Maintaining unity and coherence

When your informal or formal outline is completed, examine it for unity and coherence. **Unity** occurs when the essay's parts are closely related to the thesis sentence and to each other. Disunity occurs when irrelevant ideas creep in or, worse, when the writer moves away from the thesis sentence in mid-essay. **Coherence** occurs when the relations among ideas are clear and when each point leads easily to the one following it. Incoherence occurs when an essay jumps around, failing to guide the reader. Unity and coherence are discussed further in relation to paragraphs; see 3a and 3b.

| *The formal outline* EXERCISE **1-5**

The outline below violates formal outline form in several ways: Parallel headings are not always parallel in wording, importance, and specificity; different levels of information are not always distinguished by the level of heading; and headings are not always subdivided logically. Place an *X* in the left margin opposite each error, and revise the error by rearranging, adding, deleting, or rewording headings.

THESIS SENTENCE

Though the city has obvious drawbacks, it also provides opportunities for enjoyment of education and the arts.

OUTLINE

I. Drawbacks of the city

    A. Congestion

    B. Inconvenience

        1. Difficulty getting essential services

    C. Crime

    D. Dirty

II. Advantages

    A. Educational advantages

        1. Many colleges and universities

        2. Evening and extension courses

        3. Informal learning programs

        4. Courses at theaters and museums

B. The arts

   1. Classical music

   2. Jazz, rock, bluegrass, and so on

   3. Painting and sculpture

      a. Major collections

   4. Architecture: good examples of all significant periods

   5. Theater is especially strong

      a. College and university theater groups

      b. Legitimate theater

   6. Films

      a. First-run movies as well as the best in second-run and old movies

   7. Libraries and bookstores

|*Outlining an essay*   EXERCISE **1-6**

Prepare an outline for an essay, using the ideas you generated and arranged in Exercise 1-2. First, repeat the thesis sentence composed in Exercise 1-3. Then outline the ideas, using the form (informal or formal) specified by your instructor. Be sure the outline is unified (all its parts relate to each other and to the thesis) and coherent (the relations among ideas are logical and clear).

Thesis sentence: _____

_____

_____

Outline: _____

_____

_____

_____

_____

_____

_____

_____

_____

_____

_____

_____

_____

2 | *Writing and Revising the Essay*

Carefully developing an essay (Chapter 1) will make writing and revising it easier. But as this chapter shows, an essay will continue to evolve until you stop working on it.

2a | Writing the first draft

In working up a thesis and an outline, you have settled on a purpose, decided what you need to say to achieve that purpose, and arranged your ideas in a unified and coherent pattern. With this preparation the actual writing of the first draft can be a simple matter of phrasing ideas as sentences and stringing them together.

However, most writers do not prepare a first draft with so little thought. They do not treat their outline as unchangeable but vary from it as they discover they need to emphasize one idea, provide greater support for another, and delete yet another. If enough rearrangement seems called for, the writer may also need to revise his or her thesis so that it continues to state the essay's purpose and encompasses all the essay's content. The point is not to start over again, as if no planning had occurred, but to remain flexible.

2b | Revising the first draft

Though you may end up using substantial portions of it in the final version, especially for an in-class writing assignment, your first draft is just a start. You may, in fact, do several drafts of a single sentence, paragraph, or essay. Revision not only involves proofreading for errors in spelling, grammar, punctuation, and the like; it also, and more significantly, involves rethinking the arrangement of ideas, their support, and their effectiveness in furthering your purpose. If time allows, take a half-hour or a whole day away from the paper to clear your mind before beginning to revise.

The following checklist may be helpful in guiding your revision. If you need help in any of these areas, read the workbook or handbook discussion at the chapter and heading given in parentheses.

Revision checklist

STRUCTURAL REVISION

1. What is your purpose, and what kind of essay are you writing? How are these evident in your thesis sentence and throughout the essay? (Chapter 1)

2. How does each paragraph and sentence in your essay develop or support your thesis sentence? Have you made the relationships clear? (1d and 1f)

3. What details, examples, or reasons have you provided to support each of your ideas? Which ideas need more support? (1b and 1e)

4. How is your tone appropriate for your audience? (1e)

5. What pattern of organization have you used? Have you followed it consistently? Where have you drawn relations among elements of the essay? Which connections are *un*clear? (1f)

6. How does each sentence in a paragraph help develop the paragraph? Are the paragraphs unified, coherent, and well developed? (3a, 3b, 3c)

7. How effective are your introductory and concluding paragraphs? How can they be improved? (3d)

8. How believable are your assertions? How have you supported each one? Where have you slipped into faulty reasoning? (4a, 4b, 4c)

9. Are your sentences effective? Have you used subordination and coordination (Chapter 16) and parallelism (Chapter 17) appropriately? Are your sentences emphatic (Chapter 18) and varied (Chapter 19)?

10. Have you relied on standard diction? (31a) Do your words denote and connote what you intend? Have you avoided triteness? (31b) Is your writing concise? (31c)

PROOFREADING

11. Are your sentences grammatical? Have you avoided errors in case (Chapter 6), verb form (Chapter 7), agreement (Chapter 8), and adjectives and adverbs (Chapter 9)?

12. Are your sentences clear? Have you avoided sentence fragments (Chapter 10), comma splices and run-on sentences (Chapter 11), errors in pronoun reference (Chapter 12), shifts (Chapter 13), misplaced or dangling modifiers (Chapter 14), and mixed or incomplete constructions (Chapter 15)?

13. Is your use of commas, semicolons, colons, periods, and other punctuation correct? (Chapters 20–25)

14. Are your sentences mechanically correct in the use of capitals, italics, abbreviations, numbers, and hyphens? (Chapters 26–30)

15. Are your words spelled correctly? (Chapter 34)

2c | Preparing the final draft

Once you have revised your paper to your own satisfaction, prepare the final draft, proofread it carefully, and hand it in. When you get it back from your instructor, give close attention to his or her comments and suggestions. Be sure to ask your instructor about any comments you don't understand. If you don't ask, the planning, writing, and revising cycle may teach you less than either you want or your instructor intends.

The typewritten samples that follow show two different methods an instructor may use to correct your essay, followed by the revised paragraph. The first sample uses the correction code on the inside back cover of this book, which directs you to the chapter number and heading letter where you will find the error discussed. The second sample shows the use of correction symbols, listed on the inside front cover.

(3a)
The trouble with bank credit cards is that they prey on people where they are most vulnerable. The (banks) take a

(86)
percentage of purchases made with the card, but that is not how (it) makes its profit. Instead, the profit comes from the high interest rate on the balances people maintain over thirty days.

(13a)
Thus, the higher (your) balance over time, the more money you owe to the bank in interest. Though banks usually set a low

(13a)
limit at first on the amount (one) can charge, they just as often raise that limit as soon as the balance approaches it. Without

(10c)

(6h)
the customer (even requesting an increase. In this way the banks

(34a)
encourage (there) customers to incur large debts.

¶ un—
topic
sentence
doesn't
describe
paragraph

The trouble with bank credit cards is that they prey on people where they are most vulnerable. The (banks) take a percentage of purchases made with the card, but that is not how (it) makes its profit. Instead, the profit comes from the high

agr

interest rate on the balances people maintain over thirty days.

shift
Thus, the higher (your) balance over time, the more money you owe to the bank in interest. Though banks usually set a low

shift
limit at first on the amount (one) can charge, they just as often raise that limit as soon as the balance approaches it. Without

frag

case
the customer (even requesting an increase. In this way the banks

sp
encourage (there) customers to incur large debts.

A bank credit card can be dangerous for its holder. The bank takes a percentage of purchases made with the card, but that is not how it makes its profit. Instead, the profit comes from the high interest rate on the balance a customer maintains over thirty days. Thus, the higher a person's balance over time, the more money he or she owes the bank in interest. Though a bank usually sets a low limit at first on the amount a customer can charge, the bank just as often raises that limit as soon as the balance approaches it, without the customer's even requesting an increase. In this way the bank encourages the customer to incur a large debt.

|*Revising the first draft* EXERCISE **2-1**

Evaluate the essay below (written from the formal outline on p. 14) against the revision checklist on pages 19–20, and revise it as you think necessary. Pay special attention to the essay's structure: the effectiveness of each paragraph in contributing to the paper's purpose (expressed in the essay's thesis sentence) and the unity and coherence of the whole paper as well as of individual paragraphs. Look also for errors in spelling, grammar, punctuation, mechanics, and word choice, referring to other sections of the workbook if you need help.

Fear of Flying

I hate flying. But I am going to school a thousand miles from

home, flying is the fastest way for me to get home and back to school.

Because flying terrifies me, I have developed several techniques to help

me deal with fear both before and during a flight.

My preparations for psychological survival start the night be-

fore I have to get on the plane since I expect my fears to keep me from

sleeping, I read a book on the history of architecture. I have a good book on that subject, and I read it because I need a book that deals with solid structures that are on solid ground, the subject matter gives me comfort. I contemplate the pictures of pyramids which reminds me of stability and permanence. When I get real tired, I study photographs of flying buttresses, which remind me of both air travel and stability. Then I am able to doze off.

Reasonably well-rested the next day, calm will help me get through the next stages of the trip. On my way to the airport, I start out very nervous about the flight.

I encourage the cab driver to tell me about car accidents he has seen, then I think about how much safer flying is. I look out the window at sturdy, solid buildings and divert my eyes when we pass the cemetary. After I check in at the airport, I sit in the flight lounge and read a cheap paperback that has alot of explicit passages about sex — that keeps my mind off flying on the airplane.

The most important thing at first is to find a seat as far away from the windows as possible. If the seats are assigned, I try to choose an aisle seat — far from the windows — near the exit door at the rear of the plane, the safest part in case of a crash. If the seats are not assigned, I still try to get the same location, but I also try to sit next to someone who looks like a calm, experienced traveler, but who does not look too talkative. Because I don't want to be next to anyone as nervous as me but I also don't want to be next to someone who will try to point out sights on the ground and continually remind me how the cars look like ants. During the flight, I try to distract myself from the trip as much as possible by eating constantly, listening to music on the headphones, and by reading my paperback novel. I make sure I don't drink anything for several hours before the flight or during the flight, so that I don't have to go to the restroom. If I had to go to the restroom, then I would have to unbuckle my seat belt. Keeping the seat belt buckled throughout the trip is important to my sense of security. If I keep eating and reading throughout the trip, I am less likely to look out the window inadvertently.

I shall always believe that airplanes violate the law of gravity, but my sense of exhilaration when I get off an airplane would be something I probably would not feel if I did not go through the various stages of suppressed terror before and during a flight.

| *Writing and*
| *revising the essay*   EXERCISE **2-2**

Write the first draft of the essay you developed with ideas in Exercise 1-2, a thesis sentence in Exercise 1-3, and an outline in Exercise 1-6. Use your own paper. Then revise the draft, checking its elements against the revision checklist on pages 19–20. Work to clarify your purpose in your thesis sentence and consistently throughout the paper. Concentrate on maintaining unity and coherence (see 3a and 3b). Proofread for errors in grammar, spelling, punctuation, mechanics, and word choice. Write the final draft in the form specified by your instructor.

    When your instructor returns your corrected paper, revise it further in accordance with his or her comments and suggestions, asking questions about any comments you don't understand. Keep track of the problems and errors pointed out to you, and concentrate on these areas when you prepare your next paper.

3 | Composing Good Paragraphs

A **paragraph** is a self-contained unit of thought consisting usually of several sentences and set off from other paragraphs by the indention of its first line. To be effective, a paragraph must be unified, coherent, and well developed.

3a | Maintaining paragraph unity

A paragraph is **unified** when all its parts relate clearly to its central, controlling idea. This idea is often expressed in a **topic sentence.**

1 | Focusing on the central idea

A paragraph is a unit of thought, a central idea supported by relevant details. Its unity will be destroyed if you allow unrelated thoughts to creep in or allow the paragraph's topic to shift in midstream. Examine each paragraph you write to be sure all its parts relate to your topic sentence. You may find it useful to supplement the topic sentence with a sentence of clarification that explains or amplifies the topic or with a sentence of limitation that narrows the topic, making it more specific. With these devices you can focus the topic sentence more sharply and keep it more clearly in mind as you write.

2 | Choosing a paragraph shape

A paragraph's main idea and supporting details may be arranged in different ways. In the most common paragraph shape, the central idea (expressed in a topic sentence) falls first (sentence 1).

> *Most of the evening news programs consist of commercials, and* 1
> *most of the commercials are for products to treat the infirmities of old*
> *age.* On *The CBS Evening News* last night I watched a commercial 2
> for an iron and vitamin tonic from 6:33 to 6:34. From 6:34 to 6:35 3
> appeared a commercial for arthritis remedies. And that was fol- 4
> lowed by a thirty-second commercial for sleeping pills. At 6:40 ap- 5
> peared three more commercials: One showed an elderly man eating
> bran cereal; a second showed a hemorrhoid salve; a third showed
> a salve for aching muscles. A few minutes later another barrage of 6
> commercials came on, and two more series of them appeared still
> later. These ads dealt with such products as laxatives, life and health 7
> insurance, and pain relievers for head and stomach.

— A student

The central idea may also appear at the end of a paragraph, as in the example below.

> Harvey got two speeding tickets last week. He turned in his [1,2] psychology paper two days late. He borrowed ten dollars from me [3] and forgot to pay it back. When his girl's parents called to invite [4] him to dinner, he got the date mixed up and showed up the night after the dinner was held. *Harvey probably would not fit anyone's* [5] *definition of "responsible."*
>
> — A student

Or the central idea may appear in the middle of a paragraph.

> Slouched against the weather-beaten doorway of the Burgundy [1] Hotel ("Beds $2"), a drunk dozed, shivering in the cold, a wine bottle in a paper bag at his feet. Along both sides of the street, several [2] store windows were broken. Beer cans, gum wrappers, old news- [3] papers, broken glass, and whiskey bottles cluttered the sidewalks and gutters. *Harley Avenue was a typical street of the North Side.* In [4,5] a two-block area there were nine pawn shops, two X-rated movie houses, half a dozen bars, and an adult bookstore. Most depressing, [6] though, were the drunks, drug freaks, and raggedly dressed people who loitered near the store entrances.
>
> — A student

The central idea may appear at the beginning of the paragraph and then be restated or added to at the end. The sample paragraph on page 29 about television commercials would have such a shape if it ended with the sentence *I have quit watching television news because it makes me feel old.*

Also, the central idea may appear at the beginning of the paragraph and be amplified in the middle. This shape would characterize the paragraph about the city street if a sentence such as *The signs of decay were obvious* were added at the beginning.

Finally, the central idea may be unstated. But use this technique only if the paragraph's main idea is very obvious from the context. You should be able to sum up in writing the unstated topic sentence. If you cannot do so, the paragraph needs revision. In the following description of a class the impression of dullness, though not explicitly stated, is the central idea.

> When my biology professor walked into the room on the first [1] day of class, I first noticed his faded, threadbare herringbone jacket with leather elbow patches. His tie, a half inch wide, was fastened [2] by a large bronze clasp to his yellowing, white cotton shirt. He had [3] a burr haircut and black-plastic-framed glasses. He opened the roll [4] book and, pausing often, mumbled through the alphabetical list of class members, never looking up at the people answering. After what [5] seemed an interminable time calling roll, he began to lecture. In a [6] slow, low monotone, the professor delivered a talk on the science of biology before Darwin, staring at the light fixture on the ceiling for the remaining forty minutes of class.
>
> — A student

*Identifying
irrelevant details*   EXERCISE **3-1**

Underline the central idea (the topic sentence) in each of the two paragraphs below. Each paragraph contains sentences that are not directly
related to the central idea. Identify these sentences by circling the appropriate sentence number on the right.

1. We tend to view mosquitoes as insects with identical traits and   1
    with the primary goal of sucking human juices. But there is quite   2
    a bit of variety among mosquitoes, as their biting behavior illus-
    trates. The female mosquito tries to lay her eggs where there is   3
    water or is certain to be water. It was once thought that only fe-   4
    male mosquitoes bite, but in at least one group males also feed and
    both sexes feed only on flowers, not on animals. In another group,   5
    females feed by sticking a tube into an ant's mouth for a secretion
    the ant has collected from aphids. Mating habits also vary widely   6
    among mosquitoes. Feeding on animals, including humans, may   7
    occur after mating, when the female needs food for her eggs. But   8
    some groups of mosquitoes never do bother humans at all, getting
    their food instead exclusively from birds or other animals.

2. English pubs illustrate English character. Every neighborhood   1,2
    has a pub that serves as its social center. The local residents con-   3
    gregate in the sedate and homelike atmosphere of soft talk, warm
    lights, and comfortable furniture, drinking mostly pints of beer or
    ale. In the United States, in contrast, bars are loud with music,   4
    dark and shadowy, and furnished with hard chairs and benches.
    One can go to an American bar and expect to remain anonymous,   5
    hidden from view and free of the annoyances of human interaction.
    The pubs close their doors promptly at ten on weeknights and   6
    eleven on weekends, at which point everyone returns home. Thus   7
    the pubs almost dictate English leisure life, whose principle seems
    to be pleasure under control.

*Focusing on
a central idea*   EXERCISE **3-2**

Provide at least three details to support each of the two topic sentences below. Be sure the details relate directly to the idea expressed in the sentence. Then write two unified paragraphs using the topic sentences and your details. Position each topic sentence in its paragraph at the place where you think it is most effective.

1. Topic sentence: Crime has recently increased (or decreased) in our community.

   Details: 1. _____

   _____

   2. _____

   _____

   3. _____

   _____

   Paragraph: _____

   _____

   _____

   _____

   _____

   _____

   _____

   _____

   _____

¶
3

_____

_____

_____

_____

2. Topic sentence: Many television comedies have interesting minor characters.

Details: 1. _____

_____

2. _____

_____

3. _____

_____

Paragraph: _____

_____

_____

_____

_____

_____

_____

_____

_____

_____

_____

_____

_____

3b | Achieving paragraph coherence

An effective paragraph is not only unified but also **coherent:** the relation of its sentences is clear and easy to follow.

1 | Organizing the paragraph

The principal way to achieve coherence in a paragraph is to organize its elements so that they flow naturally and reach a conclusion logically.

One common pattern of paragraph organization, useful in description, is **spatial.** The paragraph begins at one point in space and moves from there to other points, following a logical sequence corresponding to the way we scan a scene or an object: inward or outward, up or down. For example, the following paragraph describes a person from her head to her feet:

> Aunt Carol is a prim but happy person. She usually wears a [1,2] round, gray velvet hat atop her curly gray hair, and below it her clear brown eyes peer out with kind interest through her thick glasses. Her cheeks, wrinkled with smile lines, are heavily rouged. [3] A prim, black sheath dress covers her thin, fragile frame, and black [4] leather shoes with thick, sturdy heels boost her a full inch from the floor.
>
> — A student

Another common paragraph pattern is **chronological,** relating events as they occurred over time. The paragraph on page 29 that describes a sequence of television commercials illustrates this pattern.

Paragraphs may also be arranged from specific ideas to increasingly general ones. The **specific-to-general** pattern is well illustrated by the paragraph on page 30 about Harvey, which moves from specific examples of his behavior to a general statement about his irresponsibility. The **general-to-specific** pattern is illustrated below; here, the discussion moves from generalities about the highway system to details about a specific stretch.

> Now that much of it is over twenty years old, America's inter- [1] state highway system is growing more dangerous and starting to decay. But the stretches of potholes and weakening bridges are not [2] the only evidence. As suburbs have grown, more and more entrance [3] and exit ramps have been added near metropolitan areas, and the traffic flow in many instances is increasingly heavy. An eight-mile [4] stretch of I-395, near Washington, D.C., is the most heavily traveled road in Virginia. It is almost constantly jammed, and during rush [5] hour, cars move at an average speed of thirty miles per hour. One [6] disabled car can jam up over a hundred thousand commuters for an hour or more and multiply accident hazards a hundredfold. Even [7] a light rain can add half an hour to a seven-mile commute.
>
> — A student

Finally, a paragraph may be organized in order of **increasing importance or drama,** as in the following paragraph:

The first sign I noticed of the ailing local economy was the gradual increase in the number of cars parked at the secondhand clothing store near my house. Instead of two or three cars on the usual Saturday morning, there were now six or eight. Not long after I noticed that change, our town's only car dealership closed, and the bearing manufacturing plant laid off half its twenty employees, including my next-door neighbor. A week later, my father, who operated a hardware store, made his decision to sell out and move the family to the South.

— A student

2 | Using parallel structures

The use of **parallel** or similar sentence structures within sentences or between sentences (see also 17a) can help bind a paragraph and relate its parts. In the following paragraph the parallel structures are italicized.

After her first husband died of alcoholism, Carry Nation devoted herself to eliminating consumption of alcohol in the United States. *Standing* nearly six feet tall and *weighing* nearly two hundred pounds, *she intimidated* any drinker. *Wielding* rocks and hatchets, *she destroyed* dozens of saloons. In the course of a ten-year rampage, she *terrorized* thousands of Americans but *inspired* thousands more. Though her campaign ultimately failed, she lives on as a symbol of powerful conviction and unequaled zeal.

— A student

3 | Repeating or restating words and word groups

Careful **repetition** of important words or word groups can also link sentences in a paragraph. Notice in the following paragraph how the yew tree, its huge size, and the quiet of the cemetery are echoed over and over in the repetitions and restatements.

The country cemetery today looks, I suspect, much as it did a hundred and fifty years ago, except that there are now more graves. A huge old yew tree dominates the grounds, shading the tombstones of the farmers and merchants. As the sprawling branches of the yew attract the visitor's eye, intense quiet attracts the ear. The intermittent buzzing of insects, whose sounds would go unnoticed in a busier atmosphere, accents the absence of the noises of human activity. Cattle graze silently and placidly beyond the barbed wire that fences the cemetery off from the surrounding grasslands. The scent of newly mown alfalfa from nearby fields permeates the cemetery, but the slightly bitter aroma of the yew dominates, cutting through the quiet and overriding, with the threat of death, the impression of shelter given by the tree's sprawling branches.

— A student

4 | Using pronouns

Pronouns refer to and function as nouns (see 5a-2). They allow us to discuss a single person or thing throughout an entire paragraph or paper without having constantly to repeat the subject's name. They also link sentences to each other. Notice how each sentence after the first in the paragraph on page 36 about Carry Nation contains the pronoun *she*, relating the sentences back to the first, in which Nation's name is given.

5 | Being consistent

Consistency in the person and number of nouns and pronouns and in the tense of verbs (see Chapter 13) is crucial to paragraph coherence, for a paragraph that shifts unnecessarily from one person, number, or tense to another will always be hard to follow. In the following paragraph, for example, the meaning is obscured because of inconsistency (the shifting parts are italicized).

> Some psychologists *have thought we* are basically active; others 1
> *think we* are basically passive. The "active" view says a *person has* 2
> *learned* by interacting with the environment. The "passive" view 3
> says *your* behavior *is shaped* entirely by the forces in the environment. Two schools of thought *surrounded* these conflicting views, 4
> and their members *differ* on almost everything imaginable about human behavior.

Revised to eliminate the unnecessary shifts, the paragraph is clearer and easier to follow (the revisions are italicized).

> Some psychologists *think* we are basically active; others think 1
> we are basically passive. The "active" view says *we learn* by interacting with the environment. The "passive" view says *our* behavior 2
> is shaped entirely by the forces in the environment. Two schools of 3
> thought *surround* these conflicting views, and their members differ 4
> on almost everything imaginable about human behavior.

6 | Using transitional expressions

Transitional expressions are words or word groups that connect ideas, both within sentences and between them. Some common transitional expressions are listed below by the connecting function they perform.

TO ADD OR SHOW SEQUENCE

again, also, and, and then, besides, equally important, finally, first, further, furthermore, in addition, in the first place, last, moreover, next, second, still, too

TO COMPARE

in the same way, likewise, similarly

TO CONTRAST

although, and yet, but, but at the same time, despite, even so, even though, for all that, however, in contrast, in spite of, nevertheless, notwithstanding, on the contrary, on the other hand, regardless, still, though, yet

TO GIVE EXAMPLES OR INTENSIFY

after all, an illustration of, even, for example, for instance, indeed, in fact, it is true, of course, specifically, that is, to illustrate, truly

TO INDICATE PLACE

above, adjacent to, below, elsewhere, farther on, here, near, nearby, on the other side, opposite to, there, to the east, to the left

TO INDICATE TIME

after a while, afterward, as long as, as soon as, at last, at length, at that time, before, earlier, formerly, immediately, in the meantime, in the past, lately, later, meanwhile, now, presently, shortly, simultaneously, since, so far, soon, subsequently, then, thereafter, until, until now, when

TO REPEAT, SUMMARIZE, OR CONCLUDE

all in all, altogether, as has been said, in brief, in conclusion, in other words, in particular, in short, in simpler terms, in summary, on the whole, that is, therefore, to put it differently, to summarize

TO SHOW CAUSE OR EFFECT

accordingly, as a result, because, consequently, for this purpose, hence, otherwise, since, then, therefore, thereupon, thus, to this end, with this object

For examples of transitional expressions at work, look at the paragraph on page 29 about television commercials: *and* (sentences 1, 4, 6); *a second, a third* (sentence 5); *a few minutes later* (sentence 6). Or look at the paragraph on page 36 about Carry Nation: *after* (sentence 1); *in the course of* (sentence 4); *though* (sentence 5).

7 | Combining devices to achieve coherence

No writer relies on any single device to achieve paragraph coherence. Rather, organization, parallelism, repetition, pronouns, consistency, and transitional expressions come into play together, as they are needed or useful to lead the reader smoothly from one idea to another.

¶
3

Organizing paragraphs:
spatial and chronological   EXERCISE **3-3**

The paragraph topics below are suitable for spatial (1) or chronological (2) organization. Select one topic for each pattern, or make up topics of your own. For each topic you choose, write a topic sentence, list at least three details related to the topic sentence, and write one paragraph. Use parallel structures, repetition, pronouns, and transitional expressions to achieve paragraph coherence.

1. Topics for spatial paragraph: the appearance of a neighborhood; a fair or amusement park; a stadium during a game

Topic sentence: _____

_____

Details: 1. _____

_____

2. _____

_____

3. _____

_____

Paragraph: _____

_____

_____

_____

_____

_____

_____

_____

_____

2. Topics for chronological paragraph: a wedding; a city street from dawn
to noon; studying for an examination

Topic sentence: _____

_____

Details: 1. _____

_____

2. _____

_____

3. _____

_____

Paragraph: _____

_____

_____

_____

_____

_____

_____

_____

_____

_____

_____

Organizing paragraphs: specific, general, dramatic

EXERCISE **3-4**

The topics below are suitable for paragraphs organized from specific to general and general to specific (1), or less dramatic to more dramatic (2). Select two topics, or make up topics of your own, that are suitable for two of these paragraph patterns. For each topic you choose, write a topic sentence, list at least three details related to the topic sentence, and write one paragraph. Use parallel structures, repetition, pronouns, and transitional expressions to achieve paragraph coherence.

1. Topics for specific to general or general to specific: the benefits of exercise; the benefits of gardening; the appeal of soap operas

Topic sentence: _____

_____

Details: 1. _____

_____

2. _____

_____

3. _____

_____

Paragraph: _____

_____

_____

_____

_____

_____

¶ 3

_____

_____

_____

2. Topics for less dramatic to more dramatic: why I hate (or like) family reunions; an embarrassing incident; a serious accident

Topic sentence: _____

_____

Details: 1. _____

_____

2. _____

_____

3. _____

_____

Paragraph: _____

_____

_____

_____

_____

_____

_____

_____

_____

_____

_____

| *Being consistent*

The paragraph below is made incoherent by unneeded shifts in person, number, and tense. Making corrections in the space provided, revise the paragraph so that it is consistent. (Consult Chapter 13 if you need help identifying or correcting the shifts.)

A person should be tolerant of other people's style of dress or

behavior. One chooses clothing based on what was affordable, what the

wearer's taste is, and what the current styles are. These circumstances

may be different even among neighborhoods within our town. Behavior

also varies because of people's experiences and needs. For example, you

may be brought up in a culture that discourages people from making

much noise in public. Another person may have been raised in a culture

that encouraged free expression of emotions, even in public. Differences

among individuals have often added variety to our lives. One should not

disparage them.

Identifying parallelism, repetition, pronouns, transitional expressions

EXERCISE **3-6**

Read the following paragraph, looking for the ways in which parallelism, repetition, pronouns, and transitional expressions link sentences. Then answer the questions after the paragraph.

The most notable house in Plainville has always been a large ₁ and distinguished Victorian on Grant Avenue. The house was built in ₂ the 1890s by a wealthy industrialist who claimed to see great promise in the backwater town. The promise was never fulfilled, however, and ₃ the town settled instead into permanent shabbiness and obscurity. Despite his disappointments, the industrialist and three succeeding ₄ generations of his family stayed on in the mansion, preserving it for themselves and thus for their neighbors. Standing a full story above ₅ anything else in Plainville, the house remained a source of pleasure and pride for the community. Painted royal blue with red trim, it ₆ provided a bright island in an otherwise colorless setting. Even when ₇ the house was finally abandoned in the 1970s, it still recalled Plainville's optimistic past. Last week that past was demolished along with ₈ the old house. Now all that remains in Plainville is the drab present. ₉

1. List at least five transitional expressions in the paragraph.

   a. _____   c. _____   e. _____

   b. _____   d. _____

2. Two key words in the first sentence are repeated or restated throughout the paragraph. Identify the two key words and then list five repetitions or restatements of each one in the order in which they appear in the paragraph.

   a. Key word: _____

      Repetitions or restatements: _____; _____;

      _____; _____; _____

   b. Key word: _____

Repetitions or restatements: _____ ; _____ ;

_____ ; _____ ; _____

3. The paragraph also contains three other words that are repeated in at least two sentences each. List them.

   a. _____   b. _____   c. _____

4. Pronouns substitute for three different nouns in the paragraph. Identify each noun and list the pronoun or pronouns substituting for each one.

   a. Noun: _____   Pronoun(s): _____

   b. Noun: _____   Pronoun(s): _____

   c. Noun: _____   Pronoun(s): _____

5. Two sentences in the paragraph are closely linked by parallelism. Identify the sentences by number.

   a. _____   b. _____

Name _____ Date _____

Arranging and linking sentences

EXERCISE **3-7**

The list below provides all the details needed for a unified and coherent paragraph about a volcanic eruption on the island of Krakatoa. However, the details must be rearranged. On the blanks below, write the numbers preceding the details in the order in which they should appear. Then write a paragraph with the sentences in proper chronological order. Use parallel structures, repetition, pronouns, and transitional expressions, and rearrange the information as necessary.

1. _____ 4. _____ 7. _____ 10. _____ 13. _____

2. _____ 5. _____ 8. _____ 11. _____ 14. _____

3. _____ 6. _____ 9. _____ 12. _____

1. The mountains exploded.
2. The island sank into the ocean.
3. At first the island's mountains spewed rocks and ash into the air for a day, blackening the sky.
4. The greatest volcanic eruption of modern times occurred on August 27, 1883.
5. The earth calmed down again.
6. The explosion roared.
7. The collapse of the island caused gigantic tidal waves.
8. Almost nothing remained of the island when things were calm again.
9. The great eruption occurred when the island of Krakatoa, in what is now Indonesia, blew up.
10. The sound could be heard three thousand miles away.
11. The tidal waves swallowed up coastal cities and inland towns.
12. The explosion created winds that circled the earth several times.
13. In the aftermath nearly forty thousand people were discovered to have died.
14. The waves appeared finally as unusually large waves on the English coast, half a world away.

Paragraph: _____

¶
3

3c | Developing the paragraph

An effective paragraph is **developed;** that is, the central idea of the paragraph (usually expressed in a topic sentence) is well supported with enough details, examples, or reasons to convince the reader of the point being made.

1 | Using details, examples, and reasons

A paragraph may be developed by details. Compare the following undeveloped paragraph with the one on page 30 about the professor.

> When I first saw my biology professor, he looked really old and out of fashion. He was not a dynamic speaker, and he just seemed to have boring material.

The details of the original are what provide interest and clarity. A paragraph may also be developed by using examples or reasons. For instance, the paragraph on page 30 about the city street uses examples for development, and the paragraph on page 35 about the highway system gives reasons and a specific example to develop its main point.

2 | Choosing a method of development

You can sometimes draw on the established methods of paragraph development to generate specific supporting information or to give shape to what you have. (These methods correspond to the exploratory questions on p. 2.) As we saw above, some paragraphs may be developed simply by **illustration** or **support** — that is, by well-detailed examples or reasons that explain and clarify the paragraph's central idea. Other useful methods of development include definition, division and classification, comparison and contrast, analogy, cause-and-effect analysis, and process analysis.

In **definition** you may ask and answer, "What is it?" You name the category of things to which something belongs and then distinguish it from the other members of its category. For example:

> Every class has certain kinds of students, and one kind who is   1
> always present is the hand-raiser. I mean the too-eager student who   2
> does all the required *and* suggested reading two weeks in advance
> and who needs to show off all that work. Not long after class starts, 3
> the hand goes up — not merely raised, with a slightly bent arm,
> fingers relaxed, but *waved,* arm and fingers straight as sticks, hand
> turning 180 degrees as fast as the muscles will allow. The face is   4
> bright-eyed and smiling. And the desire to say "Call on me!" is   5
> barely repressed. When the hoped-for moment comes, the answer-   6
> ing voice is full of pride. But is the answer worth hearing? Almost   7,8
> never. In the end, real thought about the reading and the question   9
> seems to get lost in the compulsion to answer.
>
> — A student

In another method of development, **division** or **analysis,** you ask, "What are its parts?" Thus you might list the ten main characteristics of all the teachers you have had. In a related method, **classification,** you ask,

"What groups can it be sorted into?" Thus, you might divide teachers into three main types on the basis of their characteristics. The following paragraph employs classification to discuss psychic phenomena.

¶
3

> Psychic phenomena — occurrences unexplained by modern laws [1] of physics and psychology — are usually classified as one of three types. The first and probably best-known is extrasensory percep- [2] tion, or ESP. A person who is supposed to have ESP receives mes- [3] sages from his or her environment, whether from people or from objects, without reasoning or using the senses of sight, hearing, smell, taste, or touch. The second category, psychokinesis, or PK, is [4] said to allow its possessor to influence the behavior of objects or people in the environment without touching them. And the third [5] category, often called spiritualism, supposedly enables its posses- sors to communicate with people who have died and who reside in a "spirit world."
>
> — A student

Comparison and contrast is a method of development for which you ask, "How is it like or different from other things?" Comparison usually shows similarities between things we perceive as different; contrast usually shows differences between things we perceive as similar. Comparison and contrast is the method of development in the following paragraph about two tennis players.

> My tennis partners, Bob and Tom, have greatly different play- [1] ing styles, but each is effective and formidable. Bob relies on a [2] straight, hard serve that darts off like a shot after it hits the court. Tom serves a high, spinning, soft arc that bounces crazily to the [3] left or right after it hits. When Bob returns a ball, he relies on a [4] powerful stroke with strong top spin, and he always aims at the opponent's base line. When Tom returns a ball, his main concern [5] is careful placement far from the opponent, and he slices the ball to give it a low bounce. Both succeed in wearing down an oppo- [6] nent — one by taxing the opponent's strength and stamina for re- turning hard shots, the other by causing the opponent to run back and forth from net to base line and to try to guess which way the ball will bounce. Basically, Bob overpowers his opponent, and Tom [7] outsmarts his.
>
> — A student

In **analogy** you ask, "Is it comparable to something in a differ- ent class but more familiar to us?" Analogy is useful for explaining some- thing complex or abstract by comparing it loosely with something sim- ple, concrete, and familiar. The writer of the following paragraph uses the analogy of washing a car to explain the lack of reward from taking a certain course.

> Philosophy class reminds me of the summer I spent washing [1] cars at a service station. A wealthy lady brought her Cadillac to be [2] washed every Saturday, whether or not the car had gotten the least bit dirty the previous week. Doing a good job of washing the car [3] seemed absolutely pointless, because I knew I would have to go

through the same motions and exert the same effort the next Saturday, regardless of how clean I got the car. In philosophy class I have to master one thinker's viewpoint each week. And each subsequent week I master another thinker's argument that logically rejects the views of the previous philosopher. The mental effort each week seems to me as pointless as washing that Cadillac. Regardless of how I work to embrace "truth," the next week my efforts are undone and I start anew.

— A student

To develop a paragraph by **cause-and-effect analysis,** you analyze the events (causes) that brought something about or the results (effects) of a sequence of events. The paragraph below examines the causes of increasing utility rates.

Utility rates will continue to increase in the near future regardless of conservation efforts. The first reason is that capital construction costs are increasing: Construction of a nuclear power plant has been delayed by lawsuits, and the original estimated construction cost of $2 billion has now risen to $3.5 billion. Second, costs for coal and oil, which had been declining, are beginning to edge upward again. Third, new utility taxes will add 3 percent to consumer bills this winter. Last year, consumers used 15 percent less power than they did the year before. A similar — and highly unlikely — reduction this year would still result in a 5 percent increase in utility bills.

— A student

Another method of developing a paragraph is **process analysis,** asking, "How does it work?" In the paragraph below, the author examines how to deal effectively with an emotionally disturbed person.

If a friend or relative loses emotional control in your presence, what should you do? The important thing is to help the person pass through the difficult moment and restore the balance between emotion and reason. First, listen carefully. Try to understand the person's view of the problem. Second, stay calm and attentive. Do not panic, and do not allow yourself to become impatient or bored or angry. Third, if you feel that the person or the problems are too much for you to cope with, by all means seek help. But, fourth, be honest. Do not mislead the person about your intentions or conspire behind his or her back, for you will lose the trust that is essential for helping.

— A student

Even when you develop a whole essay by one of the methods above, you will probably use other methods to develop individual paragraphs, and you may even *combine* methods (say, definition and comparison and contrast) in a single paragraph.

3 | Checking length

The length of a paragraph depends on the paragraph's topic and the writer's purpose. Long paragraphs are not necessarily well developed, nor are short paragraphs necessarily underdeveloped. But very long paragraphs (more than 150 words, or about eight sentences) may contain irrelevant information. And very short paragraphs (less than 100 words, or about four sentences) may lack the specific details, examples, or reasons needed to convey your point adequately.

Name _____ Date _____

Developing paragraphs with illustration or support

EXERCISE **3-8**

Drawing on the topics suggested below, or on topics of your own, develop one paragraph supported by examples (1) and one paragraph supported by reasons (2). Write a topic sentence for each paragraph, and list at least three of the items to be used in its development. Then write the paragraph.

1. Topics for examples: how newspaper ads mislead; the ideal shopping center; how graffiti is destructive (or creative)

Topic sentence: _____

_____

Examples: 1. _____

_____

2. _____

_____

3. _____

_____

Paragraph: _____

_____

_____

_____

_____

_____

_____

_____

_____

_____

_____

2. Topics for reasons: the appeal of folk (or some other kind of) music; what magazines a student should read regularly; why not to buy sweetened cereals

Topic sentence: _____

_____

Reasons: 1. _____

_____

2. _____

_____

3. _____

_____

Paragraph: _____

_____

_____

_____

_____

_____

_____

_____

_____

Name _____ Date _____

Developing paragraphs with definition; with division and classification

EXERCISE **3-9**

Drawing on the topics suggested below, or on topics of your own, develop one paragraph using definition (1) and one paragraph using division, classification, or both (2). Write a topic sentence for each paragraph, and list at least three pieces of supporting information (details, examples, or reasons) to be used in its development. Then write the paragraph.

1. Topics for definition: election primary; what an R rating for a movie should be; jealousy

Topic sentence: _____

_____

Supporting information: 1. _____

_____

2. _____

_____

3. _____

_____

Paragraph: _____

_____

_____

_____

_____

_____

_____

_____

_____

_____

2. Topics for division: a city block; a football team; a vacation spot
   Topics for classification: small towns; sales clerks; diets

   Topic sentence: _____

   _____

   Supporting information: 1. _____

   _____

   2. _____

   _____

   3. _____

   _____

   Paragraph: _____

   _____

   _____

   _____

   _____

   _____

   _____

   _____

   _____

   _____

Name _____ Date _____

Developing paragraphs with comparison and contrast; with analogy

Drawing on the topics suggested below, or on topics of your own, develop one paragraph using comparison, contrast, or both (1) and one paragraph using analogy (2). Write a topic sentence for each paragraph, and list at least three pieces of supporting information (details, examples, or reasons) to be used in its development. Then write the paragraph.

1. Topics for comparison, contrast, or both: two persons' ways of laughing; two professional athletes; a television account and a newspaper account of the same sports event

   Topic sentence: _____

   _____

   Supporting information: 1. _____

   _____

   2. _____

   _____

   3. _____

   _____

   Paragraph: _____

   _____

   _____

   _____

   _____

¶ 3

_____

_____

_____

_____

2. Topics for analogy: a classroom and a church or synagogue; dieting and being a monk; sitting in front of a television and sitting in a traffic jam

   Topic sentence: _____

   _____

   Supporting information: 1. _____

   _____

   2. _____

   _____

   3. _____

   _____

   Paragraph: _____

   _____

   _____

   _____

   _____

   _____

   _____

   _____

*Developing paragraphs
with cause-and-effect analysis;
with process analysis*   EXERCISE **3-11**

Drawing on the topics suggested below, or on topics of your own, develop one paragraph using cause-and-effect analysis (1) and one using process analysis (2). Write a topic sentence for each paragraph, and list at least three pieces of supporting information (details, examples, or reasons) to be used in its development. Then write the paragraph.

1. Topics for cause-and-effect analysis: why you never (or always) travel by bus or train; how an assembly kit defeated you; why someone bores (or delights) you

   Topic sentence: _____

   _____

   Supporting information: 1. _____

   _____

   2. _____

   _____

   3. _____

   _____

   Paragraph: _____

   _____

   _____

   _____

   _____

   _____

_____

_____

_____

_____

_____

2. Topics for process analysis: how to argue with a traffic officer; how to choose a history teacher; how to make good chili

Topic sentence: _____

_____

Supporting information: 1. _____

_____

2. _____

_____

3. _____

_____

Paragraph: _____

_____

_____

_____

_____

_____

_____

_____

_____

3d | Writing special kinds of paragraphs

The opening and closing paragraphs of an essay, transitional paragraphs, and paragraphs in dialogue serve special purposes and may not conform to the guidelines for unity, coherence, and development discussed above.

1 | Opening an essay

The introductory paragraph of your essay should arouse a reader's interest and state your purpose. You can open with a statement of the essay's subject, a brief anecdote, a startling opinion, a historical fact or event, or an intriguing or apt quotation. Here are two examples.

> During my construction job last summer, my boss often said, "As long as you look busy, whether you're really doing any work or not, I'll never get on your back." However, I have always believed that image should not be rewarded if it is not matched by performance, and maybe that is why I am bothered by the university granting the football coach a 12 percent raise this year, after the team turned in a 1–9 record. In fact, the man should be fired because he lacks interest and experience.

> Contrary to what my parents and teachers always told me, I have found daydreaming a very useful pastime. Daydreaming not only has helped me through some boring classes but also has helped me discover my career goals.

An effective opening paragraph is concise, direct, sincere, and interesting. Be sure to state your own perspective on the subject, perhaps in a thesis sentence (see 1d). Avoid simply announcing your intentions or wandering vaguely over subjects broader than or unrelated to your own.

2 | Closing an essay

A proper close to an essay indicates that you have not just stopped writing but have completed what you wanted to say. Whether in a single sentence or in several sentences, a conclusion may, among other things, summarize, ask a question, introduce a startling or weighty fact or quotation, or suggest a course of action. The first paragraph below takes the last approach. The second paragraph ends with a quotation.

> If my experiences with buying a used car have been shared by hundreds or thousands of other persons — and I do not believe it could be otherwise — then we should all be urging the Federal Trade Commission to provide regulations to protect us.

> The art of putting daydreams to practical use should be studied and encouraged by every high school counselor. Other college students can profit just as I have. "We are such stuff / As dreams are made on," Shakespeare wrote.

In writing a conclusion, avoid several common pitfalls of such paragraphs: restating the introduction, starting in an entirely new direction, concluding more than your evidence allows, and apologizing for your essay.

3 | Using transitional paragraphs

You may use a brief, one- or two-sentence paragraph to make a transition from one part of an essay to another. For example:

> The causes of child abuse are familiar to all of us, but what can we do about them? The experts have several suggestions.

Avoid using transitional paragraphs simply to mark time while you think of what to say next.

4 | Writing dialogue

In recording a conversation between two or more people, begin a new paragraph for the speech of each person, so the reader can tell when one person stops talking and another begins. For example:

> "Why should I be the one to tell him you wrecked his car?" she asked. "I wasn't even there."
>
> "That's why we want you to do it. The rest of us are too frightened."

3e | Combining paragraphs in the essay

Each paragraph in an essay should support the thesis statement (see Chapter 1). The introduction presents the main point, and the conclusion reinforces it. Paragraphs in the body develop the aspects or components of the idea. Developed ideas are necessary not only to make the essay interesting but also to make it convincing. Carefully linked paragraphs will provide *coherence* to an essay, and if each paragraph in the body supports and develops the single main idea of the entire paper, the essay will have *unity*. Note that the paragraphs in a coherent and unified essay may be and often are developed by different methods. Thus an essay on advertising ploys to sell skin cream might use *definition* of appeals to snobbery and sexuality in one paragraph, and provide *details and examples* in the next. An essay on corruption in college sports might use an *analogy* with air pollution in one paragraph, in order to suggest the seriousness of the problem, and *cause-and-effect analysis* in subsequent paragraphs.

¶
3

*Opening and
closing an essay*   EXERCISE **3-12**

Write opening and closing paragraphs for essays on two of the following topics, or on topics of your own, using different devices to begin or end in each case. For the introductions, choose from quotation, anecdote, opinion, and historical incident. For the conclusions, choose from question, fact, quotation, and suggested action.

TOPICS

an exciting play in sports   appreciating foreign visitors
raising a dog (cat, bird, etc.)   life in a small town (or big city)
improving one's manners   camping without a tent
obtaining a charge card   an embarrassing moment

1. Topic: _____

Opening paragraph: _____

_____

_____

_____

_____

_____

_____

_____

_____

Closing paragraph: _____

_____

_____

_____

¶

3

_____

_____

_____

_____

2. Topic: _____

Opening paragraph: _____

_____

_____

_____

_____

_____

_____

_____

Closing paragraph: _____

_____

_____

_____

_____

_____

_____

_____

4 | *Convincing a Reader*

In a way, whenever you write you are arguing, trying to convince readers of your point of view. An effective argument meets certain criteria of structure and content: It presents a thesis, which may be contained in a thesis sentence, and it backs up that assertion with more specific assertions and with evidence.

4a | Sounding moderate

The most convincing argument is one that sounds rational. It avoids absolute words like *all* and *never*, it avoids appealing to readers' emotions rather than their reason, and it shows that the writer has recognized and weighed all the alternatives before reaching his or her conclusions. An argument that violates these rules generally will fail to convince — and may even repel — the careful reader.

ORIGINAL It is ridiculous for elderly people, who usually do not have school-age children, to have to pay high property taxes, since most of that outrageous, legal rip-off goes to pay for schools to educate others' children.

REVISED Since most of the elderly have paid taxes all their lives, are now living on reduced incomes, and do not have school-age children, they should pay lower public education taxes.

4b | Making assertions believable

Besides taking a reasonable tone, a believable assertion distinguishes among fact, opinion, and prejudice; defines terms clearly; and confronts the issue directly.

1 | Distinguishing fact, opinion, and prejudice

A **fact** is a verifiable statement: *Shakespeare was born in 1564*. An **opinion** is a judgment based on fact: *Shakespeare was a great writer*. A **prejudice** is a generalized opinion based on too little evidence: *Elizabethan drama is boring*. An effective argument is based on facts or on opinions backed up with facts, not on prejudice.

2 | Defining terms

For your assertions to be believable, you must define your terms clearly and use them consistently. Failing to define terms makes it harder for the reader to understand and accept your argument.

65

ORIGINAL The city arts council is supposed to be supporting the arts, but the arts in our town have not improved since the council was set up.

REVISED The city arts council was created to give financial support to local performing groups, but the number of theater, music, and dance programs in our town has declined since the council was set up.

3 | Facing the question

In dealing with the central question your argument aims to answer, it is important not to oversimplify complex issues or make an emotional rather than a factual appeal. **Begging the question** treats an unproved assumption as if it were a fact: *The best solution to the energy problem, which is actually a problem of too much government regulation of the oil companies, is to deregulate oil prices.* **Ignoring the question** appeals to readers' emotions rather than reason: *Louise Smith understands our children's educational needs because she is a devoted mother herself.* Appealing to readers' snobbism or flattering them also ignores the question: *All intelligent people recognize the need for gun control.* So does the **ad hominem** argument, which criticizes the opposing view's defenders rather than the view itself: *How can you accept the commission's conclusion that marijuana should be legalized when one of the members has admitted she once smoked pot?*

4c | Supporting the assertions

Making your assertions believable requires supporting them with evidence. Details, examples, and reasons give weight to general or abstract assertions. To work effectively, evidence must meet four criteria. First, it must be an accurate, undistorted report from a reliable source. Second, it must be drawn from a source with authority on the particular topic and it must be clearly relevant to the topic. Third, it must be representative, an accurate reflection of the sample from which it is said to be drawn. And fourth, it must be sufficient to justify your conclusions.

4d | Reasoning effectively

Writing, like thinking, typically employs two types of reasoning: inductive and deductive.

1 | Reasoning inductively

Inductive reasoning involves beginning with one piece of information and adding others until enough evidence has been accumulated to justify making a general conclusion, or **generalization.** Each piece of evidence implies the conclusion, but no one piece is sufficient for it. When a detective gathers clues and infers from them who may have committed a crime, he or she is reasoning inductively. In writing, you use induction when you present a succession of relevant facts that together lead to a logical conclusion. For example:

In April, Congressman Smith told a religious coalition that he favored a total cutoff of government funds for abortions. In May, the congressman told a medical convention that he favored liberal government funding for abortions. In July, a newsletter from Smith's office stated that "abortions should be legal, but not one cent of government money should go toward paying for one." I refuse to vote for Smith because he appears unwilling to take a consistent stand on this important issue.

— A student

2 | Reasoning deductively

Deductive reasoning involves beginning with two or more related generalizations and drawing a conclusion from them. No one generalization alone implies the conclusion; information from each one is needed. If a detective knows a crime was committed in the drawing room, and the drawing room was locked until 9 P.M., he or she can deduce that the crime must have been committed after 9 P.M. or by someone with a key. In writing, you use deduction when you combine two or more generalizations to reach a conclusion:

Passenger trains have long operated in the red. Amtrak's solution for reducing its deficits was to drop routes that carried few passengers. Amtrak continued to lose money, however, so it cut services until just a few main routes were left. Still Amtrack continues to lose money. Consequently, it is time for the system to upgrade the quality of its service or find some other means to derive revenue. Apparently, cutting routes is not the answer to Amtrak's financial problems.

— A student

3 | Avoiding faulty reasoning

Fallacies are flaws in inductive or deductive reasoning that can weaken an argument. The **hasty generalization** is a fallacious assertion based on too little evidence: *Vegetarian diets are unhealthful.* One type of hasty generalization is the **stereotype,** an oversimplified characterization of a group of people: *Vegetarians are pale and unhealthy looking.* **Oversimplification** of cause and effect is an interpretation of two events that are coincidental or related in a complex way as if one were the direct cause of the other: *Giving up smoking causes people to gain weight.* The **post hoc fallacy** is an assumption that because one event followed another, the first was the cause of the second: *Every time we elect a Democratic president, the price of candy bars goes up.* The **either . . . or fallacy** sets up only two alternatives for a situation that offers more: *If we don't keep up in the arms race with the Russians, we'll be swallowed up by them.* A **non sequitur** involves following one idea with another that has no logical relation to it: *It is said that Indians never invented the wheel, but in fact much of their art includes circles.* A **false analogy** compares two situations or things that are not truly comparable: *If Rockwell Springs, Minnesota, can keep a balanced budget, why can't New York City?*

| *Convincing a reader*   EXERCISE **4-1**

A. Identify each of the following sentences as (1) fact, (2) opinion, or (3) prejudice by writing the appropriate number on the blank to the right.

Example: The energy crisis is our most serious national crisis.   *2*
—————

1. Politicians cannot be trusted.   —————

2. George Washington was the most honorable chief exec-   —————
   utive the United States has ever had.
3. Most presidents have frequent disagreements with Con-   —————
   gress.
4. The average senator is richer than the average represen-   —————
   tative.
5. The best presidents were Boy Scouts when they were   —————
   young.

B. Identify each of the following sentences as (1) begging the question, (2) emotional appeal, (3) snob appeal or flattery, or (4) *ad hominem* argument by writing the appropriate number on the blank to the right.

Example: The nation's most perceptive analysts agree that capital   *3*
punishment is necessary to control crime.   —————

1. Seat belts are unnecessary; I do not need the U.S. gov-   —————
   ernment's conscience in my car to make me a safe driver.
2. I know Ralph Nader says the Mudlark is dangerous at   —————
   high speeds, but you have to remember that he earns his
   living by making such statements.
3. How can anyone allege that a car made by dedicated   —————
   American workers in an American factory is unsafe?
4. People who really know automobiles usually prefer Brit-   —————
   ish cars.
5. Cars wouldn't be so outrageously expensive if it weren't   —————
   for all the unnecessary extras like pollution control devices, ignition locks, and padded dashboards.

C. Each sentence below illustrates one or more of the following fallacies: (1) hasty generalization, (2) stereotype, (3) oversimplification, (4) *post hoc* fallacy, (5) either . . . or fallacy, (6) non sequitur, or (7) false analogy. Identify the fallacy or fallacies of each sentence by writing the appropriate number(s) in the blank to the right.

Example: The problem with Russian novelists is that they're all so serious.   *1,2*

1. He must have been drinking, because he is always happy when he has been drinking, and he is happy now.   _____
2. If El Salvador's government is overthrown, Arizona will be next.   _____
3. Jane is a lovely, gracious woman, but she has a very sharp business sense.   _____
4. If anything can go wrong, it will.   _____
5. People's right to adequate medical care will be guaranteed only if Congress passes Senator Schmidt's health insurance bill.   _____
6. Be careful of your grammar when you talk to an English teacher, or you will be criticized.   _____
7. If scientists can send a spaceship to Mars, they should be able to cure the common cold.   _____
8. If we don't build nuclear power plants, we will be forever dependent on imported oil.   _____
9. It always snows as soon as I put my down jacket in storage.   _____
10. The game will be exciting because it is for the championship.   _____
11. Parachute jumping is just like roller skating — as long as you are careful, you will not get hurt.   _____
12. So many workers belong to unions that high-quality work is rare.   _____
13. If you light a cigarette, the bus will come right away.   _____
14. Bureaucrats are concerned only with putting in their time, not with serving the public.   _____
15. The reason our country is still respected by the Soviet Union is that we stood up to them during the Cuban missile crisis.   _____

II | Grammatical Sentences

5 | *Understanding Sentence Grammar*

Grammar is a way of describing how words work in relation to one another.

5a | Understanding the basic sentence

1 | Identifying subjects and predicates

The sentence is the basic unit of writing. It usually consists of a **subject,** which names something, and a **predicate,** which states some action or condition of the subject.

SUBJECT	PREDICATE
Alfred	lives in Kenya.
Father	calls it a country of mystery.
The chemical	leaked from the truck.
The doctors	were women.

2 | Identifying the basic words: Nouns and verbs

The important words in the sentences above are the nouns serving as the sentence subjects (*Alfred, Father, chemical, doctors*) and the verbs beginning the sentence predicates (*lives, calls, leaked, were*). Nouns and verbs are the basic **parts of speech,** or classes of words.

Nouns name people (*Alfred, Father, doctors, women*), places (*Kenya, country*), things (*chemical, truck*), and qualities or ideas (*mystery*). Most nouns add an *-s* to distinguish singular (or "one") from plural ("more than one"): *father, fathers; chemical, chemicals; doctor, doctors*. Nouns can also indicate **possession,** or ownership, of a thing or quality by adding an apostrophe plus an *-s: Alfred, Alfred's home.*

There are several kinds of nouns. **Mass nouns** name things such as *gold* that we don't usually count or qualities such as *hostility*. **Collective nouns** such as *committee* name groups of people or things. **Common nouns** such as *doctor* or *chemical* name general classes of people, places, or things. **Proper nouns** such as *Alfred* and *Kenya* name specific people, places, or things and are capitalized.

Nouns are often preceded by the **articles** *a, an,* and *the.* The appearance of one of these words signals that a noun follows.

Verbs describe action or occurrence (*live, call, leak*) or a state of being (*be, seem*). So-called **regular verbs** add a *-d* or *-ed* to indicate a change in the time of their action from the present to the past: *live, lived;*

leak, leaked. **Irregular verbs** indicate the same change in some other way: *begin, began; weep, wept.*

Verbs use the plain form (the one listed in the dictionary) to show present time with plural nouns and the pronouns *I, you, we,* and *they: members agree, I disagree.* Verbs use the plain form plus *-s* to show present time with singular nouns and the pronouns *he, she,* and *it: member agrees, she disagrees.* One exception is the verb *be,* which uses the present form *are* for plural nouns and the pronouns *you, we,* and *they* (*members are, they are*); *is* for singular nouns and the pronouns *he, she,* and *it* (*member is, she is*); and *am* for the pronoun *I* (*I am*). The forms of *be* for past time are *was* and *were* (*member was, members were*). Another exception is the verb *have,* which uses *has* for singular nouns and the pronouns *he, she,* and *it.*

Verbs often combine with **auxiliary,** or **helping, verbs** to form **verb phrases** that express complex time relationships and other attributes: *is living, has lived, will go, should call, may survive, can run.* (See pp. 87–88 and Chapter 7 for further discussion of verbs and verb forms.)

A note on form and function: A word may serve different functions in different sentences. *Support,* for instance, is a noun in "I need your *support*" but a verb in "I *support* the representative." *Work* is a noun in "She looked for *work*" but a verb in "I *work* on Sundays." Thus, determining a word's part of speech often requires examining its function in its sentence.

Pronouns function as nouns do, and most are noun substitutes. **Personal pronouns** refer to specific individuals (*I, you, he, she, it, we,* and *they*). **Demonstrative pronouns** (*this, that,* and *such,* for example) identify or point to nouns. **Relative pronouns** (*who, which,* and *that*) relate to a word or group of words and introduce subordinate clauses. **Indefinite pronouns** such as *everyone* and *somebody* function as nouns but do not substitute for any specific nouns. **Intensive pronouns** (such as *himself, themselves*) emphasize a noun or pronoun. **Reflexive pronouns** (for example, *myself*) indicate that the subject also receives the action, and **interrogative pronouns** (such as *who, what*) introduce questions. For a discussion of form changes in pronouns, see Chapter 6.

3 | Forming sentence patterns with nouns and verbs

Sentence subjects often consist simply of a noun and perhaps an article. Predicates may consist of nothing more than a verb.

> S V
> The policeman slept.

But predicates may be more complex, consisting not only of verbs but also of nouns that perform functions other than that of subject.

A **direct object** (DO) is a word that indicates who or what receives the action of the verb:

```
        S    V      DO
```
A thief cracked the *safe*.

An **indirect object** (IO) is a word that indicates to or for whom or what the action of the verb is directed:

```
          S     V     IO      DO
```
The mayor sent the *sheriff* a message.

A **subject complement** (SC) is a word that describes or renames the subject:

```
          S    V          SC
```
The mayor was also the *president* of the bank.

A subject complement may also be an adjective, as in "I was *angry*."

An **object complement** (OC) is a word that describes or renames a direct object:

```
       S    V      DO       OC
```
He called the incident a *disgrace*.

It may also be an adjective, as in "She made me *angry*."

The verbs in the predicates shown above fall into three categories. The first verb, *slept*, is called **intransitive** because it does not require an object or complement to complete its action. The verbs *cracked, sent,* and *called,* in contrast, do require objects to complete their action and are thus called **transitive.** Verbs such as *was* or any form of *be,* as well as *seem, become, feel, smell,* and several other verbs that are followed by subject complements, are called **linking verbs** because they simply connect subject and complement. The verb *be* is the most common linking verb.

Identifying subjects and predicates

In the sentences below, underline each subject once and each predicate twice.

Example: Bill drinks fruit juice every day.

1. The dead leaves blew into the swimming pool.

2. I talked to the professor after class for an hour.

3. The judge sent him back to prison.

4. She put too much faith in her ability to ski.

5. Raw garlic keeps rude people away.

6. A broken ashtray indicated the presence of my cat in the room.

7. I would rather read biographies than anything else.

8. We trained the parakeets to sing duets.

9. Elmo City has a crime problem.

10. Tom's souvenir album of Waco, Texas, rested on the top of the bureau.

11. The refrigerator contained nothing.

12. He forgot to prepare the speech.

13. The foul shots won the game for us.

14. Two reams of paper were missing from the storage cabinet.

15. The coffee table was imported from Holland.

16. The contractor is three weeks behind schedule.

17. Long sideburns have been popular in the South at least since the Civil War.

18. Coriander may be the most popular spice in Jordan.

19. Three perfect robin's eggs were in the box.

20. Tourists flock to the Clair County Sheep Festival each year.

Identifying nouns and verbs

In the passages below, underline each noun once and each verb or verb phrase twice.

Example: The <u>building</u> <u>contains</u> almost a <u>mile</u> of <u>hallways</u>.

1. The tree gave a vertical history of the storm. It rose to the height of a tall building, but the branches were few and the leaves were sparse. About halfway up, a kite dangled. Several feet higher, the remains of a hang-glider twisted in the wind. Finally, near the very top, a parachute whipped in the breeze.

2. Frederick had lived near the river all his life. His father, owner of Red Mill Grain and Rowboats, drew the energy for his business from the water. Not only his father but the entire community depended somehow on the river. But Frederick did not realize until college that the river depended for its life on how the people of the community treated it.

3. A majority of the council voted for restrictions on fences that blocked the migration of the elk. For years the movement of the animals had been free, and restrictions by humans on that movement seemed unfair.

Identifying objects and complements

In the sentences below, label each direct object (*DO*), indirect object (*IO*), subject complement (*SC*), and object complement (*OC*) by inserting the appropriate abbreviation above the word.

DO
Example: I received a new stereo for Christmas.

1. Employment is not guaranteed.

2. Without vacations, school would be pure drudgery.

3. All my friends bring me their difficult problems.

4. I bought my father a marble chess set.

5. The team was divided into squads.

6. We opened the door to a large, ugly, bearded man.

7. Jogging is a good way to destroy your feet.

8. The Japanese phrase book gives you no answers.

9. Lloyd gave Esther's advice to everyone.

10. Sue bought me a very expensive lunch.

11. As the game began, the guard passed the center the ball.

12. The prosecutor promised her immunity.

13. The movie made him unhappy.

14. Some people have taken the course twice.

15. The counselor often interrupts her clients.

16. The book has no headings or pictures.

17. The faculty considers the new grading system a disaster.

18. A fire extinguisher would be a good investment.

19. Flying is a costly way to travel.

20. Traffic jams upset Angela.

Identifying transitive, intransitive, and linking verbs

In the passage below, identify each verb as transitive (*T*), intransitive (*I*), or linking (*L*) by inserting the appropriate abbreviation above the verb.

T
Example: I bought a rare dime for a dollar.

Jonathan kept the dog in the backyard every day. When the letter carrier passed by on Tuesday morning, the dog became upset and complained loudly at the intruder in its owner's yard. That night the dog dug a hole under the fence but did not escape once it had completed the project. The next afternoon the carrier came by, and the dog scurried through the hole under the fence. The man was naturally afraid, so he dropped his mailbag and ran. The dog stopped, retrieved the mailbag, and took it to the man. Its tail wagged. When the carrier patted the dog on the head, the dog bit him.

5b | Expanding the basic sentence with single words

Most sentences we use are longer and more complex than the simple subject-predicate pattern made up of nouns, pronouns, and verbs. We regularly expand this basic pattern with single words and groups of words.

1 | Using adjectives and adverbs

An **adjective** is a part of speech that describes or modifies a noun or pronoun. An **adverb** is a part of speech that describes or modifies a verb, an adjective, another adverb, or a group of words. An adverb indicates *intensity* (*very*) or explains *how, why, where,* or *when.*

ADJECTIVES	ADVERBS
rotten mango	walked *slowly*
quick trip	*never* happy
	spoke *very carefully*

Although adverbs often end in *-ly* (*slowly, carefully*), the ending does not always signal an adverb because some adjectives also end in *-ly* (*friendly*) and some adverbs do not (*never, very*). Only a word's function in a sentence will tell you if it is an adjective or an adverb.

Adjectives, like nouns, may serve as subject complements after linking verbs and as object complements:

       S   V   SC
The house was *huge.*

       S   V   DO   OC
The critic declared the movie *pornographic.*

Adjectives and adverbs have three different forms or degrees. The **positive form** is the one listed in the dictionary: *red, bad, serious; well, stupidly.* The **comparative form** indicates a greater degree of the quality named by the word: *redder, worse, more serious; better, more stupidly.* The **superlative form** indicates the greatest degree of the quality named by the word: *reddest, worst, most serious; best, most stupidly.* (See also 9e.)

2 | Using other words as modifiers

Not only adjectives and adverbs but also nouns and some verb forms may function as single-word modifiers in some contexts.

Nouns often modify other nouns in constructions like *ticket booth, government intervention,* and *taste test.* However, they should be used sparingly as modifiers to avoid awkwardness. (See 9f.)

Special forms of verbs function as single-word modifiers: the *banging* door, *curled* hair. (See 5 c-2 and Chapter 7.)

Identifying adjectives and adverbs

In the sentences below, underline each adjective or other single-word noun modifier once, and underline each adverb twice.

Example: She entered the store and <u><u>quickly</u></u> bought a <u>paperback</u> dictionary.

1. Layla usually wore a corduroy jacket.
2. Most aids for hearing can only amplify sound.
3. The law insists on lower speed in densely populated areas.
4. Whales are an endangered species.
5. The movie about orchards was tiring.
6. The first national highway in the United States was constructed in the 1800s.
7. This problem is easier than the previous one.
8. Ed always travels first class.
9. The newest member of the committee represents a large group of lawyers.
10. The meat, tender and juicy, sizzled temptingly.
11. Zimmer often offends people.
12. An enormous iceberg ripped a hole in the keel of the ship.
13. A pattern of gold and green trumpets decorated the dress.
14. After receiving the battered box, Homer put in a claim for damages.
15. The military prosecutor demanded the death sentence.
16. The radical leaders managed to execute a thousand people.
17. A hippopotamus actually can move rapidly.
18. She asked the question impatiently.
19. The buzzing mosquito woke me from a deep sleep.
20. Cars that move slowly can be a hazard on the highway.

21. The cabinet is kept upstairs.

22. A record crop is expected in Kansas.

23. Pointed or rounded arches characterize the different styles of architecture.

24. A brick house, like a wooden house, can catch fire quickly.

25. I would not say the aircraft landed smoothly.

5c | Expanding the basic sentence with word groups

In most sentences we speak or write, groups of words function as adjectives, adverbs, nouns, or verbs. A **phrase** is a group of related words that functions as a single part of speech and lacks either a subject or a predicate or both. A **clause** is a group of related words that contains both a subject and a predicate.

1 | Using prepositional phrases

A **preposition** is a part of speech that never changes form and serves to link one word or word group to another. Common prepositions include the following:

about	beside	into	through
above	between	like	throughout
across	beyond	near	till
after	by	of	to
against	concerning	off	toward
along	despite	on	under
among	down	onto	underneath
around	during	out	unlike
as	except	outside	until
at	excepting	over	up
before	for	past	upon
behind	from	regarding	with
below	in	round	within
beneath	inside	since	without

Prepositions connect a noun, pronoun, or word or word group acting as a noun — called the **object of the preposition** — to another word that usually precedes the preposition. The entire group of preposition and its object plus any modifiers is called a **prepositional phrase.**

> We slid *down the chute.* [*Down* is the preposition; *chute* is its object. *Down the chute* is a prepositional phrase.]

Prepositional phrases may function as adjectives, adverbs, and sometimes as nouns.

> The doll is a souvenir *of Cyprus.* [Adjective phrase modifying *souvenir.*]
> A woman *in a brown shirt* stole my car. [Adjective phrase modifying *woman.*]
> A tractor ran *over my garden.* [Adverb phrase modifying *ran.*]
> The bus will leave *in an hour.* [Adverb phrase modifying *leave.*]
> *Out of sight* is *out of mind.* [Noun phrases serving as sentence subject and subject complement.]

2 | Using verbals and verbal phrases

Verbals are forms of verbs, such as *falling* and *arrived*, that can function as nouns, adjectives, or adverbs. These verb forms may combine with auxiliary verbs to form verb phrases that serve as sentence predicates:

The leaves *are falling.*
The letter *has arrived.*

n these forms function as adjectives, adverbs, or nouns, they can-
d alone as the complete verb in the predicate of a sentence.

Participles function as adjectives to modify nouns, pronouns, and
r word groups acting as nouns. The present participle is the *-ing*
the verb (*smoking, ringing*). The past participle is usually the dictionary form of the verb plus *-d* or *-ed* (*smoked*), but many irregular verbs
form their participles in other ways (*rung, understood*). (See 7-a.)

> The *whirling* kite broke from the string. [Present participle modifies
> *kite.*]
> *Stunned*, he stared at the open door. [Past participle modifies *he.*]

Gerunds function as nouns. Like present participles, gerunds
have the *-ing* form of the verb. They are distinguished from participles
only by their function in a given context. If the *-ing* form functions as a
noun, it is a gerund. If the *-ing* form functions as an adjective, it is a
present participle.

> *Flying* terrifies me. [Gerund as sentence subject.]
> *Flying* gravel struck the headlight. [Participle as adjective.]

Infinitives function as nouns, adjectives, and adverbs. They consist of the plain form of the verb listed in the dictionary, and they are
usually preceded by *to* (*to smoke, to ring*).

> I do not plan *to work.* [Infinitive as noun object of the verb *plan.*]
> That is the most economical car *to buy.* [Infinitive as adjective modi-
> fying *car.*]
> That lesson was the hardest *to learn.* [Infinitive as adverb modifying
> *hardest.*]

Infinitives, present and past participles, and gerunds can combine with subjects, objects, complements, and modifiers in **verbal phrases**
that also serve as nouns, adjectives, or adverbs. **Participial phrases** function as adjectives.

> *Sailing against the wind*, we made little headway. [Participial phrase
> as adjective modifying *we*. The participle *sailing* is modified by the
> prepositional phrase *against the wind.*]

Gerund phrases function as nouns.

> *Watching skydivers* makes me anxious. [Gerund phrase as sentence sub-
> ject.]

Infinitive phrases function as nouns, adjectives, and adverbs.

> I wanted *to win the prize.* [Infinitive phrase as noun object of the verb
> *wanted*. The infinitive *to win* has an object of its own, *the prize.*]
> The team lost its will *to finish the season.* [Infinitive phrase as adjective
> modifying *will*. The infinitive *to finish* has an object, *season.*]
> Andy worked *to overcome his handicap.* [Infinitive phrase as adverb
> modifying *worked*. The infinitive *to overcome* has an object, *handi-
> cap.*]

We urged *him to run for office.* [Infinitive phrase as noun object of *urged.* The infinitive *to run* has a subject, *him,* in the objective case (see 6f) and is modified by the prepositional phrase *for office.*]

3 | Using absolute phrases

An **absolute phrase** consists usually of a noun or pronoun and a participle. Unlike participial phrases, absolute phrases contain a subject and do not relate specifically to any word in the rest of the sentence.

PARTICIPIAL PHRASE   Forgetting the warning, we plunged into the woods.

ABSOLUTE PHRASE   The warning forgotten, we plunged into the woods.

The participle is often omitted from an absolute phrase when it is some form of *to be:*

Its body (*being*) *crushed,* the car was ruined.

Identifying prepositional phrases

In the sentences below, underline each prepositional phrase and fill in the blank to the right with the part of speech that the phrase functions as, adjective (*adj.*), adverb (*adv.*), or noun (*n.*).

Example: The fence post was embedded <u>in cement</u>.   *adv.* _____

1. Economists seem inconsistent in the way they use terms. _____

2. Against the tide is the way she prefers. _____

3. The dog can perform tricks with its tail. _____

4. The pup looked eagerly into the dish. _____

5. The zoo bought six alligators from a dealer. _____

6. The doors close after six o'clock. _____

7. The food in the dish had spoiled. _____

8. She enrolled in the course yesterday. _____

9. Only five points separated the winner from the loser. _____

10. A trophy was awarded for the best play. _____

11. The difficulty of negotiation is often underestimated. _____

12. In the winter the courts are closed. _____

13. We plan a tour of the cathedrals. _____

14. After dinner we skated for an hour. _____

15. Bruce was disqualified by the referee. _____

16. We did not attend the debate between Mailer and Vidal. _____

17. He could not understand the instructions for the clock. ⎯⎯⎯⎯⎯⎯

18. Through the mountain runs a tunnel. ⎯⎯⎯⎯⎯⎯

19. Typing can be a welcome relief from studying. ⎯⎯⎯⎯⎯⎯

gr

5

20. Included among the guests were two African students. ⎯⎯⎯⎯⎯⎯

Identifying verbals and verbal phrases

In the sentences below, underline each verbal or verbal phrase. (Note that some sentences contain more than one verbal.) Then fill the blank to the right with the part of speech each verbal or verbal phrase functions as—adjective (*adj.*), adverb (*adv.*), or noun (*n.*). If two blanks are given, fill them in the order of the verbals or verbal phrases in the sentence.

Example: A lack of <u>understanding</u> caused <u>her to fail.</u>   *n., n.*

1. To go to his class is to suffer an hour of tedium.   _____

   _____

2. Closed for the season, the camp seemed strangely empty.   _____

3. I never go to flea markets because bargaining for the best   _____
   price makes me uncomfortable.

4. After selling his last picture, the painter closed his stand.   _____

5. Before finishing dinner, we got into an argument.   _____

6. To adjust the voltage, turn the dial clockwise.   _____

7. The runner collapsed exhausted, too weak to move him-   _____
   self off the track.   _____

8. Listening carefully, I could just hear the voice inside tell   _____
   me to open the door.   _____

9. Fishing came naturally to the cub.   _____

10. She taught me that dancing adds spirit to life.   _____

11. Swimming is a useful skill as well as good exercise.   _____

12. At the gate the car halted, flashing its lights.   _____

13. A refreshing voyage changed her desire to find a new job. ———————

14. We hoped to win the game but knew our chances were ———————
slim. ———————

15. To experience Albanian cuisine is disappointing. ———————

———————

16. Crying, the child backed away from the clown. ———————

17. Karen thought raking leaves was a job for Ben. ———————

18. Robert Burns's poems, written in dialect, are the contin- ———————
uing pride of Scotland. ———————

19. Bandaged beyond recognition and mumbling incoher- ———————
ently, the patient was a pathetic sight. ———————

20. Though she objected constantly to my dating, my mother ———————
never ordered me to stay home. ———————

4 | Using subordinate clauses

A **clause** is a group of related words that contains both a subject and a predicate. A **main**, or **independent, clause** forms a sentence and makes a complete statement by itself. A **subordinate**, or **dependent, clause,** like a phrase, functions as a single part of speech and cannot stand alone as a sentence.

MAIN CLAUSE *The waves washed over their houses.*

SUBORDINATE CLAUSE *When the waves washed over their houses,* the people fled.

Subordinate clauses are connected to main clauses by subordinating conjunctions or relative pronouns. **Subordinating conjunctions** never change form. Some common ones are the following:

after	even if	since	until
although	even though	so that	when
as	if	than	whenever
as if	in order that	that	where
as though	once	though	wherever
because	rather than	unless	while
before			

The **relative pronouns** are listed below. Notice that *who* and *whoever* sometimes change form depending on how they function in their own clauses (see 6g).

which	what	who (whose, whom)
whichever	whatever	whoever (whomever)
that		

Subordinate clauses can function as either adjectives, adverbs, or nouns.

> She longed to return to the house *that she had grown up in.* [Adjective clause modifying *house*.]
> People *who can remain calm in emergencies* are well suited for medical careers. [Adjective clause modifying *people*.]
> Children should start reading *whenever they are ready.* [Adverb clause modifying *start*.]
> *As he was bowing to the audience,* the conductor fell forward. [Adverb clause modifying *fell*.]
> We all guessed *how the movie would end.* [Noun clause as object of *guessed.* Compare: *We all guessed the outcome.*]
> *Whoever destroyed the car* will be punished. [Noun clause as subject of sentence. Compare: *Jack will be punished.*]

Some subordinate clauses, called **elliptical clauses,** omit the relative pronoun *that*, *which*, or *who* or omit the predicate from the second half of a comparison, but their meaning is still clear from the context.

> I knew *(that) she meant me.*
> Monkeys are not as intelligent *as apes (are).*

Some elliptical clauses omit other elements:

> When *(I am)* in Paris, I will visit Andrew.

5 | Using appositives

An **appositive** is usually a noun or a word group functioning as a noun that follows and renames other nouns or word groups and could stand in their place.

gr

5

> The Edsel, *Ford's biggest commercial failure*, is now a classic car.
> Bob Hope and Milton Berle, *two veterans of vaudeville*, were active performers for years.

Compare:

> Ford's biggest commercial failure is now a classic car.
> Two veterans of vaudeville were active performers for years.

Identifying phrases and clauses

Identify each word group below as a phrase (*phr.*) or a clause (*cl.*) by writing the appropriate abbreviation in the blank to the right. In each clause, underline the subject once and the predicate twice.

Example: because <u>he</u> <u>was sick</u>   _____*cl.*_____

1. banned for a week from the restaurant   _____

2. the Spanish having arrived first   _____

3. from soup to nuts   _____

4. because of a flat tire   _____

5. under the tree was a book   _____

6. during the last quarter   _____

7. men in the professional ranks   _____

8. lack of understanding   _____

9. asked a question   _____

10. when the crystal broke   _____

11. who she was   _____

12. that long bench   _____

13. above the ridge   _____

14. if you save your money   _____

15. the game was lost   _____

16. why the game was poorly played   _____

17. the broken watchband   _____

18. a concise history being given   _____

19. desiring only understanding   _____

20. whoever calls my name   _____

21. money is all   _____

22. the imported tea   _____

23. while coming to a stop   _____

24. if the lights grow bright   _____

25. the owner of a Samoyed   _____

26. in a terrible, hard rain and strong wind   _____

27. the box weighed 9 kilograms   _____

28. his most recent discovery   _____

29. living in Greenwich Village   _____

30. when the lid is on the jar   _____

Identifying main and subordinate clauses

In each sentence below, underline main clauses once and subordinate clauses twice. (Note that a subordinate clause may sometimes be an indispensable element of a main clause.) For subordinate clauses, fill the blank on the right with the part of speech the clause functions as—adjective (*adj.*), adverb (*adv.*), or noun (*n.*)

Example: I understand why I made an error.   *n.*

1. The woman whom the police arrested was charged with   _____
   arson.

2. The cat's favorite hiding place, under the bed, is a quiet   _____
   spot that is also cool and dark.

3. Although our television was broken, we still heard the   _____
   game on the radio.

4. A slum that is rat-infested should receive a municipal   _____
   subsidy.

5. Oliver called the secretary, who offered him a job.   _____

6. This version of "Stardust," which is fast and slick, would   _____
   be good to dance to.

7. After the robber grabbed the cash, the manager rang the   _____
   alarm.

8. The waiter sneaked out while the after-dinner lull continued.   _____

9. The family lived in an apartment that had no fire alarm   _____
   and no extinguisher.

10. The building was erected to house an insurance com-   _____
    pany; however, when it burned down, it was uninsured.

11. Apples, which are inexpensive, are good for your gums.   _____

12. He sent her money so that she could come home, but she _____ spent it on a lavish dinner for herself and her roommate.

13. She got the best lawyer that she could find. _____

14. Frustration arose near the end of the summer program _____ when funds were cut.

15. We left on the fishing trip when the sun came up; the _____ fish, however, were already too alert to be caught.

16. More people would have survived if the waters had been _____ calmer.

17. To be eligible for student rates, you must show an iden- _____ tification card, which you do not have.

18. The owner of the College Restaurant puts Johnson grass _____ seed in the hamburger that he serves.

19. I was surprised, after reading about problems with the _____ mail, when the parcel arrived with its contents intact.

20. Lack of organization was a characteristic of all the lec- _____ tures that Mr. Donaldson gave.

| Using subordinate clauses EXERCISE 5-10

In the sentences below, underline each subordinate clause and circle each subordinating word (subordinating conjunction or relative pronoun). Then compose a complete sentence of your own that uses the same subordinating word.

Example: Elephants never forget (how) a trainer treats them.

I learned how fine fighters are trained.

1. He became a submarine commander soon after he graduated.

2. Her crying did not stop until the ceremony ended.

3. Driving a motorcycle requires a special license that you can obtain at the registry.

4. Adam jogged through the park while his cat loped behind.

5. Pedestrians are increasingly menaced by bicycles, which should be licensed like cars.

6. If the dog is not confined, it will chew on the saplings.

7. I would have passed if I had understood the question.

8. Whatever money remains goes to the children's home.

9. We will put off our trip to West Virginia until the huckleberries are ripe.

10. I knew that I should not have eaten so much.

11. The tenants, who complained regularly, found no remedy.

12. The council decided against establishing a dress code because so many students protested.

13. People who complain all the time never have time to smile.

14. The surprise is that the governor was not convicted sooner.

15. The stereo actually sold for a higher price than the store advertised.

5d | Compounding words, phrases, and clauses

Single words and groups of words may be combined to link related parts of speech or ideas and to avoid repetition. In a **compound subject,** two or more nouns or word groups join in a single subject. In a **compound object,** two or more nouns or word groups join in a single object.

> *John* and *the boy* from Nebraska played *tennis* and *darts*.

In a **compound complement,** two or more nouns, adjectives, or word groups join in a single subject or object complement.

> After exercising, I feel *healthy, strong,* and *confident.*
> The critic called the movie *thoughtless* and *dull.*

In a **compound predicate,** two or more sentence predicates or verbs join in a single predicate.

> The firecracker *sizzled* and then *exploded.*

In a **compound sentence,** two or more main clauses join in a single sentence.

> *I hoped for a good grade,* and *I got what I wanted.*

1 | Using coordinating conjunctions and correlative conjunctions

The word *and,* which links the parts of the compound constructions above, is a **coordinating conjunction.** The other coordinating conjunctions are *but, or, nor,* and sometimes *for, so,* and *yet.* As in the sentences above, these conjunctions connect words or word groups of the same kind: nouns, verbs, adjectives, adverbs, phrases, clauses, or whole sentences.

Both . . . and, not . . . but, either . . . or, and *neither . . . nor* form **correlative conjunctions.**

> *Both* John *and* the boy from Nebraska were defeated.
> After exercising, I feel *not only* healthy and strong *but also* confident.
> *Either* you *or* I will have to go.
> *Neither* sizzling *nor* exploding, the firecracker seemed to be a dud.

2 | Using conjunctive adverbs

Conjunctive adverbs are connecting words that join *only* main clauses or whole sentences — not single words, phrases, or subordinate clauses. Common conjunctive adverbs are the following:

accordingly	furthermore	moreover	similarly
also	hence	namely	still
anyway	however	next	then
besides	incidentally	nevertheless	thereafter
certainly	indeed	nonetheless	therefore
consequently	instead	now	thus
finally	likewise	otherwise	undoubtedly
further	meanwhile		

Like coordinating conjunctions, conjunctive adverbs join or relate main clauses and sentences. But unlike coordinating conjunctions, conjunctive adverbs also modify the clauses they appear in. And unlike subordinating conjunctions, conjunctive adverbs connect equal rather than unequal clauses.

> Mr. Androni talks of nothing but himself; *however,* he is one of the most interesting people I know.
>
> The season's last game was canceled. *Nonetheless,* we won the championship.

Conjunctive adverbs are unlike coordinating and subordinating conjunctions in another way: They can move around within their clauses (see also Chapter 11).

> Lee decided against taking French; *instead,* she opted for Russian.
>
> Lee decided against taking French; she opted, *instead,* for Russian.

Note that a conjunctive adverb joining main clauses in a single sentence is preceded by a semicolon and followed by a comma.

Identifying compound constructions

EXERCISE **5-11**

In the sentences below, underline each coordinating or correlative conjunction once and each conjunctive adverb twice. Identify whether each coordinating and correlative conjunction joins a compound subject (*subj.*), object (*obj.*), predicate (*pred.*), complement (*comp.*), or sentence (*sent.*) by filling the blank to the right with the appropriate abbreviation.

Example: He failed the test; however, he later studied hard and passed the course. *pred.*

1. She turned the dial clockwise, and the dial jammed. _____

2. Jagger wore a loosely fitting pink suit and yellow shoes. _____

3. The celebration was held at the disco and lasted until midnight. _____

4. Not only those who smoke but also those who are anemic should stay away from scuba diving. _____

5. She was paralyzed by the stroke, but she continued to be cheerful. _____

6. The last ticket was sold yesterday; therefore, you and I will not be able to attend. _____

7. Making cheese requires patience, or that's what I am told. _____

8. The wine had soured; hence, an additional order was necessary. _____

9. The collection includes coins from thirty countries, yet none of the coins is very valuable. _____

10. Spray and bits of dirt flew at him from passing trucks; nonetheless, he would not leave his disabled car. _____

11. The tablet should be crushed and mixed with water. _____

12. The train is both expensive and unreliable. ———————

13. The paint job will last one or two years. ———————

14. The animal shelter neither fed the creatures nor gave ———————
them exercise.

15. His first wife and his daughter ran the business. ———————

16. The party went on beyond midnight; consequently, we ———————
postponed cleaning and washing up until the next day.

17. Three of the five dollars were counterfeit, but I kept them ———————
for souvenirs.

18. After seeing the movie once, I refused to go again; I did ———————
read the book and the screenplay, however.

19. Neither the cotton nor the rayon will be suitable. ———————

20. The last album brought him fame; however, he still is ———————
not wealthy.

5e | Changing the usual order of the sentence

The basic arrangement in the sentences examined so far, subject and then predicate, may be varied to form other sentence patterns.

1 | Forming questions

We form questions by inverting the normal subject-verb order or by using a question word like *who, what, when, where, which.*

> Is the movie interesting?
> Who is in it?

2 | Forming commands

To form commands, we simply omit the sentence subject, *you.*

> Turn to the diagram on the next page.
> Don't expect much from that course.

3 | Writing passive sentences

When a sentence uses a transitive verb — a verb that takes an object — we can interchange the subject's and the object's positions by using the verb's **passive voice** rather than its **active voice** (see Chapter 7). In the passive sentence that results, the subject of the verb does not act but is acted upon.

> Charleen gave the award. [Active voice.]
> The award was given by Charleen. [Passive voice: *award*, the original object, becomes the sentence subject; and the original subject, *Charleen*, joins the predicate as part of a prepositional phrase modifying the verb.]

The passive form of the verb consists of some form of *be* plus the past participle of the verb (*was given, is acted upon*). (See 18d for a discussion of the overuse of passive sentences.)

4 | Writing sentences with postponed subjects

In some sentences the normal subject-predicate order is inverted for emphasis:

> Out the door ran Harry.

Other sentences, called **expletive constructions,** begin with *it* or *there* followed by the verb, a form of *be.* In such sentences the actual subject follows the verb.

> *There are* fifty-seven varieties. [*Varieties* is the subject.]
> *It is* unclear how they got there. [*How they got there* is the subject.]

Expletive constructions can provide variety in sentences, but they are unemphatic and should be used sparingly. (See 18e.)

5f | Classifying sentences

We can classify sentences on the basis of how many main clauses they contain and whether they contain subordinate clauses.

1 | Writing simple sentences

A **simple sentence** contains a single main clause, although it may have many modifying phrases attached to it.

> He cleaned the typewriter.
> Last June Mr. Snapp cleaned Mr. Rollo's typewriter for a small fee.

2 | Writing compound sentences

A **compound sentence** contains two or more main clauses joined by a comma and a coordinating conjunction or by a semicolon.

> Mr. Snapp cleaned Mr. Rollo's typewriter, and he removed eight candy bar wrappers from it.
> Mr. Snapp cleaned Mr. Rollo's typewriter; he removed eight candy bar wrappers from it.

3 | Writing complex sentences

A **complex sentence** contains a main clause and one or more subordinate clauses.

> After she paid the telephone bill, Paula had no money left to buy meat for dinner. [The first half of the sentence is the subordinate clause; the second half is the main clause.]

4 | Writing compound-complex sentences

A **compound-complex sentence** contains two or more main clauses and one or more subordinate clauses.

> Rodney ate chicken soup for dinner, and he felt much better than he had felt when he ate tamales. [Main clause; main clause; subordinate clause; subordinate clause.]
> After he lost the Ping-Pong game, Kendall tried his luck at Scrabble, but Merry beat him at that, too. [Subordinate clause; main clause; main clause.]

Writing compound, complex, and compound-complex sentences

EXERCISE **5-12**

The passages below are made up of simple sentences (one main clause each). Combine each group of simple sentences into the kind of sentence specified in parentheses: compound (two or more main clauses), complex (one main clause and one or more subordinate clauses), or compound-complex (two or more main clauses and one or more subordinate clauses). Use a variety of appropriate connecting words in your answers. Most items have more than one possible answer.

Example: (*Complex*) The lake was cold. It was wide. We could not swim across it.

Although the lake was cold and wide, we could swim across it.

1. (*Compound*) The camp offered riflery. It did not offer riding. It did not offer swimming.

2. (*Complex*) Some teachers grade on a curve. These teachers are fairer than those who do not.

3. (*Compound-complex*) Seven hundred sailboats entered the race. The race was 125 miles long. Almost a hundred boats failed to finish.

4. (*Complex*) All the union members went on a strike. They wanted to protest a lack of safety regulations. All of them were fired.

5. (*Compound*) Falling and freezing are dangers for mountain climbers. Heat exhaustion and dehydration are greater perils for mountain climbers.

6. (*Compound-complex*) The road commissioner owned a building supply company. His company sold materials to the government. He was fired for conflict of interest.

7. (*Compound*) The movie script was generally well written. Only one character had an unconvincing personality change.

8. (*Complex*) The motel had no swimming pool. That made us decide to go elsewhere.

9. (*Compound-complex*) Before 1967 the city seemed to have no profile. A skyscraper was built in that year. Now the skyscraper dominates the city's horizon.

10. (*Complex*) The *Glomar Explorer* was built to raise a wrecked submarine. Later it was used for oceanic research.

6 Case of Nouns and Pronouns

Self-test

Circle the correct pronouns in the following sentences.

Example: (Us, *We*) Americans often neglect our right to vote.

1. My roommate and (*I, me*) became close friends.
2. The meal was prepared especially for (*they, them*) and (*we, us*).
3. For (*we, us*) students, attendance is required.
4. There is a problem between you and (*I, me*).
5. The river rose after the Browns and (*us, we*) had safely crossed.
6. The audience did not know (*who, whom*) to applaud.
7. Either (*he, him*) or (*I, me*) will wait for the shuttle.
8. The music drew Sylvia and (*I, me*) closer.
9. The substitutes were (*her, she*) and (*I, me*).
10. Both (*he, him*) and (*her, she*) were admitted to the hospital.

Case is the form of a noun or pronoun that shows its function in a sentence. The pronouns *I, we, he, she, they,* and *who* have different forms for three cases: the **subjective,** used when the pronoun is the subject of a sentence or clause or a subject complement; the **objective,** used when the pronoun is either an object or the subject of an infinitive; and the **possessive,** used before nouns and gerunds and sometimes alone to show ownership or possession. The following list shows the case forms of the personal and relative pronouns.

PERSONAL PRONOUNS	SUBJECTIVE	OBJECTIVE	POSSESSIVE
Singular			
First person	I	me	my, mine
Second person	you	you	your, yours
Third person	he, she, it	him, her, it	his, her, hers, its

PERSONAL PRONOUNS	SUBJECTIVE	OBJECTIVE	POSSESSIVE
Plural			
First person	we	us	our, ours
Second person	you	you	your, yours
Third person	they	them	their, theirs
RELATIVE PRONOUNS	who	whom	whose
	which	which	whose
	that	that	—

All other pronouns and nouns have only a possessive case (*woman's, everybody's*) and a plain case (the dictionary form) that serves all other functions (*woman, everybody*). (See 23a for the use of the apostrophe in possessive forms of nouns and of pronouns other than personal and relative pronouns. Personal and relative pronouns never take an apostrophe.)

6a Use the subjective case for all parts of compound subjects and for subject complements.

SUBJECT *Andrea* and *I* came late.

SUBJECT COMPLEMENT The guilty person is *I*.

In speech we often use objective pronouns as subject complements in expressions like *It's me* or *It's him*, but these forms are not acceptable in formal, written English.

6b Use the objective case for all parts of compound objects.

OBJECT OF VERB We provided Josie and *him* with dry clothes.

OBJECT OF PREPOSITION The party was for Chuck and *me*.

6c Use the appropriate case form when the plural pronouns *we* and *us* occur with a noun.

The coach threw a party for *us* players. [*Players* is the object of the preposition *for.*]
We players also held a party of our own. [*Players* is the subject of the sentence.]

6d In appositives the case of a pronoun depends on the function of the word it describes or identifies.

Appositives rename nouns (see 5c-5).

Two victims, Homer and *I*, sued the company. [The appositive renames *victims*, the sentence subject.]
The company was sued by two victims, Homer and *me*. [The appositive renames *victims*, the object of a preposition.]

ca

6

6e | **The case of a pronoun after *than* or *as* expressing a comparison depends on the meaning.**

The case of a pronoun after *than* or *as* in comparisons is what it would be if the clause were completed.

> Axel likes pizza more than *I* (like pizza).
> Axel likes pizza more than (he likes) *me*.
> Axel likes pizza as much as *I* (like pizza).
> Axel likes pizza as much as (he likes) *me*.

6f | **Use the objective case for pronouns that are subjects or objects of infinitives.**

> We want *him* to learn. [Subject of infinitive.]
> To win *her* over requires patience. [Object of infinitive.]

6g | **The form of the pronoun *who* depends on its function in its clause.**

1 | **At the beginning of questions use *who* if the question is about a subject, *whom* if it is about an object.**

> *Who* ate the macaroni? [Question about a subject. Compare *He ate the macaroni.*]
> *Whom* are you kidding? [Question about an object. Compare *You are kidding them.*]

2 | **In subordinate clauses use *who* and *whoever* for all subjects, *whom* and *whomever* for all objects.**

> I do not know *who* can help me. [*Who* is the subject of the clause. Compare *She can help me.*]
> *Whoever* wants the dog can have it. [*Whoever* is the subject of the clause. Compare *He wants the dog.*]
> I know *whom* he gave the keys to. [*Whom* is the object of the preposition *to*. Compare *He gave the keys to him.*]
> I do not know *whom* to criticize. [*Whom* is the object of *criticize*. Compare *I criticize him.*]
> She will hire *whomever* she chooses. [*Whomever* is the object of *chooses*. Compare *She chooses him.*]

6h | **Ordinarily, use the possessive form of a pronoun or noun immediately before a gerund.**

A **gerund** is the *-ing* form of a verb used as a noun (see 5c-2).

> We couldn't listen to *his* singing.
> *Oxnard College's* running ruined our game plan.

Using the appropriate pronoun case

Circle the correct pronoun in each pair below.

Example: (Who, (Whom)) did the dean reprimand?

1. (*His, Him*) feeding the animals was illegal.
2. The sale was less than profitable for (*we, us*).
3. The drop in circulation left (*they, them*) confused.
4. (*We, Us*) Americans should use all the imported fuel we can get.
5. We appreciate (*you, your*) taking the job.
6. Why was (*he, him*) given the blame?
7. The traffic congestion delayed (*she, her*) and (*I, me*).
8. Ben and Bruce sold more tickets than Karen and (*I, me*).
9. The winners were really (*we, us*) and (*they, them*).
10. (*Who, Whom*) will be the one responsible for bringing the food?
11. The cameras were damaged by Linda and (*her, she*).
12. We wondered (*who, whom*) to give the assignment to.
13. To (*who, whom*) should I give the book?
14. Jamie and (*he, him*) caught the last flight.
15. The tickets are for (*whoever, whomever*) wants them.
16. The award will go to (*whoever, whomever*) prepares the best essay.
17. (*His, Him*) installing deadbolt locks deterred the burglar.
18. You and (*I, me*) should get tickets for the play.
19. One representative, either Kathy or (*I, me*), will go to the meeting.
20. We asked that (*he, him*) represent the club.
21. (*Whoever, whomever*) paid for the item forgot to claim it.
22. The tuition was more than (*we, us*) students could afford.
23. We fight harder than (*they, them*).

24. What are (*he, him*) and Jones doing here at this hour?

25. (*Who, Whom*) expected so much rain?

26. The referee had to break up a fight between (*he, him*) and (*I, me*).

27. The Lamberts and Merediths gave (*he, him*) and (*I, me*) a farewell party.

28. (*Who, Whom*) is the ecology course designed for?

29. I expected (*she, her*) to open the gifts earlier.

30. My brother is taller than (*I, me*).

Using the appropriate pronoun case

EXERCISE **6-2**

ca

6

Cross out any incorrect case form in the sentences below and write the correct form or forms on the blank to the right. If a sentence is correct as given, write *OK* on the blank.

Example: Wendy will date ~~whoe~~ver she likes.   *whomever*

1. The handmade ornament is one donated by her and I.   _____

2. I explained to the policeman, "I'd appreciate you giving   _____
   me just a warning."

3. I am not as smart as him, but my grades are just as   _____
   good.

4. We hoped that you could tell us who this car belongs to.   _____

5. Whom will the new dean be?   _____

6. Elizabeth and her were born the same day.   _____

7. It must have been them who left the books.   _____

8. When my mother sees we children watching television,   _____
   she tries to start a conversation.

9. The dispute was between he and the clerk.   _____

10. Show the map to whomever plans to drive.   _____

11. Me and my brother bought a tape deck.   _____

12. Whom can we count on to work at the hospital?   _____

13. Ed is much more willing to drive a truck than me.   _____

14. Us students all get discounts.   _____

15. Hardly any love remains between she and I.   _____

16. John lifts weights every day, so he is stronger than either   —————
Larry or me.

17. Chris tells old jokes to whoever will listen.   —————

18. After practice, the batboy brought Carl and I cold drinks.   —————

19. Dave wanted to know whom to ask about organic gar-   —————
dening.

20. The two latecomers, Judith and I, agreed on who would   —————
do the work.

21. She and the teacher disagreed over her grade.   —————

22. The police should protect you and I from peeping Marys   —————
as well as from peeping Toms.

23. Us freshmen no longer are subject to hazing from   —————
sophomores.

24. Between you and me, the play was a flop.   —————

25. We expected him to win, not Delgado.   —————

|*Pronoun case: Review*   exercise **6-3**

In the following paragraph, cross out any errors in pronoun case. Then write the correct case form above the error.

Oliver and Frank are not as clever as me in class, but they show

ingenuity in playing jokes on each other. One night in the dormitory,

Oliver decided to make trouble for Frank, who he had just argued with.

Oliver dribbled water from a bucket in front of Frank's door and then

dumped the rest of the water down the stairs. Frank, who had water

spots in front of his door, got blamed, and only Oliver and me ever knew

who was really responsible. Another time, Oliver persuaded a girl to ask

Frank to meet she and another girl at a restaurant after the football game.

Frank waited an hour for the girls, who never showed up. More recently,

Frank offered to buy Oliver's lunch. Before the check came, Frank said he was going to the restroom and then slipped out the door, sticking

Oliver with the check for both he and Frank. I do not know whom would

ca

6

believe that the two are very good friends.

7 | Verb Forms, Tense, Mood, and Voice

Self-test

Circle the correct verb form in each of the following sentences.

Example: The doctor had not (*took,* (*taken*)) too long.

1. We (*swam, swum*) the length of the pool.
2. A (*broke, broken*) chair leaned in the corner.
3. I would buy tickets if I (*was, were*) you.
4. They were surprised when the new guest (*shows, showed*) up.
5. The milk had (*set, sat*) on the table all night.
6. He would be unhappy if the test score (*was, were*) low.
7. She was (*lying, laying*) in the sun by the pool.
8. The phone had (*rang, rung*) ten times that morning.
9. The race had (*last, lasted*) all afternoon.
10. We were (*mistook, mistaken*) for intruders.

VERB FORMS

Verbs have three main forms, or **principal parts.** The first principal part is the **infinitive** form, the dictionary form of the verb. We use the infinitive form when the verb's action occurs in the **present** and the subject is a plural noun or the pronouns *I, we, you,* or *they: I go, you swim.* (For other subjects the infinitive adds *-s* or *-es* to indicate present time: *he goes, she swims.*) The **past tense,** used with all subjects, indicates action that occurred in the past: *dogs scratched, I passed, you swam.* The **past participle,** usually the same form as the past tense, combines with *have, has,* or *had: dogs have scratched, I have passed, you have swum.*

Verbs like *scratch* and *pass* that form their past tense and past participle by adding *-d* or *-ed* to the infinitive are called **regular.** Verbs like *swim* that form their past tense and past participle in some other way are called **irregular.**

	INFINITIVE	PAST TENSE	PAST PARTICIPLE
REGULAR VERBS	open	opened	opened
	close	closed	closed
IRREGULAR VERBS	bring	brought	brought
	take	took	taken

The irregular verbs *be* and *have* are unusual also in the way they indicate present time. *Be* changes to *am* with the subject *I;* to *are* with *you* and all plural subjects; and to *is* with *he, she, it,* and all other singular subjects. *Have* changes to *has* for *he, she, it,* and other singular subjects except *I* and *you.*

All verbs form a **present participle** by adding *-ing* to their infinitive form: *scratching, swimming.* This form may serve as a modifier or combine with a helping verb to form a verb phrase, but it cannot stand alone as the main verb in a sentence.

Auxiliary, or **helping, verbs** combine with other verbs in verb phrases to indicate time and other meanings. The common helping verbs are the forms of *have, do,* and *be* and the auxiliaries *shall, will, can, could, may, might, must, ought, should,* and *would.*

> We *did expect* to go.
> They *were squashed.*
> The mayor *should come.*
> The prize *will have been awarded.*

7a | Use the correct form of irregular verbs.

Because irregular verbs do not form their past tense and participle predictably, by adding *-d* or *-ed* to the infinitive, you must memorize their principal parts or look them up in a dictionary. The list below contains sixty-nine of the nearly two hundred irregular verbs in English.

INFINITIVE	PAST TENSE	PAST PARTICIPLE
arise	arose	arisen
become	became	become
begin	began	begun
bid	bid	bid
bite	bit	bitten, bit
blow	blew	blown
break	broke	broken
bring	brought	brought
burst	burst	burst
buy	bought	bought
catch	caught	caught
choose	chose	chosen
come	came	come
cut	cut	cut

INFINITIVE	PAST TENSE	PAST PARTICIPLE
dive	dived, dove	dived
do	did	done
draw	drew	drawn
dream	dreamed, dreamt	dreamed, dreamt
drink	drank	drunk
drive	drove	driven
eat	ate	eaten
fall	fell	fallen
find	found	found
flee	fled	fled
fly	flew	flown
forget	forgot	forgotten, forgot
freeze	froze	frozen
get	got	got, gotten
give	gave	given
go	went	gone
grow	grew	grown
hang	hung, hanged (executed)	hung, hanged
hear	heard	heard
hide	hid	hidden
hold	held	held
keep	kept	kept
know	knew	known
lay	laid	laid
lead	led	led
leave	left	left
let	let	let
lie	lay	lain
lose	lost	lost
pay	paid	paid
prove	proved	proved, proven
ride	rode	ridden
ring	rang	rung
rise	rose	risen
run	ran	run
say	said	said
see	saw	seen
set	set	set
shake	shook	shaken
sing	sang, sung	sung
sink	sank, sunk	sunk
sit	sat	sat
slide	slid	slid
speak	spoke	spoken
spring	sprang, sprung	sprung
stand	stood	stood
steal	stole	stolen
swim	swam	swum

INFINITIVE	PAST TENSE	PAST PARTICIPLE
take	took	taken
tear	tore	torn
throw	threw	thrown
wear	wore	worn
wind	wound	wound
write	wrote	written

7b | Distinguish between *sit* and *set* and between *lie* and *lay*.

The principal parts of *sit* and *set* and of *lie* and *lay*, shown in the preceding list, are often confused. *Sit* and *lie* are **intransitive verbs,** meaning they cannot take objects. *Sit* means "be seated"; *lie* means "recline." *Set* and *lay* are **transitive verbs,** meaning they usually take objects. Both words mean "put" or "place" something.

> They *sit* (or *sat* or *have sat*) in class like zombies. [No object.]
> We *set* (or *have set*) the pole against the wall. [Object: *pole*.]
> I *lie* (or *lay* or *have lain*) awake every night. [No object.]
> Chickens *lay* (or *laid* or *have laid*) eggs every day. [Object: *eggs*.]

7c | Use the *-s* and *-ed* forms of the verb when they are required.

The present-tense verb form *-s* (*asks*) and the past-tense and past-participle form *-ed* (*asked*) are often wrongly omitted in writing because they are not distinctly pronounced in speech. Be especially careful not to omit the ending when the verb's infinitive ends in sounds like *s, sk,* or *g* and when the ending does not add another syllable: *we supposed, she asks, he begged, they used.*

Identifying the principal parts of irregular verbs

Circle the correct form of the verb from each pair in parentheses. On the blanks to the right, fill in the principal parts (infinitive, past tense, past participle) of the correct verb. If necessary, consult a dictionary or the list of irregular verbs on pages 122–24.

Example: I had to ((lie,) *lay*) down.   *lie*   *lay*   *lain*

1. The cold wind (*blowed, blew*) up the alley. _____ _____ _____

2. Jerry had (*wrote, written*) down the directions. _____ _____ _____

3. The professor (*began, beginned*) the class with a joke. _____ _____ _____

4. He had (*ran, run*) the mile in record time. _____ _____ _____

5. That is an album you have not (*heard, heared*). _____ _____ _____

6. She (*drunk, drank*) a six-pack after the game. _____ _____ _____

7. He (*drove, drived*) the golf ball 250 yards. _____ _____ _____

8. She had not (*gave, given*) a minute of her time. _____ _____ _____

9. The problem of boarding the dog had not (*come, came*) up before. _____ _____ _____

10. The book had (*laid, lain*) on the shelf for many years. _____ _____ _____

11. She (*finded, found*) the gift on her pillow. _____ _____ _____

12. The team had (*swum, swam*) an hour that morning. _____ _____ _____

13. They (*knew, knowed*) that the class was easy. _____ _____ _____

14. The cat (*bitten, bit*) him on the wrist. _____ _____ _____

15. They had (*eat, eaten*) before going out. _____ _____ _____

16. He is (*suppose, supposed*) to arrive Monday. _____ _____ _____

17. Wilson (*bringed, brought*) a guest along. _____ _____ _____

18. The platter (*broke, breaked*) when it hit the floor. _____ _____ _____

19. They (*flew, flied*) in from Pittsburgh. _____ _____ _____

20. The patient had (*went, gone*) from the examination room. _____ _____ _____

21. The balloon had (*burst, bursted*) against the power lines. _____ _____ _____

22. The skunk has (*become, became*) Denny's favorite pet. _____ _____ _____

23. The attorney (*proved, proven*) his case. _____ _____ _____

24. No problem with cheating has (*arised, arisen*). _____ _____ _____

25. Someone has (*sat, set*) on Martha's lava lamp. _____ _____ _____

26. May and Raymond have (*took, taken*) the train. _____ _____ _____

27. The driver (*swore, sweared*) at the pedestrian. _____ _____ _____

28. He managed to (*shake, shook*) loose from the dog's grip. _____ _____ _____

29. We (*seen, saw*) the accident on our way home. _____ _____ _____

30. The shortstop (*throwed, threw*) him out. _____ _____ _____

Using the -s and -ed forms of verbs

EXERCISE **7-2**

vb

7

Cross out any verb form in the sentences below that omits a necessary -s or -ed ending, and write the correct form on the blank to the right. If the sentence is correct as given, write *OK* on the blank to the right.

Example: The stereo has been ~~fix~~   *fixed* _____

1. Lou becomes upset when he see Art.   _____

2. I am prejudice against cats.   _____

3. The punch he made tastes sour.   _____

4. Night games raise the school electric bill last year.   _____

5. The only silly question is the unask question.   _____

6. The old Plymouth last 100,000 miles.   _____

7. Was the owner ask if he would sell?   _____

8. I do not know what company first devise computer chips.   _____

9. She tries several techniques.   _____

10. A bruise palm prevented me from playing handball.   _____

11. That cheerful face mask a troubled person.   _____

12. A blind man tune the piano.   _____

13. If you want the tinted glass, it cost fifty dollars extra.   _____

14. The store owner lost an undetermine amount of cash.   _____

15. The mayor discovered he was not well like.   _____

16. Rent hikes raise the cost of living.   _____

17. Colleen and Brad dance all evening. _____

18. The coach list the rules yesterday. _____

19. Over the years the pages had yellow. _____

vb

7

20. A broken pipe cause destruction in the basement last _____ week.

21. A sleeping bag fill with feathers is quite warm. _____

22. She ran in and lock the door. _____

23. The couple finally move out of the house yesterday. _____

24. We were suppose to pay the bill. _____

25. He beg her every day to return. _____

TENSE

Tense is the quality of a verb that shows the time of its action. The **simple tenses** indicate present, past, and future. The **perfect tenses** indicate action that was or will be completed before another action or time.

SIMPLE TENSES	REGULAR VERB	IRREGULAR VERB
Present	I *use*	I *run*
Past	I *used*	I *ran*
Future	I *will use*	I *will run*

PERFECT TENSES		
Present perfect	I *have used*	I *have run*
Past perfect	I *had used*	I *had run*
Future perfect	I *will have used*	I *will have run*

The **progressive form,** or **progressive tense,** always uses the *-ing* form of the verb and indicates action continuing in the time shown; for example, *We are waiting* (present progressive), *They were stalling* (past progressive), *Others have been fleeing* (present perfect progressive).

7d | Observe the special uses of the present tense and the uses of the perfect tenses.

The present tense indicates action occurring in the present. But it can also describe habitual or recurring action (*I vote for Democrats*), state a general truth (*Oak is a hardwood*), discuss the content of a book, movie, or other creative work (*Michael Corleone is the godfather's favorite son*), or indicate future time (*We leave for Europe on the twelfth*).

The perfect tenses indicate an action completed before another action or time: *The bus had already left; By then we will have finished.* The present perfect tense also indicates action begun in the past and continued into the present: *The sun has shone every day.*

7e | Use the appropriate sequence of verb tenses.

The **sequence of tenses** is the relation between the verb in a main clause and the verbs or verbals in a subordinate clause or verbal phrase. As the following sentence indicates, the verbs in the different constructions do not have to have identical tenses to be in sequence.

Glenna *will explain* why she *is* so unhappy.

1 | When the verb in a main clause is in any tense except the past or past perfect, the verb in the subordinate clause may be in any tense required by meaning.

He *hopes* that his boss *will give* him a raise. [Present and future.]
I *have sat* through that movie more times than I *care* to admit. [Present perfect and present.]
We *know* that the doctor *meant* well. [Present and past.]

2 When the verb in a main clause is in the past or past perfect tense, the verb in the subordinate clause must also be in the past or past perfect tense.

They *thought* the dog *had spoken.* [Past and past perfect.]
Judith *had* already *called* when I *arrived.* [Past perfect and past.]
After we *posted* announcements, the opening *attracted* a large crowd. [Past and past.]

3 Use a present infinitive to express action at the same time as or later than that of the verb. Use a perfect infinitive to express action earlier than that of the verb.

The **present infinitive** is the infinitive preceded by *to: to kick, to write.* It shows action occurring at the same time as or later than that of the verb.

I *prefer to stay* right here. [Present infinitive *to stay.*]
She *would have liked to join* you. [Present infinitive *to join.*]

The **perfect infinitive** combines *to have* with the verb's past participle: *to have kicked, to have written.* It shows action that occurred earlier than that of the verb.

We now *know* human ancestors *to have existed* millions of years ago. [Perfect infinitive *to have existed.*]
My father *would like to have been* an actor. [Perfect infinitive *to have been.*]

4 Use a present participle to express action at the same time as that of the verb. Use a past participle or a present perfect participle to express action earlier than that of the verb.

Walking in the house, I *greeted* each of my relatives in turn. [Action of present participle *walking* occurs at the same time as that of verb *greeted.*]
Fanned by strong breezes, the fire *swept* through the brush. [Action of past participle *fanned* occurs earlier than that of verb *swept.*]
Having seeped through the walls, the water *left* large orange stains in the wallpaper. [Action of present perfect participle *having seeped* occurs earlier than that of verb *left.*]

Identifying verb tenses

EXERCISE **7-3**

vb

7

Underline each verb in the sentences below and write its tense on the blank to the right. Then rewrite each sentence twice, once in the past tense and once in the past perfect tense.

Example: I have repaired refrigerators.   *present perfect*

   ✓ *I repaired refrigerators.*
   ✓ *I had repaired refrigerators.*

1. Joyce will come early.   _____

2. The salesman travels frequently.   _____

3. We were expecting a large response.   _____

4. Peter is feeling inadequate.   _____

5. Charlie gets bored at parties.   _____

6. The union has terminated the agreement.   _____

7. The science of linguistics is developing.   _____

8. Ethel has a wart on her knee.   _____

9. The radio was playing too loudly.   _____

10. They will have gone by now.   _____

Using the correct sequence of tenses

For each sentence below, cross out any verb or verbal that is not in sequence with the verb in italics, and write the correct form on the blank to the right. If all verbs and verbals in a sentence are in sequence, write *OK* on the blank.

Example: Fred *quit* the game when he ~~starts~~ losing.   *started*

A. 1. We *could have bought* the boat when it is less expensive.   _____

    2. When he wants to dress well, he *wore* his striped sneakers.   _____

    3. Some scientists *believe* the human species to evolve outside Africa.   _____

    4. Exhausted from studying, I *expected* to sleep poorly.   _____

    5. Because the hot sun bleached the plant, it *will* not *bloom.*   _____

    6. As the woman pulled out of her driveway, a jogger *runs* into her car.   _____

    7. Even my friend Steve *thought* that he wants to see our play.   _____

    8. After he misses the dunk shot, we *were* two points behind.   _____

    9. The food *had cooled* when he arrives at the table.   _____

   10. We *expect* too much from them when we have given them so little.   _____

B. 1. I think people who argue for segregation of schools on the basis of states' rights *were* actually prejudiced.   _____

    2. Some churches *canceled* regular services because Christmas falls on a Sunday.   _____

3. She *had untied* the ribbon, and then she screams. _____

4. The phone *had rung* before she had come in the door. _____

5. I *did* not *see* the point of memorizing rules for apostrophes unless I am going to be a professional writer. _____

6. The band *should have refused* to have played in that club. _____

7. The special delivery letter *arrived* the same day he called. _____

8. The storm *prevented* the plane from having arrived at the scheduled time. _____

9. We *had* an hour to catch our plane, which will depart at 6:30. _____

10. I *would like* to have heard one of her lectures. _____

MOOD

The **mood** of a verb indicates the writer's or speaker's attitude toward what he or she is saying. The **indicative mood** states a fact or opinion or asks a question (*The trees are changing color. What makes the colors change?*). The **imperative mood** expresses a command or direction and omits the understood subject *you* (*Turn left at the light*). The **subjunctive mood** expresses a requirement, a desire, a suggestion, or a condition contrary to fact (*We insisted that she come. If she were present, we could finish the job faster*).

7f | Use the subjunctive verb forms appropriately.

The subjunctive mood uses distinctive verb forms. All verbs in the subjunctive use the plain form of the verb for the present tense, regardless of the subject: *They suggested that he step outside. Be* uses *be* (rather than *am, is,* or *are*) for the present tense with all subjects: *The dean requested that we be patient.* The past subjunctive form of *be* is *were* for all subjects: *I wish I were somewhere else.* These subjunctive forms are used in only a few kinds of constructions.

1 | Use the subjunctive form *were* in contrary-to-fact clauses beginning with *if* or expressing a wish.

If you *were* well, you would not have a fever.
I wish my brother *were* happier.

2 | Use the subjunctive in *that* clauses following verbs that demand, request, or recommend.

The rules required that she *start* over.
The counselor suggested that I *be* more self-confident.

3 | Use the subjunctive in some set phrases and idioms.

Far *be* it from me to interfere.
If that's the way you want it, then so *be* it.

VOICE

Verbs can indicate whether their subjects are acting or are acted upon. When the subject is the actor, the verb is in the **active voice:** *John opened three presents.* When the subject is the recipient of the action, the verb is in the **passive voice:** *Three presents were opened by John.* The passive voice consists of the verb's past participle and a form of *be.* Only transitive verbs — verbs that take objects — can form the passive voice.

	S	V	O
ACTIVE	A foul *ball*	*struck*	a *fan.*

	S	V
PASSIVE	A *fan*	*was struck* by a foul *ball.*

135

	S **V**
PASSIVE	The *toy was crushed* by the *car*.

	S **V** **O**
ACTIVE	The *car crushed* the *toy*.

vb

7

    The passive voice is useful when the actor is unknown or unimportant (*Mr. Jones was elected*). Normally, however, the active is preferable because it is more concise and forthright (see 18d).

|*Using subjunctive verb forms*   EXERCISE **7-5**

Cross out any verb in each sentence below that should be in the subjunctive mood, and write the correct form on the blank to the right. If the verb or verbs in a sentence are correct as given, write *OK* on the blank to the right.

Example: If that ✗ the case, he would have protested.   *were*

1. If I were you, I would pay less rent.   _____

2. The policeman ordered that she pulls over.   _____

3. He wishes that graduation was postponed.   _____

4. If she was smart, she would take a mathematics course   _____
   this term.

5. The coach suggested that Joel be dropped from the team.   _____

6. Lydia often wishes that she was less shy.   _____

7. If the storm was to cause a blackout, we would be in   _____
   trouble.

8. The requirement was that he pays before entering.   _____

9. If the tax was repealed, the city would go bankrupt.   _____

10. Requesting that we are seated, the instructor passed out   _____
    the tests.

11. His mouth moved as if he was speaking.   _____

12. If I was certain I could get a job in the space industry, I   _____
    would major in engineering.

13. Though she insisted that we be on time for class, the   _____
    teacher did not seem to care if we failed to show up at
    all.

14. If the president was elected by popular vote instead of _____ by the Electoral College, the country would be more of a democracy.

15. The doctor recommended that Bob went on a diet, and _____ Bob's tailor agreed.

|Using the active voice

Identify each of the following sentences as active or passive by writing an *A* for active or a *P* for passive on the blank to the right. Rewrite in the active voice each sentence that is in the passive. Sometimes you will need to supply a subject not mentioned in the original.

Example: The police chief was fired. _____P_____

The mayor fired the police chief.

1. Dance music was played by the band until midnight. _____

2. Declining circulation was suffered by the paper. _____

3. The secretary distributed the ballots at the opening _____
   session.

4. The question was not understood by the students. _____

5. The steps had been worn down. _____

6. Her car was parked in the public lot yesterday. _____

7. A heavy rain prevented us from arriving on time. _____

8. The shop was closed down a year ago. _____

9. The speech will be read over the radio. _____

10. A subscription to *Time* was given to each student. _____

11. Certain magazines were banned by the council. _____

12. The package has been mailed. _____

13. The posting of grades has been delayed for two more _____
days.

14. The waiting customers formed a line. _____

15. The suspect has been identified by two witnesses. _____

16. We were never introduced. _____

17. The sparrow snatched a crumb from the sidewalk. _____

18. A fleet of cars was owned by the corporation. _____

19. A week later the room had been rented by someone. _____

20. The building was razed on schedule. _____

Verb forms, tense, and mood: Review

In the following paragraph cross out any errors in verb forms, tense, or mood. Then write the correct verb above the error.

Nothing went right in my attempt to have a job interview last week. The interviewer had written me a letter requesting that I am on time and giving me directions to his company. I lost the directions, however, so when I was near the city, I begun looking for a service station where I could ask the way. Suddenly I heard a grinding noise coming from the right wheel. Since I knew something was broke or was about to break, I pull off the road. I knew I should have had the car inspected before the trip, but I had chose to put off the inspection so I will have money for the trip to the city. A policeman called a tow truck for me. Fortunately, I had brought along a credit card and so could pay for the repair. I ask the mechanic for directions, and I followed them easily and found the company. But I was three hours late, and the interviewer had

went home, so I had drove all that way for nothing.

vb

7

8 | Agreement

Self-test

Underline the correct choice in each of the following sentences.

Example: We (*was, were*) pleased by the election.

1. Neither Jeff nor Paula (*is, are*) willing to work hard.
2. Someone abandoned (*his, their*) cat on my doorstep.
3. The herd moved to (*their, its*) winter feeding area.
4. If anyone has (*his, their*) umbrella here, lend it to me.
5. Two parrots and a cat (*is, are*) my pets.
6. No one should leave (*his, their*) valuables in the locker.
7. Either the Smiths or John (*is, are*) responsible.
8. Three apples in a basket (*was, were*) set on the table.
9. She (*ask, asks*) that we join her.
10. Physics (*was, were*) the field she chose.

Agreement is the correspondence in form between subjects and verbs and between pronouns and the nouns or other pronouns they refer to.

8a |Make subjects and verbs agree in number.

Your meaning will always determine the subject you choose, and the subject will determine the form of the verb.

1 | Use the verb ending -*s* or -*es* with all singular nouns and third-person singular pronouns.

Adding -*s* or -*es* to a noun usually makes the noun *plural*. Adding -*s* or -*es* to a present-tense verb makes the verb *singular*. The -*s* or -*es* ending is often not distinctly pronounced in speech and thus is wrongly omitted in writing.

Elroy often asks the teacher for advice.
The monkey passes his hat when the organ grinder finishes.

2 | Subject and verb should agree even when other words come between them.

The problem with all of Riley's poems *is* that they are sentimental. [*Problem* is the subject, not *poems.*]

The goals of this construction work *are* not clear. [*Goals* is the subject, not *work.*]

3 | Subjects joined by *and* usually take plural verbs.

Even when one or more parts of a compound subject are singular, the entire subject takes a plural verb.

Howard and Emma *like* to go deer hunting together.
The Zimmers and Mrs. Rapjohn *go* to Damascus often.

Occasionally, a compound subject refers to a single person or thing or is preceded by *each* or *every.* Then the verb is singular.

The wife and mother *was* proud of her work.
Every log and stick *was* burned.

4 | When parts of a subject are joined by *or* or *nor*, the verb agrees with the nearer part.

When all parts of a subject joined by *or* or *nor* are singular, the verb is singular. When all parts are plural, the verb is plural.

Jones or Albertson *is* to be arrested on Monday.
Neither the horses nor the cows *have* been sold.

However, when one part of the subject is singular and the other plural, the verb agrees with the part closer to it.

Either the roadbed or the curbs *are* scheduled for repair next week.
Either the curbs or the roadbed *is* scheduled for repair next week.

5 | Generally, use singular verbs with indefinite pronouns.

An **indefinite pronoun** does not refer to a specific person or thing. The common indefinite pronouns include *all, any, anybody, anyone, anything, each, either, everybody, everyone, everything, neither, nobody, none, no one, one, some, somebody, someone,* and *something.* Most of them take singular verbs.

No one *knows* the real danger.
Everyone *has* caught the flu.

A few indefinite pronouns — *all, any, none,* and *some* — may be either singular or plural depending on the noun or pronoun they refer to.

All of the gas *is* held in tanks. [*All* refers to the singular *gas.*]
All of the people *are* eager to have some. [*All* refers to the plural *people.*]

6 | Collective nouns take singular or plural verbs depending on meaning.

Collective nouns such as *committee, family,* and *team* have singular form but name groups of individuals or things. Collective nouns take singular verbs when the group is considered as a unit and plural verbs when the group's members are considered individually.

> The committee *has* the power to decide.
> The committee *have* argued over every decision.

The collective noun *number* takes a singular verb when preceded by *the* and a plural verb when preceded by *a*.

> The number of highway deaths *has* decreased.
> A number of officials *attribute* the decrease to the new speed limit.

7 | **The verb agrees with the subject even when the normal word order is inverted.**

> Up the wall *run* the cockroaches. [*Cockroaches* is the subject, not *wall*.]
> There *are* three mice in the wall. [*Mice* is the subject.]

8 | **A linking verb agrees with its subject, not the subject complement.**

> Pork chops *are* the chef's selection. [*Chops* is the subject, not *selection*.]
> Sybil *becomes* three women in the movie. [*Sybil* is the subject, not *women*.]

9 | **When used as subjects, *who*, *which*, and *that* take verbs that agree with their antecedents.**

When a relative pronoun — *who, which,* or *that* — serves as a subject, the verb should agree with the noun or pronoun the relative pronoun refers to (its antecedent).

> She especially likes the man who *is* short. [*Who* refers to *man*.]
> I read all but one of the stories that *are* in the anthology. [*That* refers to *stories*.]
> Mary is the only one of the actors who *knows* her lines. [*Who* refers to *one*.]

10 | **Nouns with plural form but singular meaning take singular verbs.**

Some nouns ending in -*s*, such as *news, athletics,* and *physics*, are generally regarded as singular in meaning and thus take singular verbs. Measurements and figures ending in -*s* may also be singular when the quantity they refer to is a unit.

> Economics *is* not being offered this spring.
> Politics *takes* patience and compromise.
> Two quarts *is* the capacity of a jar.

11 | **Titles and words named as words take singular verbs.**

> The story "Swans" *is* going to win the literature prize.
> *Oxen* is a plural that is irregular.

|Subjects and verbs

EXERCISE **8-1**

agr

8

Underline the subject of each sentence or clause below and locate the corresponding verb. If the verb does not agree with the subject, cross out the verb and write the correct form on the blank to the right. If the sentence is correct as given, write *OK* on the blank to the right.

Example: There ✗ three <u>problems</u> to work out before we can pro-   *are*
     ceed.

1. The difference between twins are often surprising.   _____

2. Both the drinks and the dessert was left off the bill.   _____

3. Each of the puzzles require thirty minutes to solve.   _____

4. Neither of us enjoy the outdoors.   _____

5. The band play only original songs.   _____

6. The price of every one of the houses in our neighborhood   _____
is beyond reach.

7. The cabinet for the stereo components are made of oiled   _____
oak.

8. Good grades was her only goal.   _____

9. Delaware's two senators and one representative is its only   _____
representation in Congress.

10. Among the crowd was three pickpockets.   _____

11. Neither the ring nor the watch were stolen.   _____

12. There are a little group of houses at the curve in the   _____
road.

13. The pieces of the grandfather clock was spread over the   _____
floor.

14. Three kinds of film is sold at the shop. _____

15. When are the committee members to meet? _____

16. If the audience fail to applaud, the play will close. _____

17. Either the motorcycle or the car is to remain uninsured. _____

18. The first thing that I saw at the festival were the cheer- _____
    ful faces of the crowd.

19. One of the students who is in my class falls asleep each _____
    morning.

20. Neither the books nor the record are his. _____

21. The number of students who favor the new dean are not _____
    large.

22. Some of the statistics released by the state shows that _____
    New Brownton has a high rate of murder.

23. He is one of the many students who plays basketball well. _____

24. The style of clothes that my roommates wear are now _____
    very popular.

25. The similarity in their clothes is just one of those things _____
    that make my roommates seem like one person.

26. All of our exported wheat is not enough for all of the _____
    people who is starving.

27. The top two teams in each division gets to go to the play- _____
    offs.

28. The family eat together every evening. _____

29. Neither the sofa nor the chairs needs recovering. _____

30. Only one of the houses that were sold has a garage. _____

8b | Make pronouns and their antecedents agree in person and number.

The **antecedent** of a pronoun is the noun or other pronoun it refers to. Pronouns and their antecedents should agree in person (first, second, or third) and in number (singular or plural).

1 | Antecedents joined by *and* usually take plural pronouns.

Two or more antecedents joined by *and* take a plural pronoun even when all antecedents are singular.

> Ann and Grace sold *their* texts.

Occasionally, a compound antecedent refers to a single person or thing or is preceded by *each* or *every*. Then the pronoun is singular.

> The chief cook and dishwasher wanted *his* name on the menu.
> Every boy and man sang *his* loudest.

2 | When parts of an antecedent are joined by *or* or *nor*, the pronoun agrees with the nearer part.

When all parts of an antecedent joined by *or* or *nor* are singular, the pronoun is singular. When all parts are plural, the pronoun is plural.

> Anne or Jane left *her* umbrella behind.
> Scientists do not know how either walruses or sea cows get *their* food.

However, when one part of the antecedent is singular and the other plural, the pronoun agrees with the part closer to it.

> Neither Ms. Hogan nor the Smiths offered *their* contributions.

3 | Generally, use a singular pronoun when the antecedent is an indefinite pronoun.

> None of the Boy Scouts paid *his* dues.
> Each of the women succeeded in *her* chosen career.

Traditionally, the pronoun *he* has been used to refer to an indefinite pronoun even when the female gender is also intended. More and more writers, seeing the traditional usage as excluding females unfairly, are rewriting their sentences to avoid overreliance on *he*.

> Everyone took *his* seat.
> Everyone took *his or her* seat.
> All the students took *their* seats.

4 | Collective noun antecedents take singular or plural pronouns depending on meaning.

> The herd of wildebeests is too cramped in *its* small pasture.
> The couple divided *their* belongings evenly.

|*Pronouns and antecedents*   EXERCISE **8-2**

Underline each personal pronoun in the sentences below and draw an arrow to its antecedent. If the pronoun does not agree with its antecedent, cross the pronoun out and write the correct form on the blank to the right. If the sentence is correct as given, write *OK* on the blank to the right.

Example: Neither Tom nor Bud enjoyed their vacation.   *his* _____

1. No one can know if they will get a job in June.   _____

2. The growing complexity of economics has not lessened   _____
   their appeal to students.

3. The teachers' union lost their right to bargain.   _____

4. Anyone who turned in a late paper had their grade re-   _____
   duced.

5. The audience voiced its approval loudly.   _____

6. The herd of sheep wandered in all directions from its   _____
   pasture.

7. An elephant never eats a leaf or bark that has fungus   _____
   growing on them.

8. Bettors tend to follow his or her own whims at the race- _____
   track.

9. Every dog on the block barked themselves hoarse that   _____
   night.

10. The College of Arts and Sciences changed their entrance _____
    requirements.

11. Neither of the two cars is known for their fuel economy. _____

12. The patrol could not anticipate the danger they would   _____
    encounter.

13. The manager or the employees will get their raises, but _____
    not both.

14. The company planned to clear out the forests until a pe- _____
    tition stopped them.

agr

8

15. Ed told each of his coworkers to keep their sense of hu- _____
    mor.

16. Someone had left his shoes in my locker. _____

17. The young boy and older man who shoplifted received _____
    stiff sentences for his act.

18. If a person has no pride in their appearance, others can _____
    always tell.

19. None of the engineers bidding on the contract thought _____
    his bid would be too high.

20. Each family should install at least one smoke alarm in _____
    their home.

|Agreement: Review

In the following paragraph, cross out any verb that does not agree with its subject and any pronoun that does not agree with its antecedent. Then write the correct verb or pronoun above the errors.

Our county's mass transit system, in operation for only three

years, is already millions of dollars in debt. Each year they have lost over

a million dollars. Either the state government or the federal government

are going to have to provide a subsidy to keep the system going. There is

no alternatives. The voters in the county, like voters elsewhere in the

nation, as recently as a month ago has rejected a proposal to issue bonds

to support the system. Fare increases in the past has resulted only in

more commuters using their cars. Meanwhile the residential streets and

the highway network throughout the county is in bad repair, and it is

becoming dangerously overcrowded. Everyone in the county who commute should urge their state and national legislators to support the system. There is significant funds already invested in the system. To lose the

agr
8
system now would be foolish.

9 Adjectives and Adverbs

Self-test

Circle the correct choice in each of the following sentences.

Example: The minister preached (*serious,* ⟨*seriously*⟩).

1. The (*more, most*) successful of the three brothers is Dave.
2. We fought a (*real, really*) hard battle.
3. She felt (*bad, badly*) for a day after she fell.
4. The ice cream tasted (*good, well*) on a hot day.
5. I felt (*worse, worser*) than he did.
6. The person with the friendly smile is the (*nicest, nicer*) of the two.
7. We drove (*slow, slowly*) past the house.
8. Her ability came (*natural, naturally*).
9. The (*baddest, worst*) act won an award.
10. He set the vase (*careful, carefully*) on the table.

Adjectives and adverbs are modifiers that describe, limit, or restrict the words they relate to. An **adjective** modifies a noun or a pronoun. An **adverb** modifies another adverb, an adjective, or a verb.

9a Don't use adjectives to modify verbs, adverbs, or other adjectives.

NOT	She speaks Spanish *good.*
BUT	She speaks Spanish *well.*
NOT	We played a *real* good game.
BUT	We played a *really* good game.
NOT	They watched the children *close.*
BUT	They watched the children *closely.*

9b | Use an adjective after a linking verb to modify the subject. Use an adverb to modify a verb.

A **linking verb** connects a subject and its noun or adjective complement. The linking verbs include *be, seem, become, appear, remain,* and verbs associated with the senses such as *look, sound, smell, feel,* and *taste.* When a linking verb connects a subject and a modifier, the modifier should be an adjective. However, some of these verbs may also function as nonlinking verbs. When they do, they should be modified by adverbs.

> He felt *tired.* [Adjective.]
> He felt *tiredly* for her hand. [Adverb.]
>
> Chris appeared *calm.* [Adjective.]
> Chris appeared *suddenly.* [Adverb.]
>
> He felt *bad.* [Adjective.]
> The orchestra performed *badly.* [Adverb.]

9c | After a direct object, use an adjective to modify the object and an adverb to modify the verb.

> The mayor considered the proposal *good.* [Adjective.]
> The mayor considered the proposal *carefully.* [Adverb.]

9d | When an adverb has a short form and an *-ly* form, distinguish carefully between the forms.

Some adverbs have both an *-ly* form and a short form without the *-ly,* and the meanings of the two forms may be different.

> The ambulance arrived too *late.*
> The *lately* arrived ambassador is a tactless person.

9e | Use the comparative and superlative forms of adjectives and adverbs appropriately.

Most adjectives and adverbs have three forms. The **positive form** describes without comparing (*small, quickly*). The **comparative form** is used to indicate a difference or similarity between two items (*smaller, more quickly*). The **superlative form** is used to indicate a difference or similarity among three or more items (*smallest, most quickly*).

1 | When word length or sound requires, use *more* and *most* instead of the endings *-er* and *-est.*

Most adverbs longer than a syllable form the comparative and superlative with the words *more* and *most* instead of the endings *-er* and *-est* (*happily, more happily; nearly, more nearly*). Most one-syllable and many two-syllable adjectives can use either the *-er* and *-est* endings or the words *more* and *most* (*stealthy; stealthier, more stealthy; stealthiest, most stealthy*). Most adjectives longer than two syllables use only *more* and *most.*

2 | Use the correct form of irregular adjectives and adverbs.

Irregular adjectives and adverbs change the spelling of their positive form to show comparative and superlative.

POSITIVE	COMPARATIVE	SUPERLATIVE
good/well	better	best
bad/badly	worse	worst
little	littler, less	littlest, least
many, some, much	more	most

3 | Don't use double comparatives or double superlatives.

The *-er* or *-est* ending and the word *more* or *most* should not be used at the same time.

This is the *sharpest* (not *most sharpest*) knife I have.

4 | In general, use the comparative form for comparing two things and the superlative form for comparing three or more things.

This is the *longer* of the two plays.
The *longest* play we ever performed was *shorter* than this one.

5 | In general, don't use comparative or superlative forms for modifiers that cannot logically be compared.

Absolute modifiers like *unique, dead, perfect,* and *impossible* cannot logically be compared because their positive forms describe their only state.

NOT   That was the *most impossible* trick I ever tried.

BUT   That trick was *almost impossible.*

9f | Avoid overuse of nouns as modifiers.

Overuse of nouns as modifiers can cause writing to be wordy or confusing.

NOT   The device is a wind speed measurement instrument.

BUT   The device measures wind speed.

Using adjectives
and adverbs

EXERCISE **9-1**

In each sentence below, circle the appropriate form of the modifier from the pairs in parentheses, underline the word or words modified, and identify the modifier as an adjective (*adj.*) or adverb (*adv.*) by writing the appropriate abbreviation on the blank to the right.

Example: <u>Louisa</u> felt (*bad,* *badly*) after eating the soup. *adj.*

1. The radio played (*loud, loudly*). _____

2. The dessert tasted too (*sweetly, sweet*). _____

3. Oliver executed the pass play (*perfect, perfectly*). _____

4. She arrived too (*late, lately*) to see the show. _____

5. The jade ring is (*more expensive, expensiver*) than the opal _____
   ring.

6. The pool in the city park looks (*deeply, deep*). _____

7. The magnetic lock is the (*safer, safest*) of the three. _____

8. A (*special, specially*) designed mirror enabled him to drive. _____

9. The mailman pounded the door (*hard, hardly*). _____

10. Of the two, the second son is the (*smarter, smartest*). _____

11. My foot hurt so (*bad, badly*) that I could not walk. _____

12. Anne feels (*differently, different*) about Violet than she used _____
    to.

13. We played (*well, good*), but we didn't win. _____

14. Harry always takes arguments (*serious, seriously*). _____

15. Alex looked (*cautious, cautiously*) out the door. _____

16. Someone had treated the poor animal (*cruelly, cruel*). ⎯⎯⎯⎯⎯

17. The (*littlest, littler*) of the two boxes was damaged. ⎯⎯⎯⎯⎯

18. San Francisco's transportation system remains (*unique, uniquely*). ⎯⎯⎯⎯⎯

19. He stayed home because he felt (*bad, badly*). ⎯⎯⎯⎯⎯

20. Molly is a dog bred (*specific, specifically*) for obedience. ⎯⎯⎯⎯⎯

21. A (*normal, normally*) developed bicep is sufficient for this exercise. ⎯⎯⎯⎯⎯

22. The (*baddest, worst*) commercial got the most attention. ⎯⎯⎯⎯⎯

23. The milk tasted (*sour, sourly*). ⎯⎯⎯⎯⎯

24. Alice seems (*weak, weakly*) after her operation. ⎯⎯⎯⎯⎯

25. Mark was the (*better, best*) of the two guards. ⎯⎯⎯⎯⎯

26. The strength of a goat is (*considerable, considerably*). ⎯⎯⎯⎯⎯

27. A person should always drive (*safe, safely*). ⎯⎯⎯⎯⎯

28. Of all the snakes, Sinbad has the (*prettier, prettiest*) skin. ⎯⎯⎯⎯⎯

29. David cares for his brother (*happily, happy*). ⎯⎯⎯⎯⎯

30. That movie was the (*worse, worst*) one I have ever seen. ⎯⎯⎯⎯⎯

Using adjectives
and adverbs

EXERCISE **9-2**

In each sentence below, identify any incorrect form of a modifier by crossing it out and inserting the correct form on the blank to the right. If the adjectives and adverbs are correct as given, write *OK* on the blank to the right.

Example: July is the ~~worse~~ time to visit the Southwestern deserts.   *worst*

1. They never complained of being real lonely.   _____

2. The valley looked forbiddingly when winter came.   _____

3. She always comes dressed odd.   _____

4. Why should you feel angrily about something you can-   _____
   not control?

5. We tourists located the hotel easy.   _____

6. The difference between male and female gorillas is clear   _____
   to anyone.

7. Nancy has the more sharply defined features of all the   _____
   Mendoza girls.

8. A more neater room you will never see.   _____

9. Greg is surely going to lose his job.   _____

10. Hot grits smell well in the morning.   _____

11. The Edsel was the most unique car of the 1950s.   _____

12. My father is the more open of my parents.   _____

13. Playing bad for one game was no reason to give up.   _____

14. The old man had a friendly look.   _____

15. The car turned the corner so slow that I hit it. _____

16. Keith was one of the most brightest students to graduate _____
    from this school.

17. She always greets me cheerful. _____

ad

9

18. The bus driver applied the brakes quick to avoid hitting _____
    the bicyclist.

19. Don't speak blunt to the dean. _____

20. Beating the Hartford tennis team is near impossible. _____

21. Of the two, Reggie has the highest average. _____

22. I could not find a scarier movie. _____

23. Max has the better grades in the class. _____

24. How sudden did he stop? _____

25. The customer smiled polite at the clerk. _____

III Clear Sentences

10 Sentence Fragments

Self-test

Circle the number of each incomplete sentence in the following paragraph.

¹Police shows usually start out rather predictably with the commission of a crime. ²Normally murder or robbery. ³Murder, the most common beginning, is usually premeditated and usually carefully planned; careful planning of a crime makes its solving at least somewhat complicated. ⁴Because the police have to look very carefully for clues. ⁵What can make a show dull, though, is lack of character development of the victim. ⁶Not to mention of the murderer. ⁷If the murder victim's character is not developed, then I do not care very much about the death. ⁸Only about how the crime is solved. ⁹Oddly, robberies are often more interesting than murders. ¹⁰There being no attempt, usually, to achieve anything in murder shows other than to attract the viewer by showing outrageous violence.

A **complete sentence** consists of both a subject and a predicate, a verb that asserts something about the subject. (See 5a.) A phrase or clause that lacks a subject or a predicate or both but is set off like a sentence (with a capital letter and a period) is a **sentence fragment.** A clause that begins with a subordinating word and is set off like a complete sentence is also a sentence fragment.

FRAGMENT	For example, when I play the piano.
FRAGMENT	In a way.
FRAGMENT	Behaving strangely.

10a Don't set off a subordinate clause as a sentence.

A **subordinate clause** has both a subject and a predicate and begins with a subordinating conjunction (such as *after, although, because,* *since*) or a relative pronoun (*who, which, that*). (See 5c-4.) When set off from the main clause on which it depends for its meaning, a subordinate clause is a sentence fragment.

FRAGMENT	The return on the investment was 20 percent. *Which was higher than he expected.*
REVISED	The return on the investment was 20 percent, which was higher than he expected. [Subordinate clause linked to main clause.]
REVISED	The return on the investment was 20 percent. The earnings were higher than he expected. [Subordinate clause rewritten as main clause.]

10b | Don't set off a verbal phrase as a sentence.

A **verbal phrase** consists of an infinitive (*to spend*), a participle (*spending, spent*), or a gerund (*spending*), along with its objects or modifiers. (See 5c-2.)

FRAGMENT	I went to the convocation for one reason. *To hear the architect speak.*
REVISED	I went to the convocation for one reason, to hear the architect speak. [Verbal phrase linked to main clause.]
REVISED	I went to the convocation for one reason. I wanted to hear the architect speak. [Verbal phrase rewritten as main clause.]
FRAGMENT	He has one purpose in life. *Spending money.*
REVISED	He has one purpose in life: spending money. [Verbal phrase linked to main clause.]
REVISED	He has one purpose in life. He wants only to spend money. [Verbal phrase rewritten as main clause.]
FRAGMENT	The trip cost $400. *Money well spent.*
REVISED	The trip cost $400, which was money well spent. [Verbal phrase linked to main clause.]
REVISED	The trip cost $400. The money was well spent. [Verbal phrase rewritten as main clause.]

10c | Don't set off a prepositional phrase as a sentence.

A **prepositional phrase** consists of a preposition (*by, on, to, with*) plus its object and the object's modifiers (see 5c-1). Since it has neither a subject nor a predicate, a prepositional phrase set off as a sentence is a sentence fragment.

| FRAGMENT | The accident occurred at the main intersection. *During the evening rush hour.* |
| REVISED | The accident occurred at the main intersection during the evening rush hour. [Prepositional phrase linked to main clause.] |

10d | Don't set off an appositive or a part of a compound predicate as a sentence.

Appositives are nouns, plus any modifiers, that rename other nouns (see 5c-5).

FRAGMENT The car was a gift from her eccentric uncle. *Hubie Crumbacher.*

REVISED The car was a gift from her eccentric uncle, Hubie Crumbacher. [Appositive linked to main clause.]

REVISED The car was a gift from her eccentric uncle. Hubie Crumbacher was his name. [Appositive rewritten as main clause.]

A **compound predicate** consists of two or more verbs and their objects, if any (see 5d).

FRAGMENT The rescuers loaded their backpacks with food and bandages. *And struck out for the woods.*

REVISED The rescuers loaded their backpacks with food and bandages and struck out for the woods. [Second half of compound predicate linked to main clause.]

FRAGMENT We accepted their congratulations. *And the reward money.*

REVISED We accepted their congratulations and the reward money. [Second half of compound object linked to main clause.]

10e | Be aware of the acceptable uses of incomplete sentences.

We omit the sentence subject in commands and some exclamations: *(You) Learn these rules; (You) Forget it!* We use incomplete sentences for question-and-answer patterns in speech and sometimes in writing *(Got it? Sure)*, and we may use them to make a transition from one idea to another: *First a word of explanation.* Experienced professional writers sometimes use sentence fragments that do not fit any of these patterns and that violate the rules for avoiding fragments discussed above. But until you become quite sure of your ability to control incomplete sentences, so that you only use them effectively, you should write complete sentences with their subjects and predicates intact.

frag

10

Identifying and revising sentence fragments

Each of the following word groups is either a sentence fragment or a complete sentence. Rewrite each sentence fragment as a complete sentence by changing word forms, omitting words, or adding new words. If the word group is a complete sentence, write *OK* in the space below it.

Example: After the flood waters receded.

Or: *The flood waters receded.*
People were rescued after the flood waters receded.

1. When the ice destroys the pavement.

2. There being lots of extra features without extra cost.

3. And it was rejected.

4. A former editor, who has a sharp, critical eye.

5. On a snowy slope far from any shelter.

6. Taking the time to check.

7. Come and see our apartment.

8. Which was slimy but cool.

9. The fox looking for its mother.

10. From behind and all around.

11. But is not honest.

12. A resident of Toledo.

13. Although it was a gory film.

14. Food prices were soaring.

15. Based on historical fact.

16. Puzzled by poor sales.

17. Which looked like a passageway.

18. Afterward, the answer was challenged.

19. Having joined a band of gypsies.

20. During a tornado alert.

Revising sentence fragments

EXERCISE **10-2**

Most of the passages below contain a sentence fragment. Identify each fragment by writing the number preceding it on the blank to the right. Then rewrite the passage to correct each fragment by linking it to the preceding or following main clause, using a comma if necessary. If there is no fragment in the passage, write *OK* on the blank.

Example: [1] Johnny raised guinea pigs for a living. [2] Until recently. _____2_____
[3] He went bankrupt because he couldn't develop a large market.

Johnny raised guinea pigs for a living until recently. He went bankrupt because he couldn't develop a large market.

1. [1] Signed by the entire student council. [2] The letter ap- _____
peared on the editorial page. [3] But all the criticism had
been edited out.

2. [1] As the record companies scramble for the youth mar- _____
ket. [2] The pirates wait around for a song to become popular. [3] Then they move in.

3. [1] Chris has one quality her roommate does not have. _____
[2] Patience. [3] So patient is Chris that she is boring.

4. [1] The music was arranged well. [2] By Joel Grey. [3] The se- _____
lections are still popular today.

5. [1]Having paid $2.53 for postage, I expected prompt delivery. [2]It took six weeks. [3]I was furious.   _____

6. [1]"Society considers you an alcoholic only when you can't   _____
afford to buy liquor," says Mr. Halligan. [2]The town's
philosopher.

7. [1]Six years ago the school closed. [2]The building re-   _____
mained vacant. [3]Until it burned down last week.

8. [1]Barbara is continually humming songs by Elvis or the   _____
Beatles. [2]And she is always off-key. [3]Her humming an-
noys everyone within hearing distance.

9. [1]His days of bragging were over. [2]Once he lost the tour-   _____
nament. [3]There was no more Mr. Loudmouth.

10. [1]Andrew plays football well. [2]When he wants to. [3]But   _____
now he seems to have lost his motivation.

*Revising sentence
fragments*   EXERCISE **10-3**

Most of the passages below contain a sentence fragment. Identify each
fragment by writing the number preceding it on the blank to the right.
Then rewrite the passage to correct each fragment by making it a complete sentence, adding, changing, or deleting words as necessary. If there
is no fragment in the passage, write *OK* on the blank.

Example: [1] After studying French for three years, I tried to translate   *2*
a poem. [2] Without much success.

*After studying French for three years, I tried to
translate a poem. But I didn't have much
success.*

1. [1] The contrast between the two women is great. [2] One of   _____
   them, Roberta, being arrogant, and Patrice being shy.

2. [1] They moved into a condominium in a quiet neighbor-   _____
   hood. [2] Quiet being all they wanted.

3. [1] The National Geographic specials have been very pop-   _____
   ular. [2] Sponsored in part by an oil company. [3] PBS has
   shown several.

4. [1] The river was polluted with insecticides. [2] Funds for   _____
   cleaning it up were not available. [3] The chemical company had gone bankrupt.

5. [1]The disagreement that upset them. [2]It seemed to be over a broken date. [3]However, that was just a sign of a deeper problem. _____

6. [1]Riding the subway, I always read the advertisements above the windows. [2]Trying to figure out what gimmicks the advertisers use. _____

7. [1]I tried to be gentle with the old woman. [2]Who had insulted me the day before but now needed my help. _____

8. [1]Perry can be loudmouthed and overbearing. [2]For example, his saying he should be in a dorm with "better-quality people." _____

9. [1]The salary starting at $15,000 a year. [2]The job failed to attract qualified applicants. [3]The advertisement ran for three weeks. _____

10. [1]Mike seems to be a good father. [2]For example, taking his children to ball games or on trips, or just staying around the house teaching his children new games. _____

Sentence fragments: Review

EXERCISE **10-4**

In each passage below, circle the number preceding any word group that is a sentence fragment. Then revise each fragment by linking it to a main clause or by rewriting it as a main clause.

frag

10

A. [1] The so-called Gothic romances are criticized unfairly. [2] Just because they do not conform to some critics' ideas of what makes "literature." [3] To me the best poetry or fiction uses colorful writing and takes my mind off everyday events. [4] Making me experience things I wouldn't ordinarily encounter. [5] Or leading me to think of ideas that might not have occurred to me. [6] Gothic romances treat romantic subjects in the context of historical events. [7] Imaginary characters in real settings. [8] In Gothic romances I learn about how different people deal with different situations. [9] For example, how a poor person responds to an heiress. [10] Or how a grandfather forgives his spendthrift grandson. [11] But I also learn about the history of our country. [12] One book was set in the South after the Civil War and told of the suffering experienced by those who lost the war. [13]Another book gave me insights into early twentieth-century Texas. [14]Where Mexican immigrants, cattle ranchers, cowboys, and drifters all came together. [15]On the other hand, I find that works of "literature" deal

frag

10

with dull people in dull places and situations. [16]Such as those I experience daily. [17]"Literature" does nothing for my imagination or my curiosity. [18]Leaving me cold and bored. [19]The snobbish critics would probably enjoy reading even more. [20]If only they would stop worrying about what others think.

B. ¹In the African nation of Dahomey. ²A man's wives were put to

death at his funeral. ³Their spirits being supposed to keep him company

in the afterlife. ⁴When a king died, many attendants and wives were put

to death. ⁵The people believed that a dead person had desires and emo-

tions. ⁶Such as anger. ⁷The dead person could take revenge on the living

if his desires were not satisfied. ⁸Thus a king remained very powerful

even after death. ⁹With as much power as he had had when he was alive.

¹⁰Since the dead were so powerful, the survivors had to prevent the dead

from becoming envious. ¹¹As well as angry. ¹²So the survivors often sac-

rificed possessions. ¹³Along with attendants and wives. ¹⁴Appropriate

possessions for sacrifice being cattle, food, and jewelry. ¹⁵Such sacrifices

guaranteeing continual poverty for the people. ¹⁶War frequently resulted.

¹⁷Because through war the people renewed their wealth. ¹⁸The additional

frag

10

result, however, was the destruction of even more lives. [19] Only in this century did these mourning sacrifices disappear. [20] And now the people seem to live in a state of spiritual uneasiness.

frag

10

11 Comma Splices and Run-on Sentences

Self-test

For each sentence below, circle the letter preceding the option that correctly fills in the blank.

Example: "We waited in line for an hour," she _____ we went home."
a. said, "then   b. said "then   ©. said; "then

1. We will certainly be able to identify Bob's boat during the _____ is the only one with red and purple sails.
   a. races it   b. races, it   c. races; it
2. My morning ritual includes listening to the news while I _____ morning, however, I was in too much of a hurry to turn the radio on.
   a. shave, this   b. shave; this   c. shave this
3. He is an outstanding _____ is also a fair athlete.
   a. student he   b. student, he   c. student. He
4. She felt happy after the test was _____ and went home smiling.
   a. returned, however,   b. returned; however,   c. returned however
5. After calling the roll, my history professor tells a _____ he begins his lecture.
   a. joke then   b. joke, and then   c. joke, then
6. The car stopped _____ policeman got out.
   a. abruptly, a   b. abruptly; a   c. abruptly a
7. He is one of the kindest men I _____ will certainly help you.
   a. know he   b. know; he   c. know, he
8. The child's musical talent was _____ she was considered a musical prodigy.
   a. amazing indeed   b. amazing. Indeed,   c. amazing, indeed,
9. During the last song she pushed her way through the _____ that she could get a closer look at the band.
   a. crowd; so   b. crowd so   c. crowd. So
10. In the summer I had to do manual _____ I have to overtax my brain.
    a. labor, now   b. labor now   c. labor; now

177

Two problems commonly occur in linking main clauses in a single sentence. The first, the **comma splice,** occurs when two or more main clauses are joined only by commas (*The car was bright red, its interior was black*). The second, the **run-on sentence,** or **fused sentence,** occurs when two or more main clauses are joined with no punctuation or conjunction between them (*The car was bright red its interior was black*).

COMMA SPLICES

cs, run-on

11

11a | Don't join two main clauses with a comma unless they are also joined by a coordinating conjunction.

COMMA SPLICE   The mattress caught fire, the flames spread quickly.

REVISED   The mattress caught fire, *and* the flames spread quickly.

A comma splice can be corrected in four ways, each one establishing a different relation between the clauses.

1. Insert a coordinating conjunction (*and, but, or, nor, for, so, yet*) after the comma that separates the two main clauses (see 5d-1). This method is illustrated above.

2. Make separate sentences of the two main clauses:

   The mattress caught fire. The flames spread quickly.

3. Insert a semicolon rather than a comma between the main clauses:

   The mattress caught fire; the flames spread quickly.

4. Make one of the main clauses into a subordinate clause by using a subordinating conjunction such as *although, since,* or *when* or a relative pronoun (*that, which, who*). (See 5c-4.)

   After the mattress caught fire, the flames spread quickly.

11b | Use a period or semicolon to separate main clauses connected by conjunctive adverbs or transitional expressions.

Conjunctive adverbs include *also, consequently, however, then, thus,* and *therefore* (see 5d-2). **Transitional expressions** include *for example, in addition,* and *that is* (see 3b-6). When these words and expressions connect main clauses, the clauses must be separated by a semicolon or by a period (making two sentences). The words and expressions are themselves usually followed by commas (see 21b).

COMMA SPLICE   The house looked run down, however the inside was in beautiful shape.

REVISED   The house looked run down; however, the inside was in beautiful shape.

REVISED	The house looked run down. However, the inside was in beautiful shape.
REVISED	The house looked run down. The inside, however, was in beautiful shape. [A conjunctive adverb or a transitional expression may be placed at the beginning, middle, or end of its clause.]

RUN-ON SENTENCES

11c | **Don't run two main clauses together without using an appropriate connector or punctuation mark between them.**

A **run-on,** or **fused, sentence** joins two or more main clauses with no connecting word or punctuation between them. It can be corrected in the same ways as a comma splice.

RUN-ON	Dr. Ling is director of the hospital he also maintains a private practice.
REVISED	Dr. Ling is director of the hospital, *but* he also maintains a private practice. [Comma and coordinating conjunction.]
REVISED	Dr. Ling is director of the hospital. He also maintains a private practice. [Separate sentences.]
REVISED	Dr. Ling is director of the hospital; he also maintains a private practice. [Semicolon.]
REVISED	Dr. Ling is director of the hospital, *although* he also maintains a private practice. [Subordinate clause.]

Identifying and revising comma splices and run-on sentences

EXERCISE **11-1**

Identify each comma splice (*splice*) or run-on sentence (*run-on*) below by writing the appropriate word on the blank to the right. Correct each error by inserting a coordinating conjunction or a comma and a coordinating conjunction; by forming separate sentences; by using a semicolon; or by subordinating one of the clauses with a subordinating conjunction or a relative pronoun. If an item contains no error, write *OK* on the blank.

cs, run-on

11

Example: We installed a wood-burning stove, it heated the kitchen. *splice*

We installed a wood-burning stove that heated the kitchen.

1. The fireworks had deteriorated they had not been stored _____
   properly.

2. The visitor came to the door, however, it was too late for _____
   him to get in.

3. Bret Harte's works had great appeal to Easterners, they _____
   appreciated his attitude toward his rural characters.

4. They chattered and daydreamed the serious issue was _____
   not discussed.

5. She planned to be a chemist, but instead she wound up   _____
   in advertising.

6. The reunion was in St. Louis, I could not attend.   _____

7. The waiter piled the glasses, then the plates fell.   _____

8. I wanted to chair the committee, however, I did not have   _____
   a chance.

9. Having climbed the stairs, she rested on her suitcase.   _____

10. Blending your own tea, however, does not take much   _____
    time it saves money, too.

Revising comma splices and run-on sentences

Identify each item below as a comma splice (*splice*) or a run-on sentence (*run-on*) by writing the appropriate word on the blank to the right. Correct each error in the manner specified (to make a clause subordinate, you will have to add a subordinating conjunction or a relative pronoun).

Example: The wedding gifts had to be returned, the wax grapes   *splice*
were no loss.

Add coordinating conjunction:

The wedding gifts had to be returned, but the wax grapes were no loss.

Add semicolon and conjunctive adverb:

The wedding gifts had to be returned; however, the wax grapes were no loss.

1. The factory once employed 500 persons now there is a   _____
parking lot in its place.

    Add comma and coordinating conjunction:

    Add semicolon and conjunctive adverb:

2. She moved to Florida, however, she found the summers   _____
too sultry.

    Add semicolon:

    Make separate sentences:

3. Frederick Douglass had been an illiterate slave, he became a famous speaker and writer.

Add coordinating conjunction:

Make one clause subordinate:

4. Stevie Wonder has been a professional entertainer since the age of twelve, he was the first black Motown artist to perform overseas.

Add coordinating conjunction:

Add semicolon:

5. The airline gave a discount on the Atlanta flight, the number of passengers continued to decline.

Add semicolon and conjunctive adverb:

Make one clause subordinate:

6. The band was formed in 1971 its first hit came the same _____ year.

   Make separate sentences:

   Add semicolon:

7. Some vitamins may reduce the risk of certain diseases, _____ in high doses the vitamins are toxic.

   Add coordinating conjunction:

   Make one clause subordinate:

8. In the morning there was a rumor that the president had _____ suffered a heart attack by noon stock prices had dropped sharply.

   Make separate sentences:

   Add comma and coordinating conjunction:

9. Muhammad Ali associates with people of all races and religions, that is why he is respected worldwide. _____

   Add semicolon:

   Make separate sentences:

10. The movie got mostly positive reviews some critics found the acting unconvincing. _____

   Add comma and coordinating conjunction:

   Make one clause subordinate:

Comma splices and
run-on sentences: Review

EXERCISE **11-3**

In the following paragraph, circle the number preceding any word group that is a comma splice or a run-on sentence. Then revise each faulty sentence in the most appropriate way.

[1] From the office window I could see the cars lined up along the bridge below, the muddy river ran beneath it. [2] Traffic was backed up for several blocks on the three roads they converged at the foot of the bridge. [3] Rain started falling, the cars' lights came on. [4] Across the river was the city shrouded in fog. [5] The traffic moved even more slowly, the commuters must have hated having one more thing to delay them. [6] A few brightly colored dots gradually moved across the bridge, six pedestrians, carrying red and yellow umbrellas, moved with quickening paces. [7] Soon the traffic began to thin. [8] A gray and yellow band of sky began to show as the rain eased. [9] The sun was coming up, the rain was subsiding,

the fog was dissipating. [10] Rush hour over, the morning sky brightened

the workers were at their jobs.

12 Pronoun Reference

Self-test

In each of the following sentences, underline any pronoun whose antecedent (the noun or pronoun it refers to) is not clear, specific, or definite. If the sentence is already correct, write *OK* to the left of it.

Example: John told Dennis that <u>he</u> had a problem.

1. When I saw my teachers greeting my friends, I said hello to them.
2. The man's shadow loomed against the wall, which alarmed John.
3. After Hilda's snake escaped, Martha would not go into her room.
4. As long as the council members refused to meet the developers, there would be no end to their frustration.
5. When he saw how much the parts cost for the repairs, he decided to obtain them elsewhere.
6. Once the man met his nephew, he knew the boy was missing something in life.
7. It says on the bottle not to drink its contents.
8. In Agnes's glove compartment, she kept a revolver.
9. After my roommate insulted my father, he refused to speak to him.
10. Alice told Karen that Esther found her purse.

    A **pronoun** is a substitute for a noun. The pronoun takes its meaning from the noun it stands for and refers to, called its **antecedent.** Thus the antecedent of a pronoun must be clear.

CONFUSING	When my mother stopped speaking to my aunt, *she* rewrote *her* will. [Antecedent of *she* and *her* unclear.]
CLEAR	My mother rewrote *her* will when *she* stopped speaking to my aunt. [Antecedent of *her* and *she* is clearly *mother.*]
CLEAR	My aunt rewrote *her* will when my mother stopped speaking to *her*. [Antecedent of *her* both times is clearly *aunt.*]

    Most problems with pronoun reference occur because the pronoun could refer to more than one antecedent (as in the example above), because the pronoun is so far from its antecedent that its meaning is unclear, or because the antecedent is not specific or cannot be located at all.

12a | Make a pronoun refer clearly to one antecedent.

A plural pronoun may refer to a compound antecedent:

Smith and *Bean* doubled *their* profits.

But a pronoun will be unclear if it can refer to *either* of two antecedents.

CONFUSING   Mort told Anna that Hildy lost *her* money.

CLEAR   Mort told Anna that Hildy lost *Anna's* money. [Pronoun replaced with appropriate noun.]

CLEAR   Mort told Anna, "Hildy lost your money." [Sentence rewritten to quote Mort directly.]

12b | Place a pronoun close enough to its antecedent to ensure clarity.

Avoid separating a pronoun and its antecedent with other nouns that the pronoun could refer to.

CONFUSING   Maria almost lost her watch during a scuffle with a mugger on the subway. Fortunately, she only sprained her toe. *It* was a gift from her fiancé.

CLEAR   Maria almost lost her *watch, which* was a gift from her fiancé, during a scuffle with a mugger on the subway. Fortunately, she only sprained her toe.

A clause that begins with a relative pronoun (*who, which, that*) should generally be placed immediately after the noun it modifies.

CONFUSING   The article pointed out that the spaceships on the surface of Mars, *which* can never be recovered, form the beginning of a garbage dump on the planet.

CLEAR   The article pointed out that the spaceships, *which* can never be recovered, form the beginning of a garbage dump on Mars.

12c | Make a pronoun refer to a specific antecedent rather than to an implied one.

1 | Use *this, that, which,* and *it* cautiously in referring to whole statements.

In **broad reference** a pronoun such as *this, that, which,* or *it* refers to an entire phrase, clause, sentence, or even paragraph. Unless the meaning of the pronoun is unmistakable, avoid making a broad reference.

CONFUSING   As we watched, the two men began hitting each other and yelling for help. *This* started the riot.

CLEAR	As we watched, the two men began hitting each other and yelling for help. *This fight* started the riot.
CLEAR	We saw the riot start when the two men began hitting each other and yelling for help.

2 | Don't use a pronoun to refer to a noun implied by a modifier.

Modifiers — adjectives, nouns used as modifiers, and the possessives of nouns and pronouns — do not provide specific antecedents for pronouns.

WEAK	In the teacher's desk, *she* kept a paddle and a pint bottle.
REVISED	The teacher kept a paddle and a pint bottle in her desk.
WEAK	The sick man claimed he caught *it* from a cow at the 4-H fair.
REVISED	The sick man claimed he caught *his illness* from a cow at the 4-H fair.

3 | Don't use a pronoun to refer to a noun implied by some other noun or phrase.

UNCLEAR	After Albert studied accounting techniques, he decided to become *one*.
REVISED	After Albert studied accounting techniques, he decided to become *an accountant*.

4 | Don't use part of a title as an antecedent in the opening sentence of a paper.

TITLE	A Shortage of Locksmiths
NOT	*This* is responsible for the increase in burglaries.
BUT	Since the town's last locksmith closed his shop, the number of burglaries has doubled.

12d | Avoid the indefinite use of *it* and *they*. Use *you* only to mean "you, the reader."

Using *it* or *they* with no clear antecedent is vague and leads to wordiness.

WEAK	*It* says in the directions to open the small box first.
REVISED	The directions say to open the small box first.
WEAK	On the television advertisement *they* said science had finally conquered the common cold.
REVISED	The television advertisement said that science had finally conquered the common cold.

You is acceptable when it is used to mean "you, the reader": *You can see that I had no choice.* But *you* should not be used indefinitely in other contexts.

WEAK	Citizens of Mudburg know that *you* can have *your* car towed away for illegal parking.
REVISED	Citizens of Mudburg know that *people* can have *their* cars towed away for illegal parking.

12e | Avoid using the pronoun *it* more than one way in a sentence.

CONFUSING	*It* was an inaccurate forecast: *It* predicted rain, but *it* is snowing.
CLEAR	The forecast was inaccurate: It predicted rain, but instead we have snow.

ref

12

12f | Be sure the relative pronouns *who*, *which*, and *that* are appropriate for their antecedents.

We commonly use *who* to refer to persons and to animals that have names:

My dog Carly, *who* ran away last spring, turned up yesterday at the high school.

Which refers to animals and things:

I'd hoped to inherit the diamond stickpin, *which* my father wore at his wedding.

That refers to animals and things and occasionally to persons:

The book *that* I bought was missing seventy pages.
He studies babies *that* are just beginning to see.

(See also 21c-1 for the use of *which* and *that* in nonrestrictive and restrictive clauses.)

Unclear or remote antecedents of pronouns

ref

12

Circle each pronoun in the sentences below. Write the pronoun or pronouns whose antecedents are unclear on the blank to the right. Then revise the sentences so that all pronouns refer clearly to their antecedents.

Example: After the sick man tended (his) ailing brother, (he) developed a goiter. _____he_____

After the sick man tended his ailing brother, the brother developed a goiter.

Or:

After the sick man tended his ailing brother, the man developed a goiter.

1. After the tail pipe fell off Linda's car, Helen knew she _____ would have to take a bus.

2. The conservationists sent the senators a petition to repeal the laws, and the newspaper published an editorial on them. _____

3. As long as a group of technocrats made regulations for the students, frustration was going to plague them. _____

4. When my father was young, my grandfather regularly rubbed onions on his skin. _____

5. When I saw the dogs knock down two elderly people, I _____ ran toward them.

6. The salesman thought that the commission his partner _____ received would make him look bad.

7. I finally paid the bill for dental work that had been lying _____ around for several months.

8. Solar power promises relief from the energy shortage, _____ just as synthetic fuel does, but it would be more practical for northern climates.

9. The misspelling on the placard was unintentional, but it _____ was not noticed anyway.

10. Small foreign cars and small domestic cars are different: _____ They have a solid feel and good acceleration.

Implied or indefinite antecedents of pronouns

Circle each pronoun in the sentences below. Write the pronoun or pronouns whose antecedents are implied or indefinite on the blank to the right. Then revise the sentences so that all pronouns refer to definite, stated antecedents.

ref

12

Example: Television networks show such violent programs that   *it*
people want to try ⟨it⟩ in real life.

Television networks show such violent programs that people want to try violence in real life.

1. After being depressed for two weeks, she decided to get   _____
   over it and resume her routine.

2. When you lived in the nineteenth century, your feet and   _____
   your horses were your only private means of transportation.

3. Some toothpastes contain abrasives that whiten teeth.   _____
   However, it warns on the label that the abrasives may
   wear down tooth enamel.

4. They say that trouble comes in threes.   _____

5. After discussing the repair for the car, we knew it was   ———————
   time it was taken care of.

6. The exam was scheduled for Tuesday, which was not in   ———————
   my plans.

7. Many people shy away from the word *old* because they   ———————
   think of it as being ugly and withered.

8. The soldiers' orders in the war games left them unclear   ———————
   about where they were supposed to go.

9. The buses need more gasoline to run to distant places,   ———————
   they put on more miles, and they break down more often.
   This makes people's taxes higher.

10. He saw how expensive the supplies were for the art   ———————
    courses, which made him decide not to take them.

|*Pronoun reference: Review*   EXERCISE **12-3**

In the following paragraph, circle any pronoun whose antecedent is unclear, remote, implied, or indefinite. Then revise the sentences as necessary so that all pronouns refer clearly and appropriately to a definite and stated antecedent.

The three-story building, which had been constructed in 1935, was used for many years as a dormitory. Its wooden stairs were badly worn by the feet of thousands of students. It is a wonder that they never broke while they were hauling their heavy suitcases up to the third floor. Nothing had been repaired in it because it was deemed too costly. Then two years ago the building was turned into offices for the Arts and Sciences faculty. This causes less wear and tear on it. However, no refurbishing has ever been done to them. Recently, however, Professor Pines told Doctor Wiley that because of her efforts some funding might soon be allocated to redecorate them. I hope she is right. That will certainly please many faculty members who have found the rooms depressing.

13 Shifts

Self-test

In the following sentences, underline any unnecessary or confusing shifts in person, number, tense, mood, subject, voice, or form of quotation. If a sentence is already correct, write *OK* to the left of it.

Example: They had already left when the taxi <u>arrives</u>.

1. We entered the museum not knowing you were supposed to pay.
2. She wanted to know whether to take the job and did it pay well.
3. We planned to commute by car, but bus was found to be cheaper.
4. Oliver had no way of knowing we were there until he walks through the door.
5. The intensity of a person's feelings can cause you to act foolishly.
6. The waiter scowled at the diners, who had left a small tip.
7. A person should always have professional playing experience before they coach.
8. To revise a paper, read it through for errors, and then you should examine its structure.
9. All the members of the squad looked on me as their leader.
10. I had to decide whether to go on the trip and could I afford it?

   To be clear, a sentence, paragraph, or essay should be consistent in such grammatical elements as person, number, and tense unless grammar or meaning requires a shift. The following guidelines deal with each of these elements.

13a Keep sentences consistent in person and number.

INCONSISTENT   *We* learned before going on the desert tour that *you* should leave *your* itinerary with the park rangers. [Shift from first person to second person.]

REVISED   *We* learned before going on the desert tour that *we* should leave *our* itinerary with the park rangers.

199

INCONSISTENT	A football *player* should be in good condition even before *they* begin training. [Shift from singular to plural.]
REVISED	A football *player* should be in good condition even before *he* begins training.

13b | Keep sentences consistent in tense and mood.

INCONSISTENT	Doctors *had* no way to prevent polio until Salk *develops* the vaccine. [Shift from past tense to present tense.]
REVISED	Doctors *had* no way to prevent polio until Salk *developed* the vaccine.
INCONSISTENT	Teachers first insist that we *be* quiet in class and then that we *are supposed* to participate in discussions. [Shift from subjunctive to indicative mood.]
REVISED	Teachers first insist that we *be* quiet in class and then that we *participate* in discussions.

13c | Keep sentences consistent in subject and voice.

INCONSISTENT	If the *petition had been signed* by all of us students, *we would have won* reduced fees. [Shift in subject from *petition* to *we* and in voice from passive to active.]
REVISED	If all of us *students had signed* the petition, *we would have won* reduced fees.

13d | Don't shift unnecessarily between indirect and direct quotation.

Direct quotation reports the exact words of a speaker or writer, in quotation marks. **Indirect quotation** also reports what someone said or wrote, but not in the exact words and not in quotation marks.

INCONSISTENT	Jack asked why the Cubs kept losing and is there going to be a management change? [Shift from indirect to direct quotation.]
REVISED	Jack asked why the Cubs kept losing and whether there would be a management change. [Consistent indirect quotation.]
REVISED	Jack asked, "Why do the Cubs keep losing? Is there going to be a management change?" [Consistent direct quotation.]

|Revising for consistency

Examine each sentence below for any unnecessary shifts in person (*P*), number (*N*), tense (*T*), mood (*M*), subject (*S*), voice (*V*), or form of quotation (*Q*). If a sentence is inconsistent, identify each shift by writing the appropriate letter or letters on the blank to the right. Then rewrite the sentence to achieve consistency.

Example: The meetings were to be attended by representatives from   *S, V*
three colleges, but they could not agree on where to meet.

Representatives from three colleges were to attend the meeting, but they could not agree on where to meet.

1. He said he bought the recorder without asking would it   _____
work.

2. A person should stay clear of credit cards because they   _____
encourage you to spend more money than you have.

3. To have it printed, take it to the shop on Wednesday,   _____
and then you should call the next day.

4. Although the poet's words are fascinating, I do not know   _____
what they meant.

5. She wanted to buy flannel, but it was learned by her   _____
that she was allergic to flannel.

6. If one wants to get the most from college, you must work hard, ask questions, and keep an open mind. ————————

7. The two countries had had peaceful relations for a decade when suddenly a border dispute erupts into a war. ————————

8. An American going to a Japanese bath for the first time should have left his or her modesty at home. ————————

9. He said my face was red and was I embarrassed? ————————

10. When someone receives repeated nuisance phone calls, they have no choice but to change their number. ————————

11. After a mugger attacked the elderly man, he was taken to the hospital by police. ————————

12. To get the dog to swallow the pill, place it in the dog's mouth, and then one should stroke the dog's throat. ————————

13. A person should be aware of how poor night vision can endanger your life. ————————

14. The crowding one experiences at a beach can make you wish you had stayed home. ————————

15. The characters in the movie are average people, but they had more than average problems. ————————

|Shifts: Review

In the following paragraph, underline any unnecessary or confusing shifts in person, number, tense, mood, subject, voice, or form of quotation. Then revise the paragraph to achieve appropriate consistency both within sentences and from sentence to sentence.

shift

13

Our trip to the beach got off to a bad start when the car has two flat tires a mile from home. You can always count on some trouble with our car, but nothing so annoying. We arrived at the motel late, but, fortunately, our reservations had not been canceled by the manager, who remembers us from last time. He asked how long we would be staying and do we want the seafood special for dinner. We checked into our room, and our luggage was unpacked. Everything was going smoothly. Then we went to dinner and turned in for the night. One would have expected that the rest of the vacation should be routine if not fun. But that night each one of us gets sick from their seafood dinner. The next morning the rain came, and for the next three days we just sat in the room playing cards

until it was time that our trip home had to be made.

14 Misplaced and Dangling Modifiers

Self-test

In the following sentences, underline any words or phrases that do not clearly modify the words intended or that relate nonsensically to other words. If a sentence is already correct, write *OK* to the left of it.

Example: The man said he thought the car was in good condition <u>during his sales pitch</u>.

1. Art only walked to the campus once last month.
2. Looking in the mirror, the new suit was very becoming.
3. She kept the dog in the closet that was housebroken.
4. After calling the repairman, the furnace started working.
5. He kept the marble cups that he bought in Taiwan during his tour last spring in the closet.
6. Having hired an attorney, the lawsuit was under way.
7. Never again in his life did he want to travel by boat.
8. Two teams were in the play-offs that were undefeated.
9. To gain entry, a special pass is necessary.
10. Six of us ordered drinks at the bar that tasted like after-shave lotion.

MISPLACED MODIFIERS

A **misplaced modifier** does not clearly modify the word intended by the writer.

14a | Place prepositional phrases where they will clearly modify the words intended.

CONFUSING The teacher said that she expected us to do well on the exam *during her lecture.*

CLEAR *During her lecture,* the teacher said that she expected us to do well on the exam.

14b | Place subordinate clauses where they will clearly modify the words intended.

CONFUSING   The house was in the woods *that burned last night.*

CLEAR   The house *that burned last night* was in the woods.

14c | Place limiting modifiers carefully.

Limiting modifiers such as *almost, even, just, only,* and *simply* modify the words or word groups that immediately follow them.

Aaron sold *only* one car today. [He sold no more than one.]
Only Aaron sold one car today. [No one else sold one car.]

14d | Avoid squinting modifiers.

A **squinting modifier** may refer to either a word preceding it or a word following it.

SQUINTING   The ambassador invited them *before leaving* to visit her.

CLEAR   *Before leaving,* the ambassador invited them to visit her.

CLEAR   The ambassador invited them to visit her *before leaving.*

14e | Avoid separating a subject from its verb or a verb from its object or complement.

We frequently interrupt a subject and its predicate or a verb and its object or complement with modifiers relating to one of the parts, as in *The people who take that attitude deserve to be friendless.* However, a long modifier in such a position may make a sentence awkward or confusing, especially if it precedes the word it modifies or relates to the whole sentence.

AWKWARD   The old papers were, *just as I had suspected when I found them in the attic,* valuable.

REVISED   The old papers were valuable, *just as I had suspected when I found them in the attic.*

14f | Avoid separating the parts of a verb phrase or the parts of an infinitive.

AWKWARD   The boys *had,* with the money made from shoveling snow, *bought* firecrackers. [Verb phrase split.]

REVISED   With the money made from shoveling snow, the boys *had bought* firecrackers.

AWKWARD   The aides are expected *to* without delay *do* whatever the nurses ask. [Infinitive split.]

REVISED   The aides are expected *to do* without delay whatever the nurses ask.

Note that it is sometimes natural and acceptable to split an infinitive with a single-word modifier when the alternative would be awkward: *To openly shun younger students is not only arrogant but rude.*

DANGLING MODIFIERS

14g | Avoid dangling modifiers.

A **dangling modifier** is one that does not relate sensibly to any word in its sentence.

> DANGLING · To win the marathon, the weather should be cool. [The modifying phrase *To win the marathon* seems, illogically, to describe *weather*.]

A dangling modifier usually appears at the beginning of a sentence, and it is usually a participial phrase (*screaming for help*), an infinitive phrase (*to arrive on time*), a prepositional phrase in which the object of the preposition is a gerund (*after riding the subway*), or an elliptical clause in which the subject is understood (*while in school*). (See 5c.) Since these constructions do not name their subjects, they appear to modify the subject of the following main clause. If the two subjects are different, the modifier dangles.

> DANGLING · *After riding the subway,* my wallet was missing. [Prepositional phrase appears to modify *wallet*, so that the wallet rather than a person appears to have been riding the subway.]
>
> REVISED · *After I had ridden the subway,* my wallet was missing. [Prepositional phrase made into a subordinate clause with an expressed subject.]
>
> DANGLING · *Screaming for help,* his cries were heard throughout the building. [Participial phrase appears to modify *cries*, so that the cries appear to have been screaming.]
>
> REVISED · *Screaming for help,* he was heard throughout the building. [The subject *he* in the main clause is now the same as the unnamed subject of the participial phrase.]

|Revising misplaced modifiers EXERCISE **14-1**

In the sentences below, identify each misplaced modifier by underlining it. Then rewrite the sentence, placing the modifier where it belongs. If the sentence is already correct, write *OK* in the space below it.

mm, dm

14

Example: I entered the frog <u>in the contest</u> that can jump sixteen feet.

In the contest I entered the frog that can jump sixteen feet.

1. She remembered the heroine in the play with a sense of humor.

2. The charter flight he wants to take on Monday will be canceled.

3. The catcher threw to second base and got the runner out as soon as the third strike had landed in his mitt.

4. Tobacco companies suggest that cigarettes are good for us in their ads.

5. The tragedy shocked us all that occurred in the stadium.

6. Seven people came to the dance in a jeep.

7. The man purchased perfume in the store that smelled of lilacs.

8. Those of us who expect raises soon will be surprised.

9. The fans were devoted to John Lennon who crowded the streets during the memorial service.

10. They just bought gasoline before starting for the mountains.

11. Those who get average grades occasionally drop out of school.

12. Students only were allowed one helping at the dinner.

13. Mary wanted to have lunch in the park under the trees.

14. The rude woman blew smoke in our food that smelled like burning tires.

15. The man who committed the theft recently was caught.

|*Revising misplaced modifiers*   EXERCISE **14-2**

In the sentences below, underline the modifiers that cause awkwardness or confusion because they separate subject from predicate, verb from complement or object, parts of a verb phrase, or parts of an infinitive. Then rewrite each sentence, placing the modifier where it belongs.

Example: Maria had ever since junior high school planned to be a teacher.

Ever since junior high school, Maria had planned to be a teacher.

1. The chairs had been placed near the edge of the pool in order to with ease allow us to watch the children.

2. To have, with energy to spare, the ability to run as far as the courthouse is his goal.

3. The bicycle hit at high speed, with the front wheel wobbling crazily, the curb, throwing the rider into the hedge.

4. People drive ten miles hoping to, at the rate of a few cents a gallon, save themselves money.

5. Henry chose to, after a great deal of consideration, buy a violin that cost $2000.

6. The law requires, for the safety of the drivers behind you, that your brake lights be in working order at all times.

7. They held, on nearly any issue of importance, a difference of opinion.

8. You will see that the new building, after the ceremonies have ended and the bills have been paid, was absurdly expensive.

9. Mark Twain never made, during all his years as a writer, as much money as a professional quarterback makes in a year.

10. Arthritis tends to slowly and painfully swell a person's joints.

11. I always found she made, whenever asked to do something, excuses and objections.

12. He, unfortunately, because he had little money, could not pay for the dinner.

13. A model train set can, no matter how simple or complex a system it is, allow a person to use his or her dramatic imagination.

14. The players were able to expertly and for several minutes stall the game.

15. The relations between the two for over six years had been strained.

Name _____ Date _____ Score _____

|*Revising dangling modifiers*   EXERCISE **14-3**

Most of the sentences below contain dangling modifiers. Rewrite each incorrect sentence so that it is clear and correct. If a sentence is already correct, write *OK* in the space below it.

mm, dm

14

Example: To operate a citizen's-band radio, the fee is no longer required.

To operate a citizen's-band radio, one no longer needs to pay a fee.

1. When reading poetry, rhythm often contributes to meaning.

2. After selecting an entrée, a wine should be ordered.

3. To recover from the surgery, the vet recommended leaving our puppy overnight.

4. When painting the walls, care should be taken to protect the floor from dripping brushes.

5. After adding three cups of ground chickpeas, the pot should be heated.

6. Taking a look at the gifts, the smallest box was the one the child selected.

213

7. Going for a touchdown, the quarterback lofted the ball.

8. Being a nonconformist, a multicolored wig was what she chose to wear.

9. With no concern that the audience was bored, the lecture continued for two hours.

10. To get the employer's attention, your résumé should be attractive and informative.

Misplaced and dangling modifiers: Review

Underline any misplaced or dangling modifiers in the following paragraph. Then revise the paragraph by moving modifiers, adding words, or rewriting sentences as necessary.

To successfully and calmly wait at a dentist's office before having your teeth drilled, a little preparation can make a great difference. First, select for taking along to the dentist's office your own book. Never plan to read old magazines dentists set around their waiting rooms that are always dog-eared, dated, and boring. Such magazines cannot provide you any escape from anticipating the pain that awaits you. Second, because you only by arriving early can increase your anxiety, arrive exactly on time and hope your wait will be brief. Third, have a good joke that you can tell the dentist in mind, because a dentist will be less likely to hurt you who is not feeling tense. By keeping the dentist at ease, the most important step will be achieved. A big pain, however, comes when the

dentist finishes. It is then that you must pay the bill.

mm, dm

14

15 | *Mixed and Incomplete Sentences*

Self-test

Write *M* on the blank to the right of any sentence that has mixed structure (parts that do not fit together in grammar or meaning). Write *I* on the blank if the sentence has an illogical or incomplete comparison. If a sentence is already correct, write *OK* on the blank.

Example: Getting a puppy is when you are up all night. ___*M*___

1. The reason we lost was because of a weak center. _____

2. Physics is where you apply mathematics to theory. _____

3. Joyce likes Sam better than Carol. _____

4. The Civil War era was a period of economic strain. _____

5. Cigars are more dangerous to inhale than any tobacco product. _____

6. Some kinds of gasoline have higher octane. _____

7. After the test relaxed all of us. _____

8. The ones who are opposed or uninterested in participating stayed away from the rally. _____

9. A problem that came up was my stereo when the speaker blew out. _____

10. The catcher dropped the ball is why the runner is safe. _____

MIXED SENTENCES

A **mixed sentence** is one whose parts do not fit together, either in grammar or in meaning.

15a | Be sure that the parts of your sentences, particularly subjects and predicates, fit together grammatically.

A mixed sentence will occur if you begin a sentence with one grammatical construction and end it with another.

MIXED	During the worst part of the storm frightened all of us.
REVISED	During the worst part of the storm, all of us were frightened.
REVISED	The worst part of the storm frightened all of us.

15b | Be sure that the subjects and predicates of your sentences fit together in meaning.

A mixed sentence will also occur if its subject and predicate are incompatible in meaning, especially if a subject and its complement are not sensibly equated by the linking verb between them.

MIXED	A prank that irks me is my brother when he jumps out from behind corners. [The prank is not the brother.]
REVISED	A prank that irks me is my brother's jumping out from behind corners.
MIXED	The reason for her failure is because she was ill. [A noun clause is needed to complement the subject *reason*, but *because* signals an adverb clause.]
REVISED	The reason for her failure is that she was ill.

INCOMPLETE SENTENCES

15c | Be sure that omissions from compound constructions are consistent with grammar or idiom.

INCOMPLETE	My grandparents' generation was indoctrinated in conventional morality and strong-minded as a result.
REVISED	My grandparents' generation was indoctrinated in conventional morality and *was* strong-minded as a result. [The first *was* is part of a passive construction; the second is a linking verb.]
INCOMPLETE	Most of us lack knowledge or comfort with science.
REVISED	Most of us lack knowledge *of* or comfort with science. [Idiom requires different prepositions with *knowledge* and *comfort*. (See also 31b-3.)]

15d | Be sure that all comparisons are complete and logical.

1 | State a comparison fully enough to ensure clarity.

UNCLEAR	Mars is nearer to us than Pluto.
CLEAR	Mars is nearer to us than *it is to* Pluto.
CLEAR	Mars is nearer to us than Pluto *is*.

2 | Be sure that the items being compared are in fact comparable.

| UNCLEAR | The chimpanzee's thumb is smaller than a *human*. |
| CLEAR | The chimpanzee's thumb is smaller than a *human's*. |

3 | In comparing members of the same class, use *other* or *any other*. In comparing members of different classes, use *any*.

ILLOGICAL	The Pacific is larger than *any* ocean in the world.
LOGICAL	The Pacific is larger than *any other* ocean in the world.
ILLOGICAL	Toyotas are more popular than *any other* American car.
LOGICAL	Toyotas are more popular than *any* American car.

4 | Avoid comparisons that do not state what is being compared.

| NOT | That restaurant is *better*. |
| BUT | That restaurant is *better than the other one we went to*. |

15e | Be careful not to omit articles, prepositions, or other needed words.

Writers sometimes omit necessary words because of inattentive proofreading.

| INCOMPLETE | She sat moodily in front the fireplace. |
| REVISED | She sat moodily in front *of* the fireplace. |

Writers often omit *that* when it introduces a noun clause: *We realized (that) Joe was responsible.* But sometimes such an omission may cause an initial misreading: *Karen knew the flower vendor on the corner would leave by dark.* (At first reading, we think that Karen knew who the flower vendor was rather than what time the vendor would leave.)

Revising mixed sentences EXERCISE **15-1**

Revise each mixed sentence below, changing, adding, or deleting words as needed to make its parts fit together in grammar and meaning.

Example: The team that won was the result of bad refereeing.

The team's winning was the result of bad refereeing.

1. While bargaining for a discount was how she made the clerk angry.

2. The appliance cost $300, and which was too much for an automatic dishwasher, I thought.

3. A candle-making kit was the way she made the designs.

4. Hesitation is when we lost our chance.

5. The toy department, which hired only women, which I thought was discrimination.

6. In his attempt to get good grades was how he started cheating.

7. For someone who knows that fighting and sports are not necessarily related could be very disappointed at a hockey game.

8. The hardware store that burned down on First Street was caused by an arsonist.

mixed, inc

15

9. Our living-room window cracked was caused by the noise from jet airliners.

10. The reason he was lonely was because he had a quick, violent temper.

Revising
incomplete sentences

Adding or changing words as necessary, rewrite the following sentences to provide any carelessly omitted words or to complete the compound constructions and comparisons.

Example: The apartment was as roomy as any other house.

The apartment was as roomy as any house.

1. We suspect that Judy is more devoted to music than Andy.

2. The administration claims to believe and plan for the college's future.

3. Some brands of vodka contain more alcohol than any beverage.

4. I was going seventy miles per hour and stopped for speeding.

5. The Hilton's room service is as good as the Astor.

6. They were fond and totally devoted to their grandchild.

7. The second-night audience found the play more impressive than the opening-night audience.

8. He left the art book in the car or the basketball practice.

9. Aspirin does more good and less harmful to you than some other nonprescription drugs.

10. Faulkner's novels are more complex than any author's.

11. He fears death more than his sister.

12. Fruit juice stains are harder to remove than grass.

13. All the voting members are consulted regularly and present at every meeting.

14. The living room was larger than any other house she had ever seen.

15. All those opposed or in favor of the resolution raised their hands.

Mixed and incomplete sentences: Review

EXERCISE **15-3**

Circle the number preceding any mixed or incomplete sentence in the following paragraph. Then revise the paragraph by changing, deleting, or adding words as necessary.

[1] During the first day at college was somewhat frightening for me. [2] I was unsure of my ability to meet new people and do well in my classes. [3] I began feeling more secure when I met my roommate, who was friendlier than any student I had met so far. [4] The second day I met my classes and learned the professors and my classmates were all human. [5] Most seemed nice. [6] When I got the assignments and heard what was expected of me gave me even more security. [7] By the third day, I felt relaxed. [8] I knew my schedule very well, and I was beginning make friends. [9] Although I had planned to go home on the first weekend, I stayed on campus. [10] Now I do not plan to home until Thanksgiving.

IV | Effective Sentences

16 | *Using Coordination and Subordination*

Self-test

In each set of sentences below, circle the letter preceding the sentence that most effectively establishes relations among ideas in the sentence.

coord, sub

16

Example: a. The 3:30 flight, which crashed on the runway, had engine problems.
 b. The 3:30 flight, which had engine problems, crashed on the runway.

1. a. Because the doctor had moved from the town, 325 persons had nowhere to go for emergency treatment.
   b. The doctor moved from the town, and 325 persons had nowhere to go for emergency treatment.
2. a. The islanders once practiced cannibalism and infanticide, and they now operate hospitals.
   b. The islanders, who once practiced cannibalism and infanticide, now operate hospitals.
3. a. Roland, an accomplished pole-vaulter, won three national championships.
   b. Roland was an accomplished pole-vaulter, and he won three national championships.
4. a. The box had a locked, blue lid, and he carried it with him everywhere.
   b. He carried the box, which had a locked, blue lid, with him everywhere.
5. a. I had read twenty reports of rabies, and I was quite wary of the raccoon.
   b. Having read twenty reports of rabies, I was quite wary of the raccoon.
6. a. As he was missing the ball game, the child hunched angrily over the keyboard.
   b. Because he was missing the ball game, the child hunched angrily over the keyboard.

227

7. a. The donation went to refugee orphans, who were suffering from malnutrition.
   b. The donation went to refugee orphans, and they were suffering from malnutrition.
8. a. We finally finished rehearsing the song, but the polls had already closed, so I didn't have a chance to vote.
   b. Because the polls had already closed by the time we finished rehearsing the song, I didn't have a chance to vote.
9. a. The woman decided to rake the leaves even though they were blowing against the fence.
   b. The woman decided to rake the leaves, and they were blowing against the fence.
10. a. The test, which I failed and which made me want to quit school, was given on Monday.
    b. Because I failed the test on Monday, I wanted to quit school.

Use **coordination** to give equal emphasis to the meanings contained in two or more sentence elements: *The conductor fainted, but the orchestra played on.* Use **subordination** to emphasize the meaning in one element over that in another: *When the conductor fainted, the orchestra played on.*

16a | Coordinating to relate equal ideas

Coordination is achieved by linking sentence elements with the coordinating conjunctions *and, but, or, nor,* and sometimes *for, so,* and *yet* (see 5d-1); by linking elements with conjunctive adverbs such as *however* and *therefore* (see 5d-2); or by expressing elements in the same grammatical construction (see Chapter 17 on parallelism). By linking ideas, coordination shows a relation between them that simple sentences alone rarely can.

> Men in the Middle Ages granted women few political rights. Men idolized women in literature. [No relation established.]
> Men in the Middle Ages granted women few political rights, *but* they idolized women in literature. [Coordinating conjunction.]
> Men in the Middle Ages granted women few political rights; *however,* they idolized women in literature. [Conjunctive adverb.]
> Men in the Middle Ages *excluded women from politics* but *idolized them in literature.* [Parallelism and coordinating conjunction.]

1 | Avoiding faulty coordination

Faulty coordination occurs when two ideas that are coordinated do not seem related in fact.

> FAULTY   The crash occurred at night, and all the passengers were rescued.

REVISED	Because the crash occurred at night, the rescuers had a difficult job. However, they rescued all the passengers.

2 | Avoiding excessive coordination

Though coordination can establish relations between ideas, it does not do so as effectively as subordination does. Since strings of compounded elements may blur relations, use subordination to clarify relations and to vary sentence structure.

EXCESSIVE COORDINATION	I spent Easter vacation at the beach, and I met my future wife, and three months later we were married.
REVISED	During my Easter vacation at the beach, I met my future wife. After three months we were married.

16b | Subordinating to distinguish the main idea

As the example above shows, subordination allows you to play down less significant information and to stress your important points by placing them in main clauses. Subordinate information may be conveyed in a subordinate clause (introduced by a subordinating conjunction like *although* or *when* or a relative pronoun — *who, which,* or *that*), in a phrase, or in a single word.

coord, sub

16

The dog snarled at me, and it ran to the fence. [Compound sentence gives equal emphasis to both ideas by placing both in main clauses.]
After it snarled at me, the dog ran to the fence. [Subordinate clause reduces emphasis on the dog's snarling.]
Snarling at me, the dog ran to the fence. [Participial phrase further subordinates the dog's snarling.]
The *snarling* dog ran to the fence. [Adjective gives minimum emphasis to the dog's snarling.]

1 | Avoiding faulty subordination

Faulty subordination occurs when the idea expressed in a subordinate clause or a phrase seems more important than the idea expressed in the main clause.

FAULTY	Elephants and their ancestors have ruled the plains for millions of years, although they are now being squeezed out by humans.
REVISED	Although elephants and their ancestors have ruled the plains for millions of years, they are now being squeezed out by humans.

2 | Avoiding excessive subordination

Excessive subordination occurs when too many subordinate constructions, containing details only loosely related, are strung together in a single sentence. The result is not only awkward but confusing. A common kind of excessive subordination occurs with the use of a succession of modifying *which* clauses. Use other modifying structures to simplify the sentence.

EXCESSIVE SUBORDINATION We waited to hear the announcement, which was scheduled for noon, over the intercom, which had speakers in the halls, which we congregated in.

REVISED We congregated in the halls, waiting to hear the announcement that was scheduled to come over the intercom at noon.

16c | Choosing clear connectors

1 | Avoiding ambiguous connectors: *as* and *while*

Because the subordinating conjunction *as* can indicate a relation of time or cause (as well as comparison), its meaning in a sentence may be unclear.

coord, sub

16

UNCLEAR *As* I was awaiting a visitor, the telephone's ringing surprised me.

CLEAR *When* I was awaiting a visitor, the telephone's ringing surprised me.

CLEAR *Because* I was awaiting a visitor, the telephone's ringing surprised me.

Similarly, the subordinating conjunction *while* can indicate a relation of time or concession. If the meaning of *while* is not unmistakably clear, use a more precise connector.

UNCLEAR *While* the downtown stores were renovated, customers flocked to the shopping malls.

CLEAR *Until* the downtown stores were renovated, customers flocked to the shopping malls.

CLEAR *Although* the downtown stores were renovated, customers flocked to the shopping malls.

2 | Avoiding misused connectors: *as*, *like*, and *while*

As is a nonstandard substitute for *whether* or *that: I was pleased that* (not *as*) *he singled me out.*

Like should be avoided as a subordinating conjunction in writing, even though it is common in speech and in advertising: *She drove as if* (or *as though*, but not *like*) *someone were chasing her.*

The subordinating conjunction *while* should not be used to substitute for the coordinating conjunction *and* or *but: Chaucer wrote a great deal of poetry, but* (not *while*) *none of it is drama.*

|Using coordination   EXERCISE **16-1**

Combine each pair of simple sentences below into one sentence, using the coordinating conjunction that is most appropriate for meaning. Choose from *and, but, or, nor, for, so,* and *yet.* Try to use each conjunction at least once.

Example: The novels have richly varied characters. The philosophy contained in all the novels is the same.

The novels have richly varied characters, but they all contain the same philosophy.

1. Television announcers want to look appealing on color sets. They usually wear bright clothing.

2. Gretzky broke the record for the number of goals in a single season. He is also likely to break the lifetime record.

3. She exercises for several hours a day. She sleeps well at night.

4. Winter driving is hazardous. More accidents occur in summer than in winter.

5. Rush hour is my favorite time to drive. I enjoy the challenge of heavy traffic.

6. You should go to sleep now. You won't be able to play in the game tomorrow.

7. I do not enjoy physics. I do not enjoy the other sciences either.

8. The reporter was fired from the newspaper. She has now been unemployed for a year.

9. Woody Allen is our favorite film director. We have seen all of his films.

10. A set of tennis gives me ample exercise. The running burns off hundreds of calories.

|Using subordination   EXERCISE **16-2**

Combine each pair of simple sentences below into one sentence by placing the less important information in a subordinate clause, a phrase, or a single word, as specified in parentheses.

Example: Many Americans favor handgun control. Congress has not enacted any laws requiring it. (Subordinate clause beginning with *although.*)

Although many Americans favor handgun control, Congress has not enacted any laws requiring it.

1. His shoulders are slightly stooped. He still looks energetic. (Subordinate clause beginning with *although.*)

2. Tonight he played his greatest role. It was Lothario. (Single word.)

3. We were nearly at the end of our trip. Then we were stopped by the state police. (Phrase beginning with *nearly.*)

4. The meeting ended. The hall was again deserted. (Subordinate clause beginning with *after.*)

5. Sparrows are unwelcome pests. They may eat as much as 6 percent of a grain crop. (Phrase beginning with *unwelcome*.)

6. She wore jogging shoes. The waiter refused to seat her. (Subordinate clause beginning with *because*.)

7. The patient was recovering. He was depressed and irritable. (Single word.)

8. He felt embarrassed. He could not get a word out. (Phrase beginning with *feeling*.)

9. German stereo components are often of high quality. They are usually more expensive than Japanese components. (Subordinate clause beginning with *although*.)

10. I did not know how to interpret the question. It had four possible answers. (Subordinate clause beginning with *because*.)

*Using coordination
and subordination*   EXERCISE **16-3**

Revise each passage below to use both coordination and subordination effectively in establishing relations among ideas and in distinguishing main ideas from less important ones.

1. A good example of corruption occurred in the U.S. Navy. The event occurred recently. A Washington columnist told the story. An officer was demoted. He had reported some of his fellow officers. The officers were responsible for training recruits. The officers had sold the recruits uniforms. The uniforms were supposed to be issued free.

coord, sub

16

_____

_____

_____

_____

_____

_____

_____

_____

_____

2. A triangle was tattooed on the back of his hand. He got the tattoo when he was sixteen. It was a symbol of the instrument he had played. He had played in a rock band. His instrument had been a brass triangle.

_____

_____

_____

_____

_____

_____

_____

_____

_____

coord, sub

16

3. The night was black, and the road was slippery, and the car, which ran up an embankment, rolled over twice, an action that caused the occupants to be thrown out, while no one was injured. The car was a total loss.

_____

_____

_____

_____

_____

_____

_____

_____

_____

17|Using Parallelism

Self-test

Some of the following sentences could be made more effective if words and phrases with parallel importance and function were given parallel grammatical form. If a sentence seems ineffective because of a lack of parallelism, underline those words or phrases that should be given parallel form. If a sentence uses parallelism effectively, write *OK* to the left of it.

Example: I spent the evening <u>reading</u> and <u>with music.</u>

1. Going to a professional football game is better than to watch one.
2. The Episcopalians and those who are Catholics have more ritual in their services than Methodism has.
3. In the spring I took economics, and in the fall I took statistics.
4. Men's clothing styles and the clothes that women wear have grown similar in recent years.
5. In both the campus and in the town, sentiment for drug control was strong.
6. Field trips are required not only for biology but also for geology.
7. The seniors, juniors, and the sophomores all helped raise money.
8. To coach professional baseball and coaching professional football were both career possibilities for him.
9. Listening to records and attendance at live concerts are both enjoyable.
10. In many aspects of technology, the Japanese excel over England.

Parallelism is the duplication of grammatical form between two or more coordinate elements:

I was beckoned by	the	broad	blue	horizon
and	the	straight	open	road.

Parallelism gives the same grammatical form to elements with the same function and importance. It also emphasizes important points and gives a sentence coherence.

17a | Using parallelism for coordinate elements

1 | Using parallelism for elements linked by coordinating conjunctions

The coordinating conjunctions *and, but, or, nor,* and *yet* should link words, phrases, and clauses that are the same grammatically.

> **FAULTY**   A commercial should be *of interest* and *informative.*
>
> **REVISED**   A commercial should be *interesting* and *informative.*
>
> **FAULTY**   The rookie pitched an uneven game, *allowing only three hits,* but *he walked seven batters.*
>
> **REVISED**   The rookie pitched an uneven game, *allowing only three hits* but *walking seven batters.*

2 | Using parallelism for elements linked by correlative conjunctions

Correlative conjunctions (such as *not only . . . but also, either . . . or, both . . . and*) should always link parallel elements. Be sure to include prepositions and the word *to* with an infinitive after the second part of the connector.

> **FAULTY**   The poet wrote not only *of Greece* but also *Asia Minor.*
>
> **REVISED**   The poet wrote not only *of Greece* but also *of Asia Minor.*
>
> **FAULTY**   He said either *to wait* or *go* without him.
>
> **REVISED**   He said either *to wait* or *to go* without him.

3 | Using parallelism for elements being compared or contrasted

> **FAULTY**   *Riding* in a parade is better than *to watch* one.
>
> **REVISED**   *Riding* in a parade is better than *watching* one.

4 | Using parallelism for items in lists or outlines

> **FAULTY**   The most dangerous forms of transportation are *riding motorcycles, cars,* and *riding a bicycle.*
>
> **REVISED**   The most dangerous forms of transportation are *motorcycles, cars,* and *bicycles.*

17b | Using parallelism to increase coherence

Parallelism helps to strengthen the relation between elements in a sentence.

> **FAULTY**   As the curtain opened, *three actors moved on stage to simulate* a sword fight, and *behind them was slipped a backdrop that showed* a castle's walls.
>
> **REVISED**   As the curtain opened, *three actors moved on stage to simulate* a sword fight, and *a backdrop slipped behind them to show* a castle's walls.

//

17

|Identifying parallelism

Identify the parallel elements in each sentence below by underlining them.

Example: Fitzgerald was a novelist of the <u>1920s</u> and <u>1930s</u> who wrote <u>colorful short stories</u> and <u>romantic novels</u>.

1. The people crowded the main street, pouring from cars, trucks, buses, and subways.

2. In the lawn, in the garden, in the orchard — gypsy moths were everywhere she looked.

3. The Baptists and the Methodists have similar doctrines.

4. Some patients played checkers, others played cards, and still others played shuffleboard.

5. One bit of old-fashioned advice warns against baths in the morning and instead urges baths in the evening.

6. I think that self-help books, which not only peddle common sense but also inflate expectations, do more harm than good for their readers.

7. The kitchen doors squeaked on their hinges, plates clattered on the tables, and diners chattered throughout the small room.

8. Cigarette smoking is unhealthful not only for the smokers themselves but also for the nonsmokers around them.

9. Her clasped hands, her taut shoulders, and her tense face showed her concern.

10. I will go out of my way to see an old movie or to watch a puppet show.

11. Peering into the room and pushing against the windows, the children stared eagerly at the Christmas display.

12. Looking both at the exam paper and at the assignment sheet, she threw up her hands.

13. Last week I claimed that I would never again take an English course, but this week I find that I enjoy English.

//

17

14. His cheerful face, caked, chapped, and hardened, revealed not only the nature of his work but also the strength of his character.

15. Grease spots and tobacco stains made a curious design on his pink tie.

//
17

|Achieving parallelism   EXERCISE **17-2**

The sentences below are weakened by a lack of parallelism for coordinate elements. Locate the coordinate elements and revise the sentence to make the elements parallel.

Example: I would much rather have an older model Corvette than a new one because of the older one's body style and the engine is more powerful.

I would much rather have an older Corvette than a newer one because the older one has a better body style and a more powerful engine.

//

17

1. Replacing Chevrolet engine parts costs more than replacing the parts of an Oldsmobile.

2. With a lack of cash and not having a credit card, we could not fill the gas tank.

3. Neither a paper clip nor should a knife be used for cleaning a stereo needle.

4. She left the thermostat on high, took long showers, and she was a waster of energy.

5. Either by entering the side gate without paying or stealing tickets, they get in for free.

6. The bill could have been determined either at the hourly rate or determined at the job rate.

7. The corporation agreed to recall the cars and make the repair or is refunding the cost of replacement.

8. Different persons respond to different types of music, such as folk, rock, or they like to listen to blues.

9. The statistics were either unavailable or they were inaccurate.

10. There are many sports in which Americans excel over Europe.

| *Parallelism: Review*   EXERCISE **17-3**

Combine each set of sentences below into a single sentence, using parallel structures wherever appropriate.

Example: Cattle management is being mechanized. Strip-mining consumes the rangelands. The rangelands are also being consumed by housing developments.

Because cattle management is being mechanized and the rangelands are being consumed by strip-mining and housing developments, cowboys are becoming an endangered species.

//

17

1. Our school has put on several musicals. In May we put on *Godspell.* We put on *Hello, Dolly* in February. Two months before that, we did *Jesus Christ, Superstar.*

2. We paid $30 for steaks. The drinks cost $3.60. We spent $40 for the picnic.

3. The heat was stifling. Also stifling was the humidity. Thus we stayed indoors.

4. He often read aloud from Robert Frost's poetry. He also read from novels by Ernest Hemingway. He also read from plays written by Harold Pinter.

243

5. Elizabeth collected only commemorative stamps. Foreign stamps were all her father collected. They both collected only canceled stamps to keep their hobbies inexpensive.

6. During the summer easterly trade winds make the air feel pleasant. The air during the winter feels chilly because of dampness.

7. Civil defense may be a good use of our money. Or the money we spend on it may be wasted.

8. Sunlight reflected off the glass sides of the building. Drivers had difficulty seeing the traffic lights. The Walk/Don't Walk signs were hard for the pedestrians to see.

9. Many of the pictures were underexposed. A few of the pictures were exposed too much. Only one was exposed properly.

10. On his first trip to New York, he was mugged. He was hit by a taxi on his second trip. Someone stole his camera on his third trip.

18 Emphasizing Main Ideas

Self-test

In each set of sentences below, circle the letter of the sentence that better emphasizes the main point.

Example: a. Crime affects thousands of people each day, and few crimes are solved.

      (b.) Although crime affects thousands of people each day, few crimes are solved.

1. a. Because of a heavy snow and icy roads, the delivery truck did not make its rounds.
   b. The delivery truck did not make its rounds because a heavy snow fell and the roads were icy.
2. a. The first year his batting average was .220, the second year it was .300, and the third year it was .200.
   b. The first year his batting average was .220 and the third year it was .200, but the second year it was .300.
3. a. The manager forgot the cash box in the desk.
   b. The cash box in the desk was forgotten by the manager.
4. a. It is her desire to run her own architectural firm.
   b. She wants to run her own architectural firm.
5. a. When the city legalized pornography, the tax revenue increased and the population doubled.
   b. The population doubled when the city legalized pornography, and the tax revenue increased.
6. a. It is probable that the telephone company will introduce inexpensive telecopiers for residential customers.
   b. The telephone company will probably introduce inexpensive telecopiers for residential customers.
7. a. A man should seek to know in order to live instead of seeking to live in order to know.
   b. A man should seek to know in order to live, not seek to live in order to know.
8. a. Some spectators were angry, some were disappointed, but all wanted refunds.
   b. All the spectators wanted refunds, some were disappointed, and some were angry.

emph

18

9. a. The defendant left the building by a rope ladder, according to a witness who testified on the first day of the trial.

   b. According to a witness who testified on the first day of the trial, the defendant left the building by a rope ladder.

10. a. Hovering around me, his brother watched everything I did by looking over my shoulder.

   b. His brother watched everything I did, hovering around me and looking over my shoulder.

Use sentence construction to emphasize your main ideas.

18a | Arranging ideas effectively

1 | Using sentence beginnings and endings

The most emphatic positions in a sentence are the beginning and the ending. Don't bury an important idea in the middle of a sentence.

> UNEMPHATIC Because its winds sometimes exceed 500 miles per hour and it has more energy than an atomic bomb, *the tornado is one of the most destructive forces on earth*, and it can strike without warning.

> REVISED *The tornado is one of the most destructive forces on earth* because its winds sometimes exceed 500 miles per hour, it has more energy than an atomic bomb, and it can strike without warning.

> REVISED Because its winds sometimes exceed 500 miles an hour, it has more energy than an atomic bomb, and it can strike without warning, *the tornado is one of the most destructive forces on earth*.

The first revision above is a **cumulative,** or **loose, sentence:** The main point comes first and is followed by explanation. The second revision is a **periodic sentence:** All the explanation comes first, and the main point comes at the end. Since the main clause is withheld until the end of the sentence, the periodic sentence creates suspense.

2 | Arranging parallel elements effectively

Elements in a series using parallel constructions (see Chapter 17) should be arranged in order of increasing importance.

> UNEMPHATIC The friends he had, in general the life he led, the books he read, the sports he played — all brought him satisfaction.

> REVISED The books he read, the sports he played, the friends he had, in general the life he led — all brought him satisfaction.

A **balanced sentence** — one made up of directly parallel clauses — can be very emphatic.

> The screen filled with color; the hall filled with music.
> The climb was painfully difficult; the descent was refreshingly simple.

18b | Repeating ideas

Needless repetition will weaken a sentence, but careful repetition of a key word or phrase can effectively emphasize that word or phrase.

> Cholera, which kills by dehydration, should be treated *by giving* the victim huge amounts of water, *not by giving* food intravenously and *not by giving* a drug.

18c | Separating ideas

Setting a statement off from the ideas to which it relates emphasizes it.

> The uncontrolled fire destroyed stores, offices, and homes.
> The fire — uncontrolled — destroyed stores, offices, and homes.
> The fire was uncontrolled. It destroyed stores, offices, and homes.

emph

18

18d | Preferring the active voice

In the active voice the subject acts; in the passive voice the subject is acted upon. (See Chapter 7.) Active constructions are usually more direct and emphatic than passive constructions.

> PASSIVE   The game was watched with great interest by the scout.
>
> ACTIVE   The scout watched the game with great interest.

18e | Being concise

Unnecessary words weaken sentences. Concise sentences convey the essential meaning in as few words as possible and thus help emphasize ideas. (See also 31c.) Examine your sentences for empty phrases as well as for needless repetition.

> WEAK   It is unlikely that a complete resolution of the conflict between the Arabs and Israelis will be achieved.
>
> EMPHATIC   The Arab-Israeli conflict probably will not be resolved.
>
> WEAK   She behaved in such a way as to alienate her friends.
>
> EMPHATIC   She alienated her friends.
>
> WEAK   A problem of communication arose between the roommates, who did not speak to each other.
>
> EMPHATIC   The roommates did not speak to each other.

|*Revising for emphasis*   EXERCISE **18-1**

Rewrite each sentence or group of sentences below to emphasize the main idea, following the instructions in parentheses. Make your sentences as concise as possible.

Example: Sea gulls quarrel frequently over food. They quarrel noisily. But they are graceful in flight. (Make one sentence with the main idea at the end of the sentence.)

Though they quarrel frequently and noisily over food, sea gulls are graceful in flight.

emph

18

1. The prize will probably be awarded by the foundation for the first time in fifty years. (Use the active voice.)

2. Legal gambling can increase tax revenues. It can increase tourism. It can also increase crime. (Make two sentences with the main idea in a separate sentence.)

3. The kitchen contains poisons that can kill instantly. It is a room filled with perils. It also contains appliances that can be heated to 500 degrees. (Make one sentence with the main idea at the end.)

4. He had only six dollars left for his heart medicine, to buy food for his cat, and for his dinner. (Use parallelism for series elements and arrange them in order of importance.)

5. It was the winning point that was scored by Shank. (Use normal word order and the active voice.)

6. Carrying its prey in its beak, the hawk swooped upward. The hawk was flapping its wings. (Make one sentence with the main idea at the beginning of the sentence.)

7. A lock was placed on the warehouse door by the guard, who was afraid of theft. (Use the active voice and place the main idea at the beginning or end of the sentence.)

8. Because of the steady downpour, the ball could not be held on to by the players, three players tore ligaments, and the uniforms were ruined by the players. (Use parallelism for series elements and arrange them in order of importance.)

9. For three hours the speaker discussed nutrition in a monotonous voice. (Place the main idea at the beginning of the sentence.)

10. There is some likelihood this year that raises may be withheld by management. (Use normal word order and the active voice.)

| *Revising for emphasis* | EXERCISE **18-2** |

Combine each group of sentences below into one or two sentences that emphasize the main idea of the group. Make your sentences effective with an appropriate combination of effective beginnings and endings, parallelism, arrangement of elements in order of increasing importance, careful repetition, separation, and the active voice. Be concise.

Example: She does not own a crystal ball. She does not understand sports. She won the baseball pool. A four-leaf clover was not found by her.

She does not own a crystal ball or a four-leaf clover, and she does not understand sports. Yet she won the baseball pool.

emph

18

1. The largest bank cut its lending rate. The other large banks followed. The experts thought the rates would keep dropping. The rates held steady.

2. My telephone does not work during a rain. I receive calls for wrong numbers. I got twenty-seven calls for an ice-cream shop one rainy afternoon. I was trying to study.

3. Summer jobs were hard to find. There was no construction work in town. The gas stations were going broke. No businesses were hiring.

4. A policeman has to keep his car keys handy. He has to know how to drive at high speed. A policeman needs special driving skills and habits. He has to know how to drive with caution. He must always remember to park facing an exit.

5. The old woman had white hair. Her face had many wrinkles. She pulled a revolver and took my wallet. Her blue eyes twinkled. She looked innocent.

6. A visit to a nursing home can be depressing. It does not have to be. Taking time to smile and say hello cheers up the residents. Bringing along a small child cheers up the residents.

7. *Breakout* by Ron LeFlore is an inspiring story. It describes his life in prison. It is my favorite biography. He used his skill at baseball to rejoin society.

8. Twelve head of cattle died in the fire. Gasoline spread across the highway and ignited a field. The tanker truck overturned.

9. The last issue of the magazine described Leon Spinks. He could have been a champion for several years. He seemed to lose faith in himself.

10. Dachshunds shed very little. They are great pets. They are obedient. Dachshunds are gentle with children.

19|*Achieving Variety*

Self-test

Circle the number preceding the paragraph in each pair below that conveys its meaning more clearly by varying the lengths or structures of sentences.

1.   a. Backpacking in the wilderness is a gratifying experience, but it can also be dangerous. Besides contending with rough terrain and watching out for predatory animals, the backpacker must be self-sufficient because the wilderness by definition contains few people. Minimum survival equipment includes food, a canteen filled with water, a knife, a compass and maps, wooden matches in a watertight container, extra woolen clothes, and a poncho or tarpaulin. In addition, a first-aid kit can save a life in an emergency.

       b. Backpacking in the wilderness is a gratifying experience, but it can also be dangerous. The backpacker must contend with rough terrain, and he or she must also watch out for predatory animals. The wilderness by definition contains few people, so the backpacker must also be self-sufficient. Minimum survival equipment includes food, a canteen filled with water, a knife, a compass and maps, wooden matches in a watertight container, extra woolen clothes, and a poncho or tarpaulin; and a first-aid kit can save a life in an emergency.

2.   a. Crossword puzzles have been around since early in this century. They were introduced as space filler in newspapers, and they were primitive at first. Now they are more complex; some can be completed only by experts. The typical square puzzle with blank and darkened boxes and numbered clues is still most common. A more sophisticated puzzle is one with numbered clues but no diagram, and another sophisticated puzzle has a diagram but unnumbered, scrambled clues.

       b. Crossword puzzles have been around since early in this century. Introduced as space filler in newspapers, the puzzles were primitive at first. Now some are so complex that they can be completed only by experts. The typical square puzzle with blank and darkened boxes is still most common. More sophisticated are the puzzles with numbered clues but no diagram or with a diagram but unnumbered, scrambled clues.

Sentences work together to convey your meaning. A string of similar sentences is not only dull but also potentially confusing because important ideas do not stand out. To enhance your ideas, your sentences should vary in length, emphasis, and arrangement of elements to reflect the importance and complexity of your thoughts.

19a | Varying sentence length and emphasis

A paragraph filled with sentences of the same length lacks variety, especially if the sentences are all very short (say, ten or fifteen words) or very long (thirty or more words). Check your sentences to be sure you have not relied primarily on similar lengths.

1 | Avoiding strings of brief and simple sentences

A series of brief, simple sentences can be choppy and dull. Use connecting and subordinating words to combine sentences, emphasizing important ideas and de-emphasizing lesser ones.

WEAK   The lab is modern and bare. It is almost frightening. It has fluorescent lights. The walls are green. The floors are gray. The equipment is shiny. All these produce a cold atmosphere. They remind the visitor of the work done here.

REVISED   The lab is modern, bare, and almost frightening. Its fluorescent lights, green walls, gray floors, and shiny equipment produce a cold atmosphere that reminds the visitor of the work done here.

2 | Avoiding excessive compounding

A string of compound sentences can be just as monotonous as a string of simple sentences. Vary the sentences and emphasize important ideas by changing some main clauses into modifiers and varying their positions.

WEAK   I opened the door, and a salesman stood on the porch. He began his pitch, but he seemed drowsy. His voice was expressionless, and it finally trailed off in midsentence. I was startled, but I did not know what to do. He clearly was not going away, so I just shut the door on him.

REVISED   I opened the door to a salesman on the porch. Though he began his pitch, he seemed drowsy, and his expressionless voice finally trailed off in midsentence. I was startled. Not knowing what to do and seeing that he was not going away, I just shut the door on him.

19b | Varying sentence beginnings

Most English sentences follow the standard pattern of subject followed by verb followed by object or complement. But a series of sen-

var

19

tences all beginning with their subjects can be dull. Vary the pattern by beginning some sentences with elements other than subjects. An adverb modifier can postpone the subject:

> *Mercilessly,* the loan shark's agents pursued her. [Adverb.]
> *Because she had no money,* she could not pay the interest on the loan. [Adverb clause.]

A participial phrase can postpone the subject:

> *Sitting on the bench,* Oscar plucked his guitar.

A coordinating conjunction or transitional expression (see 3b-6) not only varies a sentence beginning but also links two sentences containing related ideas:

> He started a rumor about me. We have not met.
> He started a rumor about me. *But* we have not met.
> He started a rumor about me. *Even so,* we have not met.

Occasionally, you may want to vary sentence beginnings by using an expletive construction such as *there is* or *it is* (see 5e-4), although frequent use of expletives will make your writing wordy.

> *There were* nine invitations in the mail.

19c | Inverting the normal word order

Sentences that reverse the normal order of subject-verb-object should be used sparingly but can give strong emphasis to an idea.

> Through the glass *came* his *fist.* [Subject and verb inverted.]
> *Spiders* he feared greatly. [Object placed first.]

19d | Mixing types of sentences

Since most sentences we use in writing are statements, a question, command, or exclamation can introduce variety if used sparingly. Questions, especially, can raise the central issue of a discussion or emphasize an important point.

> Visitors appreciate the warmth of Homer's hotel. But why, they wonder, is it called the Hairless Raccoon? Legend has it that Homer once demonstrated a hair-growth tonic of his own invention on the back of a raccoon. The raccoon lost its hair, and Homer lost his business. In his next venture, operating a hotel, Homer immortalized his victim.

var

19

IVarying sentence beginnings   EXERCISE 19-1

Each sentence below begins with its subject. Rewrite each sentence or pair of sentences as specified in parentheses to postpone the subject.

Example: The union remained on strike after the votes were counted. (Begin with *After.*)

After the votes were counted, the union remained on strike.

1. Penicillin can cure the disease she has. She is allergic to penicillin though. (Begin one sentence with a coordinating conjunction or a transitional expression.)

var

19

2. The bamboo basket, which looks frail, is really quite sturdy. (Begin with *Although.*)

3. The speech was priced at one dollar a copy, and not one copy was sold. (Begin with *Because.*)

4. The crane crashed five stories to the street and smashed a truck. (Begin with a participial phrase.)

5. The party invitations omitted the address. Just a few people came. (Begin one sentence with a transitional expression.)

6. He never became a great architect, but he was not obscure. (Begin with *Even though.*)

7. Johnson won the game by sinking a shot from thirty feet. (Begin with a participial phrase.)

8. Money for travel is in the budget. (Begin with *There.*)

9. Being a good photographer certainly requires skill. It also requires money. (Begin one sentence with a transitional expression.)

10. We were swimming in the pond when we heard a shot from across the meadows. (Begin with *While.*)

| *Varying sentences in paragraphs* | EXERCISE **19-2** |

The paragraphs below lack sentence variety. Rewrite each paragraph to stress main ideas by changing some main clauses into modifiers and by varying sentence lengths and beginnings.

Example: Almost everyone is afraid of something. Some people are paralyzed by multiple phobias, however. They cannot leave the house for fear of an emotional collapse. Treating such people is a slow process. They have to become comfortable with each feared object or situation. The treatment may occur in a laboratory. It may also occur in natural surroundings. The phobias are eliminated one at a time. The patient can often resume a normal life at the end of treatment.

var

19

Although almost everyone is afraid of something, some people are so paralyzed by multiple phobias that they cannot leave the house for fear of an emotional collapse. Treating such people is a slow process, for they have to become comfortable with each feared object or situation. The treatment, which may occur in a laboratory or in natural surroundings, eliminates the phobias one at a time. At the end of the treatment, the patient can often resume a normal life.

1.   The army has spent over $3 million to evaluate the intelligence of its recruits. The results were satisfying in some respects. They were disappointing in other respects. The army discovered that it was recruiting many people of above-average intelligence. It was also recruiting many people with below-average intelligence. The army is planning to spend another $15 million this year to educate recruits. Its education programs have not had much success in the past.

2.   Almost 4 billion domesticated chickens exist in the world today, and they produce almost 400 billion eggs every year. The modern chicken descends from a wild Southeast Asian bird. Humans first tamed the wild bird over five thousand years ago, and they were breeding and raising them some time later. Spanish explorers first brought domesticated chickens to the New World, and later the Pilgrims also brought them. Chicken meat and eggs are a staple of the diet throughout the world, but Americans eat more of both than anyone else. A disproportionate share of the world's chickens are in the United States. Chicken farming is a major United States business.

var

19

V | Punctuation

20 | *End Punctuation*

Self-test

Add periods, question marks, or exclamation points wherever needed in the sentences below, and circle any punctuation marks that are not needed. If a sentence is already punctuated correctly, write *OK* to the left of it.

Example: What points should I consider before I make my decision **?**

1. The sign on the mailbox read, "William Morris, Esq.."
2. He asked whether I had played varsity
3. UNESCO is quite active in Africa.
4. "Did you return the package?," she asked.
5. They think the legislative delay is intolerable.
6. Hiram P Luce, BA, edited the anthology.
7. Her former home is Washington, D.C..
8. "Ready!!!" he shouted.
9. The talk was titled "When Will We Have Rights"
10. The report will be available at noon

. ? !

20

THE PERIOD

20a | Use the period to end sentences that are statements, mild commands, or indirect questions.

> STATEMENT The crisis resolved itself.
>
> MILD COMMAND Turn to the illustration on the next page.
>
> INDIRECT QUESTION They asked whether I intended to vote.

20b | Use periods with most abbreviations.

> Dr., Mr., Mrs., Ms., B.A., A.M., B.C., p., George H. Packer

Periods are commonly omitted from abbreviations for organizations and agencies (CBS, FDA). They are always omitted from **acronyms,** which are pronounceable words made from the first letters of the words in a name (UNESCO, NATO). (See Chapter 28 for a discussion of abbreviations that are or are not acceptable in most writing.)

Use only one period when an abbreviation comes at the end of a sentence: *Our speaker was G. Maurice Dunning, M.D.*

THE QUESTION MARK

20c | Use the question mark after direct questions.

Do we know what caused the fire?

After indirect questions, use the period: *He asked whether I knew what caused the fire.* (See 20a.)

Note: Never use a question mark with another question mark, a period, or a comma.

FAULTY   He asked, "Which way to the dance hall?."

REVISED   He asked, "Which way to the dance hall?"

20d | Use a question mark within parentheses to indicate doubt about the correctness of a number or date.

At the time of Chaucer's birth in 1340 (?), only a few people could read.

THE EXCLAMATION POINT

20e | Use the exclamation point after emphatic statements and interjections and after strong commands.

EMPHATIC INTERJECTION   Oh! I wish I had my camera.

EMPHATIC STATEMENT   We must not allow it!

EMPHATIC COMMAND   Stop talking!

Note: Never use an exclamation point with another exclamation point, a period, or a comma.

FAULTY   "He stole my wallet!," I yelled.

REVISED   "He stole my wallet!" I yelled.

20f | Avoid overusing exclamation points.

Don't use exclamation points to express amazement or sarcasm or to stress important points. Avoid using multiple exclamation points (!!!).

FAULTY   These facts prove that women office workers are discriminated against in this city!

REVISED   These facts prove that women office workers are discriminated against in this city.

|Using end punctuation

Circle the place in each sentence below where punctuation should be added or is used incorrectly, and write the correct punctuation, along with the adjacent words, on the blank to the right. If the sentence is already punctuated correctly, write *OK* on the blank.

Example: "Why must I have an address⟨?⟩" he asked.　　*address?" he*

1. She screamed, "Get it right!!!" 　　_____

2. A cloud of dust from the track settled on the crew from NBC. 　　_____

3. We puzzled over the question of how to find the square root of 1109? 　　_____

4. Stay away from the quarry. 　　_____

5. Did he say, "Never"?? 　　_____

6. The lecture was titled "Why Are Citizens Alienated from Government." 　　_____

7. I do not understand why the applause was so weak 　　_____

8. Mr Schmidt got a new wig after Christmas. 　　_____

9. The dean said the dorms would be painted, but we knew better! 　　_____

10. Covered with mud, the dog made a horrible mess 　　_____

11. Did he ask, "When?" 　　_____

12. They wanted to see if there had been an accident? 　　_____

.?!

20

13. The snow continues to fall throughout May   _____

14. We called to ask whether the snowstorm had   _____
    closed the airport?

15. NATO is not in danger of collapse.   _____

16. I demand to see him in person!!!   _____

17. The physician studied what causes lycan-   _____
    thropy to strike the aged?

18. "Get out of my yard!," screamed the woman   _____
    to the costumed children.

19. Sgt Meyer changed his tactics.   _____

20. She asked, "Why are you late?."   _____

21. The Greek philosopher Aristippus died in   _____
    356 (?) B.C..

22. Always take a good knife on a camping trip   _____

23. The governor told the demonstrators to clear   _____
    out of his path!

24. The Future Farmers of America formed a   _____
    chapter here in 1953; since then the FFA has
    been quite active.

25. A one-armed man built this chair!   _____

26. A nutritionist with an MS degree selected the   _____
    school menu.

27. Is there a single reason why I have to tolerate   _____
    my neighbor's late-night parties? No!

28. Does Dr Felson charge reasonable fees?   _____

29. The speaker came all the way from Washing-   _____
    ton, D.C..

30. Her autobiography was published in 1903 by   _____
    St James Press.

21 | *The Comma*

Self-test

Add commas wherever they are needed in the sentences below, and circle any commas that are not needed. If a sentence is already punctuated correctly, write *OK* to the left of it.

Example: The owners preferred to negotiate with Zusky,who had broken his contract.

1. Some walls in the old house were painted yellow and others were covered with dark paneling.
2. Before the mail arrived this morning we were waiting impatiently for word.
3. Tuition of course is high this year.
4. He claimed that the lawnmower was defective.
5. The vandalized dilapidated building was the gym.
6. At sixty workers are eligible for retirement.
7. "I can't" she said, looking apologetic.
8. The voters elected a woman who had served three terms in Congress.
9. The time to act, is now.
10. The rally ended with the familiar song, "We Shall Overcome."

The comma is often essential to separate parts of a sentence and to provide clarity.

| COMMA NEEDED | Seventy stories below the basement caught fire. |
| REVISED | Seventy stories below, the basement caught fire. |

However, overuse of the comma can also make writing unclear.

UNNEEDED COMMA	My father and I, began collecting the sap when snow was still on the ground.
REVISED	My father and I began collecting the sap when snow was still on the ground.
UNNEEDED COMMA	My sister and I decided, that we would not go to the game.
REVISED	My sister and I decided that we would not go to the game.

21a | Use the comma before a coordinating conjunction linking main clauses.

The coordinating conjunctions are *and, but, or, nor,* and sometimes *for, so,* and *yet.* When one of them links main clauses, it should be preceded by a comma.

> I had three accidents, *and* my insurance costs doubled.
> The book listed poisonous plants, *but* it did not mention poison ivy.
> My high school teachers did not help me learn to write, *nor* did they encourage me to read extensively.
> The movie went way over budget, *for* the director insisted on shooting most of it in the jungle.
> I bought the text secondhand; *yet* it cost over $20.
> The book included all the information I could use; *so* I didn't need to consult other sources.

Exceptions: Some writers prefer to use a semicolon before *so* and *yet.*

> I bought the text secondhand; *yet* it cost over $20.
> The book included all the information I could use; *so* I didn't need to consult other sources.

A semicolon may clarify the division between long main clauses that contain internal punctuation (see 22c).

> The trip was six hours long, involving three plane changes, two hours waiting in airports, and two taxi rides; *but* I arrived feeling fresh.

A comma may be omitted between main clauses when they are short and closely related in meaning.

> We give little *and* we expect much.

21b | Use the comma to set off introductory phrases and clauses.

Modifying phrases and subordinate clauses that begin sentences should be set off with commas.

> Although the bank offered "free checking," it tripled the charge for printing checks.
> Expecting a green and tree-filled campus, I was shocked to find it surrounded by highways and parking lots.

If the introductory element is short, especially if it is a short prepositional phrase, the comma is often omitted.

> At times it seems the children have little in common.

Remember, however, that clarity may require the comma.

> COMMA NEEDED   At three thoroughbred horses are eligible to run in the Kentucky Derby.
>
> REVISED   At three, thoroughbred horses are eligible to run in the Kentucky Derby.

A verbal or a verbal phrase is set off by a comma.

> Singing, he skipped down the hall.

| *Using commas between main clauses and after introductory elements* | EXERCISE **21-1** |

Place a caret (∧) at each place in the following sentences where a comma is required. (Some sentences may require more than one comma.) If the sentence is already punctuated correctly or if an introductory element does not need to be set off, write *OK* to the left of the sentence.

Example: The snow was so deep that I could not get to class∧nor could I even get out the front door.

1. Shaking his head in amazement Jessup headed for the bench.
2. The hamburger was extended with oatmeal and the oatmeal seemed to be made of sawdust.
3. Lacking rating symbols the guidebook was difficult to follow.
4. If something is upsetting you might dream about it.
5. After witnessing Jones's third slam-dunk the crowd had new respect for him.
6. President Coolidge was not a great speaker nor was he a wise administrator.
7. As the light turned yellow the accident flashed through my mind.
8. The audience was receptive but the comedian made a poor effort.
9. In the old days a woman could be suspended for coming in a half-hour past curfew.
10. On the hood of the dragster the trophy gleamed in the sunshine.
11. If more people become unemployed housing prices will fall.
12. When the council changed the zoning law the mayor resigned in protest.
13. The pianist played a medley of Cohan tunes after the applause subsided.
14. Margaret had not yet learned about the theft for she had not yet been home.
15. If I had to bet I would place my money on the Yankees but it is a tough choice.
16. Paying a dollar for a bottle of water will always seem ridiculous to me.
17. Showing up late for practice the coach looked exhausted.

∧
,

21

18. The estate was not for sale but it remained unoccupied for many years.

19. A new set of luggage and a camera were stolen but the jewelry was overlooked.

20. In a single season attendance at professional hockey games dropped 15 percent.

21. Since it takes at least a week to obtain a passport you should get one in advance if you might have to take a trip suddenly.

22. The beagle discovered the rabbit's hole and cornered the animal before we caught up.

23. Having taught for thirty years Professor Whitbeck looks as if he could use a rest.

24. Receiving a gift certificate to Woody's would make her happy.

25. When you go to sleep after intense mental activity your dreams may carry on with that activity and allow you to rest at the same time.

26. With winter coming everyone wants to get away.

27. About a month before school started in the fall I got a letter from the college.

28. Once a week the subway has broken down and I have been on it every time.

29. Not everyone who uses a pesticide reads the directions on the label and the result is a large number of preventable deaths and illnesses.

30. Four-wheel-drive vehicles have increased in popularity and also in price.

∧
,

21

21c | Use the comma to set off nonrestrictive elements.

Restrictive elements limit the meaning of the word or words they refer to and thus cannot be omitted without changing meaning. They are not set off by commas. **Nonrestrictive elements** add information but do not limit meaning and thus are optional in the sentence. They are set off by commas.

> RESTRICTIVE All the students *who graduated in June* found jobs.
>
> NONRESTRICTIVE The school library, *which now has 500,000 books*, is adequate for most undergraduates.

1 | Use the comma to set off nonrestrictive clauses and phrases.

> RESTRICTIVE The car *that was stolen* was mine.
> The police officers *on the case* didn't know that.
>
> NONRESTRICTIVE The gallery, *which opened two years ago*, has been very successful.
> Its location, *on the new pedestrian mall*, has helped it attract customers.

2 | Use the comma to set off nonrestrictive appositives.

An **appositive** is a noun, or a word or word group acting as a noun, that describes another noun (see 5c-5).

> RESTRICTIVE The jazz pianist *Keith Jarrett* will perform here next year.
>
> NONRESTRICTIVE The concert will be held in Hadley Hall, the place in which most music events are held.

3 | Use the comma to set off parenthetical expressions.

Parenthetical expressions interrupt a sentence to explain or make a transition or to add extra information. Brief parenthetical expressions are sometimes set off with commas. (See also Chapter 25 on the uses of dashes and parentheses to set off parenthetical elements.)

> The cost of living, *believe it or not*, actually declined this month.
> The bus, *for example*, has not been on time once in twenty days.
> The tail, *almost twenty inches long*, acts as a fly swatter.

4 | Use the comma to set off *yes* and *no*, tag questions, words of direct address, and mild interjections.

> We said *yes*, we would be willing to perform for the patients.
> You went to the interview, *didn't you?*
> *Harriet*, we appreciate your support.
> *Well*, I didn't expect to receive an A.

21d | Use the comma to set off absolute phrases.

An **absolute phrase** usually consists of a noun or a pronoun and a participle. (Sometimes the participle *being* is omitted.) An absolute phrase relates to a whole main clause rather than to a specific word in a main clause.

> *The old car refusing to start*, I am without transportation.
> *The meeting (being) over*, the reporters called their papers.

21e | Use the comma to set off phrases expressing contrast.

> We saw the play, *not the movie*.

The use of the comma is optional for contrasting phrases that begin with *but*.

> The dean invited faculty *but not students* to the reception.
> The dean invited faculty, *but not students*, to the reception.

Using commas with nonrestrictive elements, absolute phrases, phrases of contrast

EXERCISE **21-2**

Place a caret (∧) at each place in the following sentences where a comma is required. (Some sentences may require more than one comma.) If the sentence is already punctuated correctly, write *OK* to the left of it.

Example: The poster∧a picture of a singer∧cost $4.98.

A.
1. The trial, which lasted for three days ended with a verdict of guilty.
2. No one who is related to a police officer would say police work is easy or safe.
3. The American director who may be most popular now is Steven Spielberg.
4. All the banks I hear, refuse to lend money to students.
5. Two men one of them wearing a ski mask robbed the small grocery store where I work.
6. The woman who called me claimed to work at the White House.
7. We are after all here to get an education.
8. There were few surprises I thought, in tonight's game.
9. Senator Cumo who chairs the finance committee voted against tax reform.
10. Her health failing Sarah called her children around her.
11. The audience becoming impatient the theater manager asked for a little more time to get the sound system working.
12. My dog whose name is Jasper eats two rawhide bones a day.
13. The tax forms six pages of figures were mailed yesterday.
14. The delay during which the pitcher's arm tightened up lasted an hour.
15. The famous New York restaurant Four Seasons has many imitators.
16. I replied, "Yes I would like to play music professionally."
17. Every morning I drink grapefruit juice which contains vitamins and eat a brownie which tastes good.
18. Hypnotism still not allowable in court testimony is a fertile method for developing one's memory.
19. The songs of birds for instance, are more complex than they sound.
20. The music blaring next door I was unable to concentrate on my reading.

∧
,

21

B. 1. We must report on three books one being a biography.

2. It was geometry not algebra that gave me the most trouble in high school.

3. Some local newspapers such as the *Times*, the *Enquirer*, and the *News* which is a weekly failed to carry the story.

4. We waited only two days not the four suggested before walking on our new concrete steps.

5. Even then fifty years ago the house was run-down.

6. After defeating his opponent, who was much smaller than he, the wrestler retired.

7. Shakespeare's *Hamlet*, the world's best tragedy drew a record crowd at the college theater Saturday.

8. He answered, "Yes the price is reasonable isn't it?"

9. Mathematics which she believes is a pure science is her major.

10. Children under ten years old should not be exposed to violence.

11. My father reads only one magazine *The New Yorker* regularly.

12. We learned that a microbiologist Dr. Allen raises white mice for profit.

13. My cousin who has the same name that I do is in jail for bank robbery.

14. There is only one intersection in town that has a stoplight, and it is the scene of the most accidents.

15. Mrs. Kim who spoke little English wanted written directions.

16. When you wake up, remember to mail your application Richard.

17. He agreed, of course, that two more hours of play would be tiring.

18. Compared with the interstate highway, Route 460 is shorter not safer.

19. A specialist in fractures the physician studied the X rays.

20. Color photographs unlike black and white will fade in about ten years.

^
,

21

21f | Use the comma between words, phrases, or clauses forming a series and between coordinate adjectives not linked by conjunctions.

A **series** consists of three or more items of equal importance.

The sauce contained *mustard*, *ground cloves*, and *sherry*.

The comma is optional before the *and* that connects the last two items in the series (. . . *mustard, ground cloves and sherry*). However, it can prevent confusion by clearly indicating that the last two items are separate, so using the comma consistently is the best practice.

> CONFUSING   The house had no storm windows, shoddy plumbing and electrical outlets in inconvenient places.
>
> CLEAR   The house had no storm windows, shoddy plumbing, and electrical outlets in inconvenient places.

When the elements in a series are long, grammatically complicated, or internally punctuated, they should be connected with semicolons (see 22d).

Sylvia had three brothers: Jim, 16; Alfred, 14; and Billy, 2.

Coordinate adjectives are two or more adjectives modifying equally the same word. Such adjectives may be separated either by a coordinating conjunction or by a comma.

The *rickety*, *old* swing could not support the child's weight.
The *rickety* and *old* swing could not support the child's weight.
The *old*, *rickety* swing could not support the child's weight.

As these examples show, two adjectives are coordinate (1) if they can be reversed without a change in meaning or (2) if *and* can be inserted between them. (Note that a comma is not used between the final adjective and the noun.) If these changes cannot be made, then the adjectives are not coordinate and they should not be separated by a comma.

> FAULTY   My father owned a pair of unique, rubber boxing gloves.
>
> REVISED   My father owned a pair of unique rubber boxing gloves.

21g | Use the comma according to convention in dates, addresses, place names, and long numbers.

> August 23, 1943, is the day she was born. [The second comma is required to complete setting off the year.]
>
> She was born on 23 August 1943. [No commas when day precedes month.]
>
> She moved here from Axtel, Kansas, in 1975.
>
> He lived at 1321 Cardinal Drive, Birmingham, Alabama 35223, for only a year. [No comma before zip code.]

If a date is given only as month and year, no comma is necessary: *The battalion landed in April 1945.*

The comma separates long numbers into groups of three, starting from the right: *83,745,906*. The comma is optional in four-digit numbers: Both *4,215* and *4215* are acceptable.

∧
,

21

21h | Use the comma with quotations according to standard practice.

1 | Ordinarily, use the comma to separate introductory and concluding explanatory words from quotations.

> Ginott tells parents, "Resist the temptation to preach."
> "Get out of my life," she said coldly.

Don't use a comma when the quotation ends in a question mark or exclamation point: *"Did they go?" I asked.* (See 20c and 20e.) Use a colon to introduce a quotation when the quotation is long or weighty (see 25a).

2 | Use the comma after the first part of a quotation interrupted by explanatory words. Follow the explanatory words with the punctuation required by the quotation.

> "Our attitude toward money," Harvey Cox says, "is unrealistic in the extreme." [The explanatory words interrupt a sentence in the quotation.]
> "We have been drifting for years," the speaker said. "It is almost too late." [The explanatory words fall at the end of a sentence in the quotation.]

3 | Place commas that follow quotations within quotation marks.

> "No split infinitives," she muttered in her sleep.

For further guidance on punctuating quotations, see 24g.

21

21i | Use the comma to prevent misreading.

Even when a comma is not required by a rule, it may be necessary to prevent words from running together in ways that cause confusion.

CONFUSING   Still a baby Mary needs full-time care. [The short introductory phrase does not require a comma, but clarity does.]

CLEAR   Still a baby, Mary needs full-time care.

| *Using commas with series, coordinate adjectives, dates, addresses, long numbers, quotations* | EXERCISE **21-3** |

Place a caret (∧) at each place in the following sentences where a comma is required. (Some sentences may require more than one comma.) If the sentence is already punctuated correctly, write *OK* to the left of it.

Example: Our team played tournaments last year in Canada∧Japan∧and Australia and lost only in Canada.

A.
1. A high-priced skimpy meal was all that was available.
2. After testing 33107 subjects, the scientist still thought she needed a bigger sample.
3. "Please, can you help me?" the old woman asked.
4. "I need fifty volunteers, now" the physical education teacher said ominously.
5. The excited angry bull was shot to death after it destroyed the garden.
6. The shop is located at 2110 Greenwood Street Kennett Square Pennsylvania 19348.
7. Many athletes believe that they are more important vital people than those who come to watch them.
8. The open mine attracted children looking for adventure couples needing privacy and old drunks seeking a place to sleep.
9. The aged exotic dancer gave the arresting police officer a phony address.
10. I bought a CB radio on July 2 1982 and I still have not received the missing warranty from the manufacturer.
11. The area around Riverside California has some of the most polluted air in the country.
12. The records disappeared from the doctor's office in Olean New York yesterday.
13. Seven lonely desperate people come to the neighborhood center for counseling every night.
14. The lantern has a large very heavy base.

∧
,

21

15. The town council designated the area's oldest largest house as a landmark.
16. The evil day of 24 October 1929, when the stock market crashed, marked the beginning of the Great Depression.
17. The office is located at 714 W. Lincoln Harlingen Texas.
18. The November 17 1944 issue of the *Times* carried the submarine story.
19. The team lost its final games by scores of 72–66 72–68 and 72–70.
20. Through the wide-open door I could hear them by turns squabbling laughing and crying.

B.
1. The strangely spiced soup contained asparagus carrots and coriander.
2. The first line reads "I never said I wanted you to come."
3. In August 1982 over 36500 people saw the exhibit at the museum.
4. Dangerous experimental drugs are readily available in Europe.
5. Dozens and dozens of children lined up for lessons at the hot steamy poolside.
6. Squealing tires roaring engines yelling fans and black-and-white flags are my dominant images of the auto race.
7. I expected long classes lots of reading and difficult examinations when I entered college but not boring courses.
8. The 1982 team's record-breaking winning streak is unlikely to be matched.
9. We expected one more blanketing snow before spring.
10. The car's headlights were smashed its hood was badly dented and muddy and its convertible top was ripped.
11. "Hand in your tests" the examiner said "and then file singly out of the room."
12. The runner, fresh eager and well rested, took his starting position.
13. "What will happen if we lose the series?" the coach asked.
14. Only a foolish thoughtless person would leave the door unlocked.
15. He will never never agree to the proposal.
16. The *Journal* for September 28 1979 carried fourteen advertisements for adult movies.
17. She is young inexperienced and unfit for the position.
18. "Fertilizer" the consultant agreed "should have been applied in the fall."
19. Having old worn-out tires did not help the resale value of the car.
20. My mother yelled "Wash the sand off your feet!"

21

21j Avoid misusing or overusing the comma.

1 Don't use the comma to separate a subject from its verb, or a verb or a preposition from its object, unless the words between them require punctuation.

FAULTY   The bearded man, was the one the police arrested.

REVISED   The bearded man was the one the police arrested.

FAULTY   Washington quartered, his troops in the fields nearby.

REVISED   Washington quartered his troops in the fields nearby.

In the following sentence the appositive (*my uncle*) requires commas between subject and verb.

The bearded man, my uncle, was arrested for demonstrating.

(See also 21c for use of commas with nonrestrictive elements.)

2 Don't use the comma with words or phrases joined by coordinating conjunctions.

FAULTY   The concerts in the chapel, and other musical events are all free.

REVISED   The concerts in the chapel and other musical events are all free.

FAULTY   I found the book on Thursday, and returned it to the library.

REVISED   I found the book on Thursday and returned it to the library.

(See also 21a for use of commas with coordinating conjunctions linking main clauses and 21f for use of commas in a series.)

3 Don't use the comma to set off restrictive elements.

FAULTY   The miner, who contracts black lung disease, is eligible for compensation.

REVISED   The miner who contracts black lung disease is eligible for compensation.

See also 21c.

4 Don't use the comma before the first or after the last item in a series unless a rule requires it.

FAULTY   Tragedies, comedies, and tragicomedies, are represented in the text.

REVISED   Tragedies, comedies, and tragicomedies are represented in the text.

5 | **Don't use the comma to set off an indirect quotation or a single word unless it is a nonrestrictive appositive.**

FAULTY   He asked, who was responsible.

REVISED   He asked who was responsible.

FAULTY   My roommate pronounces, "Washington," as, "Warshington."

REVISED   My roommate pronounces "Washington" as "Warshington."

$\wedge$
,

21

Correcting misused and overused commas

In the sentences below, circle each comma that does not belong. Note that not all the commas are wrong. If a sentence is already punctuated correctly, write *OK* to the left of it.

Example: The characters in the novel, are not very believable.

A. 1. The dark clouds in the east, indicated the storm was near.
2. He declined the drink, saying he was sleepy.
3. The one who committed the crime, got away.
4. "What seems to be your problem?," the doctor asked.
5. The children, Oscar, and Bo, are cared for in the afternoons by their aunt.
6. The most valuable, beautiful stone in the world, is the diamond.
7. Architects, who design houses, should know better than to put the back and front doors on the same side of a house.
8. Anyone who earns honors, in this college has to work very hard.
9. She thought, that the old book was a valuable, first edition.
10. The first karate belt is white, and the next, is orange.
11. The Monte Carlo, is one of General Motors' most luxurious cars.
12. Our training exercises, consisting of wind sprints, push-ups, jumping jacks, and a three-mile run, leave us too tired to play.
13. Dressed in Navajo garb, he made a very, impressive entrance.
14. The new cars will not run as fast as the old ones because, they have too much pollution-control equipment.
15. I was one of two, unfortunate participants in the race, who had to drop out because of muscle cramps.
16. The sizes of the tanks used to make moonshine can vary, but, they usually hold fifty gallons.
17. Soon, there were six trout on the line.
18. I could not have a ruder, or meaner roommate.
19. The tourism bureau, it appeared, had closed for the summer.
20. At the end of our vacation, the refrigerator contained, two slices of salami, a bottle of soda, and half a jar of mustard.

B. 1. We promote people on the basis of seniority, not merit.
2. The threat of aggression, is constant.
3. We were angry at the kid who yelled at us, but my friend said, to let him go.
4. Both of us qualified for the job, that only one of us could have.
5. We played, in a noisy, dark, café, for people who could not even see or hear us.
6. Hate derives from troubling experiences such as, an unhappy, strife-torn, home life.
7. The air, hazy and damp, drifted over the valley.
8. Divisive issues dominated the long, tedious, meeting.
9. Monkeys make bad pets because they have, bad tempers, long nails, and sharp teeth.
10. The best stories, in the literary magazine, are those by Muscante and Rowling.
11. The visitors' register, showed that our last call had been exactly, a year ago.
12. No one, of course, seeks humiliation, but some do ask for it.
13. Athletic shoes such as sneakers, which have been around for decades, seem more popular today than ever.
14. A dozen cats crowded eagerly, in front of the chipmunk's hole.
15. Just before the gun blast, the dove, wheeled sharply.
16. She said, that all of us would have to take the test over because one person cheated.
17. The, elusive, eccentric professor, usually kept his office door firmly shut.
18. In winter I do not have to cut the grass, or rake the leaves.
19. The word, *taco*, means different things to different people.
20. Buried 1000 years ago, the urn was unearthed in 1925.

|*Commas: Review I*

The sentences below both contain unneeded commas and omit needed ones. (They also contain commas that are used correctly.) Circle every unneeded comma and insert a caret (∧) where a comma is needed. If a sentence is already punctuated correctly, write *OK* to the left of it.

Example: For Sue∧Joe is a friend who can be relied on.

1. Each time the train stopped the sudden, sharp, jolt awakened the, old, tired, porter.
2. People, who claim to feel sympathy for the poor but do not want to pay tax money to help the poor, are hypocrites.
3. Going back to school, is something that can frighten a veteran.
4. The competition scored a total of 1103 points against our 974 in 1982.
5. "Besides" he said "our success depends on our practicing."
6. *King Lear* the only tragedy we staged last fall, was a sellout.
7. A less successful effort, was that of the tennis team.
8. We know, however, that the markup on the car was 30 percent.
9. The movie, which was seen by the largest audience ever grossed millions of dollars.
10. Long an admirer of the actress, John, saw each of her pictures twice.
11. However long it may take you be certain to prepare thoroughly.
12. He said, that term insurance is the best buy.
13. If as predicted the storm had turned out to sea the trailer would still be in one, large piece instead of in two, smaller ones.
14. The main guest room, which is the largest room on the second floor, was once occupied by Mark Twain.
15. The photographs had double images so, we took them back to the store.
16. After the plate went through the dishwasher the design faded.
17. Men's hats very popular in the 1930s are finally making a comeback.
18. The victim having been shoved inside the door the windows were nailed shut.
19. The third ship the *Aquinas* left three weeks later.
20. Cokes popcorn candy — that was her diet for two weeks.

∧
,

21

21. The forms, that we were supposed to turn in on Friday, were not distributed until Thursday.
22. After a restless adolescence my sister has grown to be an active, responsible, concerned young woman.
23. We lost the tournament not the game.
24. Her address 3004 Westcott, Brunswick Maine 04011 was stenciled on the old leather bag.
25. Her duties which did not include making coffee did require skills in stenography and telex operation.
26. The poet Byron lived a romantic life to parallel a romantic age.
27. Our new neighbors moved from Reno Nevada to Columbia South Carolina to Atlanta Georgia to Davis California before arriving here.
28. The ledger dated July 1 1946 showed the city's finances to be in a condition, that many would envy today.
29. The one, Spanish-style house, is a refreshing change from the boxy houses that dominate the street.
30. Neither the class schedule, nor the examination schedule allows me to take all the courses I need and the registrar will not grant me special approval.

21

|*Commas: Review II*

The following paragraph contains unneeded commas and omits needed ones. Circle every unneeded comma and insert a caret (∧) wherever a comma is needed.

Since John and I had been friends for years we decided to enroll in the same college, and to room together. John and I also asked another friend Tim to live with us and share expenses. The three of us, moved into a house at 120 Locust Street, Greenburg, Virginia on August 31. A little over a month later, two of us, John and I moved out. Tim had argued violently with us over paying his share of expenses, and doing his share of the work. After John and I moved into a dormitory we began searching, bulletin boards, newspapers, and housing lists, for notice of another, better, place to live. A month later, we located another house that we could afford and it was within walking distance of campus. However we could not move out of the dormitory until the end of the semester. We heard that Tim could not find any, new roommates. Not being able to afford the Locust Street house by himself Tim had to move to a dormitory.

∧
,

21

22 | *The Semicolon*

Self-test

In the sentences below, add semicolons wherever they are needed or where they should replace commas and circle any semicolons that are not needed. If a sentence is already punctuated correctly, write *OK* to the left of it.

Example: Finley was quite popular;she was more popular than Alger.

1. A foreign coin jammed the vending machine, however, the coin was soon dislodged.
2. Although we found the atlas, the map of Iowa was missing.
3. She called to say she would arrive at noon, therefore, we ran out for groceries.
4. His face tightened with tension, he clenched his fists.
5. Hoping that he would be able to play the entire game, Smith practiced diligently.
6. They had met twice before, nevertheless, he did not remember her.
7. The horse, which was not used to a saddle, bucked, kicked, and shook its head; but still the rider stayed on.
8. The other driver offered an apology; then he sped off.
9. The following gave generously: E. E. Edwards, a broker, R. Zikowicz, a contractor, and L. Peters, a banker.
10. After repairing the carburetor, the mechanic worked on the transmission.

;
22

22a | Use the semicolon to separate main clauses not joined by a coordinating conjunction.

A main clause is one that contains a subject and a predicate and can stand alone as a sentence. When two main clauses in a sentence are not linked by a coordinating conjunction (*and, but, or, nor, for, so, yet*), they should be separated by a semicolon.

There are six museums in the city; the largest is the Museum of Fine Arts.

The college motor pool has several cars; none is available for student activities.

22b | Use the semicolon to separate main clauses joined by a conjunctive adverb.

The conjunctive adverbs include *however, indeed, moreover,* and *nonetheless.* (See 5d-2 for a more extensive list.)

The reporters waited for an explanation of the policy change; *indeed,* they felt they were entitled to it.

Manufacturers each year recall more cars with defects; the number of faulty and even dangerous cars on the road, *however,* is still alarming.

Notice that the conjunctive adverb may fall in several places in its clause. If it follows the semicolon, it is generally followed with a comma. If it falls elsewhere in the clause, it is generally preceded and followed with a comma.

22c | Use the semicolon to separate main clauses if they are very long and complex or if they contain commas, even when they are joined by a coordinating conjunction.

Though a comma is normally sufficient to separate main clauses joined by a coordinating conjunction (see 21a), a semicolon signals a longer pause and can make the clauses easier to read when they are complicated or punctuated by commas. Many writers prefer to use a semicolon to separate clauses joined by *so* and *yet,* even when the clauses are not complex or internally punctuated.

The caterer arrived on time, and the food she served was delicious; *but* the guests had to drink from plastic cups because she forgot to bring glasses.

The announcement that classes were canceled had been posted all over campus; *yet* dozens of students missed it and showed up anyway.

22d | Use the semicolon to separate items in a series if they are long or contain commas.

The staff especially wishes to thank N. M. Matson, mayor; "Lima Bean" Horton, deputy mayor; Axel Garcia, police chief; and Norma Smith, school provost.

Logan charged $370 for repairing the steps and the fence gate; Rogers charged $800 for painting the exterior of the house; and Morris charged $200 to replace the doors and $300 to fix the plumbing.

22e | Avoid misusing or overusing the semicolon.

1 | Don't use the semicolon to link subordinate clauses or phrases to main clauses.

FAULTY   After he read the story; he gave his analysis of it.

REVISED   After he read the story, he gave his analysis of it.

FAULTY   I do not see how I can get good grades; with such a heavy course load.

REVISED   I do not see how I can get good grades with such a heavy course load.

2 | Don't use the semicolon to introduce a list.

FAULTY   Three of our team's players made the all-star team; the quarterback, the center, and the middle linebacker.

REVISED   Three of our team's players made the all-star team: the quarterback, the center, and the middle linebacker.

(See 25a and 25b for use of colons and dashes with lists.)

3 | Don't overuse the semicolon.

A series of sentences whose clauses are linked by semicolons often indicates repetitive sentence structure.

REPETITIVE   Several times they called to him; each time only their own echoes answered back. They had expected to rescue him before nightfall; now they hoped he could keep himself alive until morning.

REVISED   Several times they called to him; each time only their own echoes answered back. Although they had expected to rescue him by nightfall, they now hoped he could keep himself alive until morning.

;

22

|*Using the semicolon*

Insert a caret (∧) in the following sentences where a semicolon is needed or where it should replace a comma. (Some sentences may require more than one semicolon.) If a sentence is already punctuated correctly, write *OK* to the left of it.

Example: I have not studied French, in fact, I have not studied any foreign languages.   ∧

1. An ostrich is unable to fly, it can run at speeds of up to 40 miles per hour, however.
2. The town zoning laws are under the control of Mrs. Ida Balat, who owns much of the property in town, Mr. Luke Balat, her son and the town's mayor, Mrs. Ethel Goines, her daughter and a member of the town planning board, and Mr. Harold Goines, Ethel's husband and a member of the zoning board.
3. The telegram announcing his arrival on Tuesday was delivered Monday night, therefore, we had to scurry to have the house ready.
4. Most of the guests had left or fallen asleep from boredom, a few others read magazines, and one was cooking something in the kitchen, but the four remaining guests kept things going until three in the morning.
5. I do not understand why Mr. Nelson, for example, does not get tenure.
6. Never fix a leaky pipe if you can afford a plumber, that is my father's motto.
7. The chipmunk lived on crab apples, it stored them under the porch.
8. Horses prosper in our county because the soil has a high lime content.
9. In the 1950s many screenwriters were prevented from working because they were supposedly Communist sympathizers, some excellent scripts never got made into films as a result.
10. The advisory board comprised the manager, Martins, the foreman, and Travers, the engineer.

;

22

11. The two-day blackout of electricity affected three thousand houses, two hundred businesses, and thirty schools, yet no one can explain how it happened.

12. The trip was scheduled for Niagara Falls, I had been there, however, and so did not sign up.

13. The breakup of a marriage is usually upsetting, however it comes about.

14. My high school did not offer Latin, consequently, I am taking first-year Latin in college.

15. The doctor examined the child with great care, then he ordered additional tests.

16. The blueprints for the house showed a second bathroom the builders, apparently, had forgotten about it.

17. The police investigation was sloppy, several important leads were overlooked.

18. Oil exploration efforts are leveling off, however, energy shortages are worsening.

19. Brodhead has changed his open-shirt, chains-around-the-neck look and replaced it with a conservative, three-piece-suit look that makes him seem middle-aged.

20. I enjoy deep-sea fishing after trying it twice I could never go back to stream fishing again.

21. Japanese technology is superior to ours in several areas, including industrial robots.

22. The stores are refusing to accept credit cards, nevertheless, sales continue to grow.

23. The taxpayers will have to bail out the auto industry, it will be very expensive.

24. The three old brass keys, each at least six inches long, were found years ago in the attic, they have puzzled the family ever since, for no one can figure out what they open.

25. Reassuring though the promise sounded, few thought she could keep it.

;

22

The comma and the semicolon: Review I

Insert a comma or a semicolon, as appropriate, above each caret (∧) in the sentences below. If no punctuation is required at the caret, cross it out.

Example: When you drive into my hometown of Centerton, Nevada∧you see Dr. Ming's office first∧and then the Dairy Queen.

1. The museum∧which needs 300 visitors a day to meet costs∧will close in the spring∧no tax subsidy is available.
2. Dennison∧the former director∧and Ellis∧the current one∧were indicted for embezzlement.
3. The process consists of cutting the felt∧shaping it∧pressing it with steam∧and decorating the finished hat with a ribbon.
4. The pilot∧angry∧nervous∧and tired∧stood at the top of the ramp.
5. Moving in was annoying∧my roommate spent all morning hanging her favorite print∧while I rearranged furniture∧and carried heavy suitcases.
6. The computer system has been reliable∧however∧it will soon be obsolete.
7. The ceremony∧which started at ten o'clock∧was over∧before anyone thought to take pictures.
8. My roommates are my good friends∧and they are careful about sharing expenses.
9. The weather had been beautiful for four days in a row∧leading us to expect a perfect day∧for the season's biggest game∧instead∧we got rained out.
10. The Greek alphabet has one drawback∧to me∧it is incomprehensible.
11. The station∧which sold discount coupon books for $20∧raised its prices at the pump∧by 4¢ a gallon.
12. After searching through the atlas∧I located Bogotá∧Colombia∧ Caracas∧Venezuela∧and San Juan∧Puerto Rico.
13. The fire crackled noisily∧its glow and its warmth spread∧to the dark corners of the room.

;
22

14. The huge∧ornate∧carving∧which was made from cork∧rested on the top of the piano∧it overwhelmed the small room.

15. However∧only fifty∧unspirited∧people turned up.

16. My friend∧an insurance agent∧advised me∧to cut my car insurance back to the compulsory level∧and save the rest of the premium cost∧for statistics show that I would almost certainly save enough to replace the car∧before an accident ever occurred.

17. The new ignition shows major improvements∧however∧it still is not on the market.

18. They met eight times∧nevertheless∧they were no closer to agreement∧after the eighth meeting∧than they were after the first.

19. If we had been Plains Indians in our past lives∧we would more greatly appreciate∧understand∧and respect∧the natural world.

20. Spiders used to bother me until I learned∧that they keep down the populations of other insects∧that bother me more.

21. One can make fun of the overweight men and women∧who pay high fees∧for memberships in health spas∧but at least they are trying to help themselves.

22. Thousands∧who bought Stevie Wonder's first albums∧remain his faithful fans today.

23. Expecting to be elected president∧Mary Lou left the campaigning to her friends.

24. Whereas I feel∧that I can go in any direction∧when I graduate from college∧my mother felt∧that she had but one route to follow∧that of homemaker.

25. The students offered the dean a feeble∧half hearted apology∧then they left to plot their next prank.

;

22

The comma and the semicolon: Review II

EXERCISE **22-3**

Insert a caret (∧) in the following paragraph wherever a comma or semi-colon is needed, and then insert the appropriate mark above the caret.

Beneath her red woolen cap the old woman's bloodshot eyes looked searchingly at me as she held out one hand the other clutching a fat shopping bag. She looked to be dressed for a snowstorm it was however the middle of summer. "You got money?" she asked. "No" I said. She stared at my food which I had been enjoying at an outdoor café then she lifted her eyes to gaze at the other diners and tables of food. Again turning her stare on me she said "Give me your watch." I shook my head and looked down at my plate wishing she would go away. Suddenly a vagabond child ran up knocked off her hat and sprinted away laughing. "Brat!" she yelled at the child before shuffling off in the afternoon heat. I looked back at my plate but I had no appetite.

',
∨

23

23|*The Apostrophe*

Self-test

Add apostrophes wherever they are needed in the sentences below. If a sentence is already punctuated correctly, write *OK* to the left of it.

Example: Alfred's dog has heartworms.

1. The princes reputations have been impugned.
2. At todays prices, we cant afford to eat out.
3. The womens coats were left in the pew.
4. The child asked how many *s*s are in *Mississippi*.
5. Karen will graduate in the spring of 86.
6. The cat lost its collar.
7. The geometry texts are hers.
8. Students privileges are limited.
9. Childrens art will be featured.
10. "Its a big job," she said.

23a | Use the apostrophe to indicate the possessive case for nouns and indefinite pronouns.

The **possessive case** indicates the possession or ownership of one person or thing by another (see Chapter 6).

1 | Add -'s to form the possessive case of singular or plural nouns or indefinite pronouns *not* ending in *s*.

The *men's* claim was honored.
That *person's* car was towed away.
Everyone's ears were ringing.

2 | Add -'s to form the possessive case of singular words ending in -s.

Morris's career is prospering.
The *business's* files were confiscated.

Since we usually do not pronounce the possessive -*s* of a few singular nouns ending in an *s* or *z* sound, add only the apostrophe to indicate possession: *for science' sake; for conscience' sake; Jesus' teaching.*

295

3 | **Add only an apostrophe to form the possessive case of plural words ending in -*s*.**

Students' rights are a big issue on this campus.
The *Sheldons'* stables caught fire.

4 | **Add -'*s* only to the last word to form the possessive case of compound words or word groups.**

My *brother-in-law's* arguments bore me.
The *attorney general's* dismissal was overdue.

5 | **When two or more words show individual possession, add -'*s* to them all. If they show joint possession, add -'*s* only to the last word.**

Fink and *Schlenk's* restaurant went bankrupt. [The restaurant was jointly owned.]
Wyatt's and *Surrey's* contributions to the sonnet form have long been acknowledged. [The two writers made different contributions to the sonnet form.]

23b | **Don't use the apostrophe in forming noun plurals or the possessive case of personal pronouns.**

Only an -*s* is needed to indicate the plural of most nouns.

FAULTY   The three *car's* were sold yesterday.

REVISED   The three *cars* were sold yesterday.

His, hers, its, ours, yours, theirs, and *whose* are already possessive and do not need apostrophes.

FAULTY   The victory was *their's.*

REVISED   The victory was *theirs.*

23c | **Use the apostrophe to indicate the omission of one or more letters, numbers, or words in standard contractions.**

doesn't	does not
who's	who is
it's	it is
you're	you are
'69	1969

23d | **Use the apostrophe plus -*s* to form the plurals of letters, numbers, and words named as words.**

Legal prose is filled with *wherefore*'s.
Instead of drawing circles over your *i*'s, just use dots.

(See 27d on the use of italics or underlining for letters, numbers, or words named as words.)

|*Forming the possessive case*   EXERCISE **23-1**

Form the possessive case of each noun and pronoun below by adding an
apostrophe, adding an apostrophe and an *-s,* or changing form as needed.

Example: Mike Smith   *Mike Smith's*

1. princess   _____

2. desks   _____

3. James   _____

4. everyone   _____

5. Ed Knox   _____

6. the Miles   _____

7. vice president   _____

8. fox   _____

9. community   _____

10. Mr. and Mrs. Slocum   _____

11. they   _____

12. women   _____

13. no one   _____

14. who   _____

15. Sally Mendez   _____

16. St. Louis   _____

17. father-in-law   _____

23

18. Terre Haute   _____

19. sheep   _____

20. you   _____

21. the Bahamas   _____

22. committee member   _____

23. oxen   _____

24. *Denver Post*   _____

25. wrens   _____

'
v

23

|*Using the apostrophe*

Insert an inverted caret ($\vee$) in the following sentences where an apostrophe is required. (The caret will often have to be inserted between the letters of a word.) If the sentence is already punctuated correctly, write *OK* to the left of it.

Example: We think it˅s time for united action.

A.
1. The Hongs divorce has not been announced.
2. Thirty years on the same job will dull anyones approach to life.
3. The cows disease will kill it but wont affect the rest of the herd.
4. The mens club has voted to admit women.
5. The Smiths and Schmidts houses are as similar as their names.
6. Frances prime minister addressed the delegations.
7. The best term paper is yours.
8. IBMs technological progress has outstripped Wang's.
9. How many *ifs* are in the agreement?
10. She put in a full days work.
11. The dog ran around in circles chasing its tail.
12. I can't recall whos speaking, but I do remember being excited when I heard who it is.
13. He told me that the car was yours and Teds.
14. Last Sundays sermon was better than this Sundays.
15. Everyones pay will increase because of the strike.
16. Theyre sure that the seats are theirs.
17. Its too late for an appointment.
18. The twins likeness is not surprising.
19. The class of 21 held a reunion last June.
20. The childrens habits need reforming.

B.
1. Sheep and oxen grazed near the lakes edge.
2. The decision was theirs and they made it, so theres nothing we can do.
3. Bruces cats preferred meal is lettuce and tomato.
4. The flooded apartment was ours.
5. We left Sandras house at midnight.

23

6. The shopping malls attraction is their concentration of widely varied stores.
7. Olivers run in the marathon seemed unwise after his recent illness.
8. Larrys rooms were broken into.
9. The lecture lasts two hours each Tuesday.
10. Theirs was a difficult task.
11. Television shows seem to be getting better; at least, its possible to watch something worthwhile every night.
12. The Joneses and Whites boats are moored in the same cove.
13. The ends of both races were uneventful.
14. I did not know whose coats were left.
15. Mr. Princes son has to walk because of the bus strike.
16. The tops of the bottles had broken off.
17. The thickness of caterpillars fur indicates the severity of the coming winter.
18. She asked how many *t*s are in Cincinnati.
19. This years rainfall was greater than last years.
20. Dans kennel is always crowded because its the best in the city.

23

24 | *Quotation Marks*

Self-test

In the sentences below, add single or double quotation marks wherever they are needed, being careful to place the marks correctly in relation to letters and other punctuation. If a sentence is already punctuated correctly, write *OK* to the left of it.

Example: He said, "Did you call?"

1. Were the books damaged? he asked.
2. Jeff said Okay when I asked him, Peg remarked.
3. Moon Drool is the title of her latest song.
4. Asia, Burke wrote, will remain a puzzle eternally.
5. Blake's poem The Tiger was not assigned.
6. The audience shouted Bravo! each time she came on stage, her agent reported.
7. Did the waitress say, As soon as I can?
8. He asked, Why are you home?
9. A pile of ashes, he said, is all that's left.
10. There are two reasons the poet wrote O Eager Bleat: to celebrate the sheep industry and to earn money.

" "

24

Quotation marks are used primarily to enclose direct quotations from speech and writing. They always come in pairs: one before the quotation and one after.

24a | Use double quotation marks to enclose direct quotations.

> Shirer wrote that Hitler "remains, so far, the most remarkable of those who have used modern techniques to apply the classic formulas of tyranny."

Indirect quotations — reporting what a speaker said but not in his or her exact words — are not enclosed in quotation marks: *He said that he would not be late again.*

24b | Use single quotation marks to enclose a quotation within a quotation.

"Graham said 'No way!' each time the coach asked him to go into the game," the reporter for the *Messenger* wrote.

24c | Set off quotations of dialogue, poetry, and long prose passages according to standard practice.

Begin a new paragraph for each speaker when quoting a conversation.

"Why did you come?" the instructor asked.
"Because the course is supposed to be easy," answered the student.
"And besides, the subject interests me."

When you quote a single speaker for more than one paragraph, place quotation marks at the beginning of each paragraph but at the end of the last paragraph only.

Poetry quotations of one line are normally run into the text and enclosed by quotation marks. Poetry quotations of two or three lines may be run into the text and enclosed by quotation marks or set off. If the quotation is run in, separate the lines with a slash (/).

Coleridge's beginning places the poem in an exotic land: "In Xanadu did Kubla Khan / A stately pleasure-dome decree."

Always set off poetry quotations of more than three lines. To set off a poetry quotation, separate the lines from the text and indent them ten spaces from the left margin. Triple-space above and below the quotation, and double-space the quotation itself. A quotation that is set off from the text needs no quotation marks.

Emerson's poem opens with an indication of his worship of nature:

Think me not unkind and rude
   That I walk alone in grove and glen;
I go to the god of the wood
   To fetch his word to men.

Prose quotations of up to four lines should ordinarily be run into the text and enclosed in quotation marks. Quotations of four lines or more should be set off from the body of the paper and indented ten spaces from the left. Triple-space above and below the quotation, and double-space the quotation itself. Don't enclose a set-off quotation in quotation marks.

24d | Put quotation marks around the titles of songs, short poems, articles in periodicals, short stories, essays, episodes of television and radio programs, and the subdivisions of books.

The song "Night and Day" is one of Cole Porter's best.
"Anecdote of the Jar" is a poem by Wallace Stevens.
The article entitled "The Perceptive Abilities of Rats" put me to sleep.
Mansfield wrote the short story "The Fly."

I still remember an essay we read, called "The Spider and the Wasp."
An episode called "Red Baiter" was one of the show's best.
Chapter 24, "Quotation Marks," was fascinating.

24e Occasionally, quotation marks may be used to enclose defined words and words used in a special sense.

The "correct" version actually included fifteen errors.
Determining the meter of a line of poetry is called "scanning."

Note: Italics may also be used in definitions. (See 27d.)

24f Avoid using quotation marks where they are not required.

Don't enclose the titles of your papers in quotation marks unless they contain or are themselves direct quotations. Common nicknames, technical terms not being defined, slang, or trite expressions should not be enclosed in quotation marks. If slang or trite expressions are inappropriate, rewrite the sentence.

NOT   "Rites of Passage in One Story by William Faulkner"

BUT   Rites of Passage in One Story by William Faulkner

OR   Rites of Passage in "The Bear"

NOT   The government should "get its act together" on national health care.

BUT   The government should develop a comprehensive program for national health care.

24g Place other marks of punctuation inside or outside quotation marks according to standard practice.

1 Place commas and periods inside quotation marks.

They sang "America the Beautiful."
It replaced "The Star-Spangled Banner," which no one could sing.

2 Place colons and semicolons outside quotation marks.

He said his footing was "precarious": he was on a high wire.
The label said "for relief of itching"; so we bought a bottle.

3 Place dashes, question marks, and exclamation points inside quotation marks only if they belong to the quotation.

The lawyer's one comment — "Immaterial" — sent a buzz through the courtroom.
Did I hear you say, "No"?

BUT

Did I hear you ask, "Why?"

|Quotation marks EXERCISE **24-1**

In the following sentences, insert an inverted caret (∨) and single or double quotation marks as required. Be sure to place the caret or carets correctly in relation to other punctuation marks. If a sentence is already punctuated correctly, write *OK* to the left of it.

Example: How many of you, the instructor asked, have read the assigned story, Araby?

A. 1. He made the following comment: I am determined to win.

2. Did Cohan write You're a Grand Old Flag?

3. The nucleus of a cell is its center, where its vital work goes on.

4. Did I hear you say, The show is sold out?

5. America would be a more appropriate national anthem than the Star-Spangled Banner is, the committee declared.

6. When asked how he felt about guarding Jones, Geiger answered: He has to check me, too.

7. The student replied that she hadn't noticed it.

8. Never take Route 1 unless you like traffic jams, he stated.

9. African man, writes Mbiti, lives in a religious universe.

10. Dickinson's poem first sets the mood: A quietness distilled, / As twilight long begun.

11. I have been trying to shed my nickname, Bernie, ever since I acquired it.

12. Truman stated, I fired General MacArthur because he would not respect the authority of the President.

13. Do you have to be macho to love Minnesota's winters? the visitor asked.

14. Remember the Alamo! was first used as a battle cry at San Jacinto.

15. Dandruff is the code name that CB operators give to snow.

" "

24

B. 1. Coleridge was ridiculed for writing I hail thee brother in his poem To a Young Ass.

2. Her only response was Maybe! my father shouted.

3. The Congo is a poem that experiments with rhythmic effects.

4. Why did you shout Eureka! as you left? she asked.

5. The band played Auld Lang Syne from midnight until two in the morning, and no one seemed to notice.

6. The waitress asked, Did you leave me a tip?

7. We spent a whole class discussing the word moral; yet we never agreed on its meaning.

8. The characters in the story are, in the author's words, anti-heroes; however, none is realistic.

9. Huckleberry Hawkins played center for three years.

10. Her article, The Joy of Anguish, was reprinted in six languages.

11. Sotweed is a synonym for tobacco.

12. Ray owns twenty different recordings of Stardust.

13. How many of you know the To be or not to be speech from *Hamlet?* asked the drama coach.

14. He said that the test would be challenging; he should have said that it would be impossible.

15. William Blake's poem The Fly includes this stanza:

> Am not I
> A fly like thee?
> Or art not thou
> A man like me?

25 | *Other Punctuation Marks*

Self-test

In the sentences below, add colons, dashes, parentheses, brackets, ellipsis marks, or slashes wherever they are needed or wherever they should replace other punctuation marks. When more than one mark would be correct in a sentence, choose the mark that seems most appropriate. If a sentence is already punctuated correctly, write *OK* to the left of it.

Example: The speaker dwelled on a single problem; the destructive power of ideals.

1. J. S. Mill 1806–1873 was considered the brightest man of his time.

2. A good student, he still lacks an important quality patience.

3. First editions especially rare ones can be costly.

4. The pool will be closed on the following days July 4 and September 2.

5. "The movie . . . is truly his worst effort in years," wrote one critic.

6. "The lessor and-or the agent is responsible," the attorney stated.

7. The rebate $250 prompted her to buy the car.

8. The ad read, "Buy now for tremendous saveings [*sic*]."

9. We were given a choice of 1 a term paper, 2 five book reports, or 3 a lab project.

10. Of the cities we investigated, three cities Rockville, Monroe Heights, and West Greenway had a surplus of rental housing.

:—( )[ ].../

25

THE COLON

25a | Use the colon to introduce and to separate.

1 | Use the colon to introduce summaries, explanations, series, appositives ending sentences, long or formal quotations, and statements introduced by *the following* or *as follows.*

Note that a complete main clause precedes the colon.

307

SUMMARY

The essence of his warning was this: Obey the law or lose the funds.

EXPLANATION

Pedestrians risk their lives to cross the city's streets: Even when a sign says "Walk," they stand a good chance of being run over by drivers who assume red lights do not apply to them.

SERIES

The winners could choose one of three prizes: a new car, a trip to Europe, or a lifetime's supply of canned crab meat.

FINAL APPOSITIVE

A good career has one essential quality: challenge.

FORMAL OR LONG QUOTATION

The senator issued the following statement: "I repudiate those who question my honesty, and I call on my constituents to do the same."

STATEMENT INTRODUCED BY *THE FOLLOWING* **OR** *AS FOLLOWS*

The winners were as follows: Harriet Joyce, Bonnie Chapman, and Charleen Oliver.

2 | **Use the colon to separate subtitles and titles, the subdivisions of time, and the parts of biblical citations.**

TITLE AND SUBTITLE *Poetry: Sound and Image*

TIME 5:45, 9:00

BIBLICAL CITATION Luke 5:12

3 | **Avoid misusing the colon.**

Don't put a colon between a verb or a preposition and its object or when a formal introduction (such as *the following*) is lacking.

FAULTY The subjects of the painting were: a cow, a bear, and a zebra.

REVISED The subjects of the painting were a cow, a bear, and a zebra.

THE DASH

25b | **Use the dash or dashes to indicate sudden changes in tone or thought and to set off some sentence elements.**

1 | **Use the dash or dashes to indicate sudden shifts in tone, new or unfinished thoughts, and hesitation in dialogue.**

Jasper's sense of humor might appeal to you — if you are as witless as he is.
In response I said — well, my reply is unprintable.
"My father —" she blurted out and then stopped.

2 | Use the dash or dashes to emphasize appositives and parenthetical expressions.

Many animals — for example, the elephant — are in danger of extinction.

3 | Use the dash to set off introductory series and summaries.

Care, tenderness, a sense of humor — Gunther possessed all of these.

4 | Avoid misusing or overusing the dash.

Don't use a dash when a comma, semicolon, or period is more appropriate. Keep in mind that too many dashes can give writing a choppy or jumpy quality.

> FAULTY   The envelope — torn and scuffed — arrived on Tuesday — my birthday — and when I opened it, I found a bent birthday card — and a torn check.
>
> REVISED   The envelope, torn and scuffed, arrived on Tuesday, my birthday. When I opened it, I found a bent birthday card and a torn check.

PARENTHESES

25c | Use parentheses to enclose nonessential elements within sentences.

1 | Use parentheses to enclose parenthetical expressions.

Parenthetical expressions include explanations, examples, and minor digressions that are not essential to meaning.

> The zoo places animals in settings that simulate their natural environments (forest, desert, swamp, and so forth).
> William Butler Yeats (1865–1939) was not only a poet but also a playwright and essayist.

2 | Use parentheses to enclose letters and figures labeling items in lists within sentences.

The course has three requirements: (1) an oral report, (2) a midterm examination, and (3) a final examination.

BRACKETS

25d | Use brackets only within quotations to separate your own comments from the words of the writer you quote.

Brooke writes that "the essence of the religion [Islam] is legalism."

Use the word *sic* (Latin for "in this manner") in brackets to indicate that an error in a quotation appeared in the original and was not introduced by you.

> The manual pointed out that "proofreading is an important job that must be performed caerfully [*sic*]."

: — ( ) [ ] ... /

25

THE ELLIPSIS MARK

25e Use the ellipsis mark to indicate omissions within quotations.

The **ellipsis mark** is three spaced periods (. . .).

ORIGINAL "Riley's works must be read aloud for the reader to get the fullest possible enjoyment."

WITH ELLIPSIS "Riley's works must be read aloud for . . . the fullest possible enjoyment."

When the ellipsis mark follows a sentence, it is used in addition to the period that ends the sentence: *"The plans went awry. . . . The 'perfect' crime was a failure."*

THE SLASH

25f Use the slash between options and to separate lines of poetry that are run in to the text.

OPTION We faced an either/or situation: either sell or be taken to court.

POETRY Wallace Stevens paints autumn differently: "The rain falls. The sky / Falls and lies with the worms."

Unless you are writing a legal document, avoid use of *and/or* and *he/she*.

:—()[]...*/*

25

| *Using the colon, the dash, parentheses, brackets, the ellipsis mark, the slash* | EXERCISE **25-1** |

Circle the place in each sentence below where punctuation should be added or is used incorrectly, and write the correct punctuation, along with the adjacent words, on the blank to the right. (The mark may be used to replace another mark that is used incorrectly.) When more than one mark would be correct in a sentence, choose the mark that seems most appropriate. If a sentence is already punctuated correctly, write *OK* on the blank.

Example: Adams was fascinated by one thing in the exhibit⊙the power of steam.　　　*exhibit : the*

1. Of the nine regions surveyed, only one New England had a low suicide rate.　　_____

2. The ring was priced reasonably ($200).　　_____

3. "Iamb," "trochee," "spondee" all are terms for poetry analysis.　　_____

4. "The penalty is a $500 fine and or a year in jail," the lawyer said.　　_____

5. There are two basic defenses: 1 the zone and 2 the man to man.　　_____

6. A good worker, he lacks only one quality tact.　　_____

7. Our savings $100 are not enough for the trip.　　_____

8. The recipe my aunt's favorite calls for three eels.　　_____

9. The discount on the new car was insignificant only $50.　　_____

10. Two of the contestants (Perry and Hughy are my roommates.　　_____

:−()[]…/

25

11. In two lines of the poem, Robinson portrays Richard Cory as "a gentleman from sole to crown, / Clean favored, and imperially slim." _____

12. The paper said, "People waved from the poop-site (*sic*) shore." _____

13. I got a high grade in only one course; Elementary Education 101. _____

14. The kit contained the following items, a flare, a wrench, two screwdrivers, one hammer, and a fan belt. _____

15. The life of Ernest Hemingway 1899–1961 was exciting by almost anyone's standards. _____

16. His new title [associate fireman] brought no increase in pay. _____

17. The hide — (alligator) — could not be imported. _____

18. The assignment for Friday was a long one pages 200–290. _____

19. The cathedral, built in 1295?, was open to tour groups. _____

20. "The state's largest drinking fountain" that is what Mayor Belotti called the new reservoir. _____

21. However, she then said, "Let's not forget how difficult it was to bring this water here and . . how much it means to us." _____

22. Among the recruiters were IBM, Olivetti, and TRW. _____

23. Tolstoy's *Works* [volumes 2 and 3] were on sale for $7.95. _____

24. The course depended on only one assignment . . . the term paper. _____

25. The teacher, actually, his assistant wrote that my paper was "flabby and pointless." _____

Punctuation: Review
of Chapters 20–25

In the following passages, insert a caret (∧) wherever punctuation is wrong or missing and write the correct punctuation above the caret.

A. On September 30 1982, I wrote to a manufacturer Johnson's Curds, Inc, in Lockhaven Kentucky to complain about a cup of blueberry yogurt, that had a pebble in it. I told the company, that I had complained to the manager, of the store in which I bought the yogurt, however I got no satisfaction. You cant prove the pebble was in the cup when you bought it I reported the manager as saying. Why are you trying to cheat me. Since the manager would not refund my money I told Johnsons that I expected a prompt refund. Having waited three months I have no answer but I will be patient.

B. The diary, which I found in the trunk ended with the following entry; "Two squalls struck the coast on 31 June *sic,* destroying the candle factory." There were no further entries except for a reference to a Bible verse [John 3;16]. The diary was in the handwriting of my mother's father whom I had never met. It contained historical information valuable to our community as well as several entries important to my family history I let the county historian borrow it however I could not part with it permanently.

VI | Mechanics
26 | *Capitals*

Self-test

In the sentences below, draw a line *through* any letter that *should not* be capitalized, and draw a line *under* any letter that *should* be capitalized. If the capitalization in a sentence is already correct, write *OK* to the left of it.

Example: Horace Met Angela in june.

1. He has a fondness for asian art.
2. Woodworth's lyric entitled "the old oaken bucket" gives me chills.
3. My Mother sent Grandfather a box of Cuban cigars.
4. He is the president of the American Sculpture Society.
5. "The worst season here is Summer," doctor Ellis said.
6. Joan, a Professor of Music, owns many Classical music tapes.
7. The East side of the woods borders Claytor lake.
8. His latest book is *The Era of the Frog: a Study in Green.*
9. She has thirty copies of "Ode to my Bunny."
10. Elmo majored in Physics at Greenburg state college.

cap

26

26a | Capitalize the first word of every sentence.

The snows came early.
Why must we go?

26b | Follow standard practice in capitalizing the titles of your own papers and of books and their parts, periodicals, articles, films, television and radio programs, poems, plays, and other works.

In titles, capitalize the first and last words, any word after a colon or semicolon, and all other words except articles (*a, an, the*) and prepositions and conjunctions of fewer than five letters.

Pope: A Metrical Study
Albee: His Position Among Tragedians
"How a River Got Its Name"
"Sexist Language in Television Commercials"

26c | **Always capitalize the pronoun *I* and the interjection *O*.**
Don't capitalize *oh* unless it begins a sentence.

"But O heart! heart! heart!" wrote Whitman on the death of Lincoln.
My interview was short, but, oh, did I have to answer hard questions.

26d | **Capitalize proper nouns, proper adjectives, and words used as essential parts of proper nouns.**

1 | **Capitalize proper nouns and adjectives.**

Common nouns name general classes of persons, places, and things. **Proper nouns** name specific persons, places, and things. **Proper adjectives** are formed from some proper nouns. Capitalize all proper nouns and proper adjectives but not the articles (*a, an, the*) that precede them.

COMMON NOUNS	PROPER NOUNS	PROPER ADJECTIVES
country	Mexico	Mexican
man	Milton	Miltonic
building	Arizona State Prison	—

SPECIFIC PERSONS AND THINGS

Joe Smith   the Liberty Bell

SPECIFIC PLACES AND GEOGRAPHICAL REGIONS

Louisville, Kentucky   the Gulf of Mexico
the South   the West

DAYS OF THE WEEK, MONTHS, HOLIDAYS

Tuesday, March 13   Labor Day

HISTORICAL EVENTS, DOCUMENTS, PERIODS, MOVEMENTS

the Civil War   the Bill of Rights
the Magna Carta   the War of 1812
the Stone Age   the Reformation

GOVERNMENT OFFICES OR DEPARTMENTS AND INSTITUTIONS

Atomic Energy Commission   Department of Defense
Centerville High School   State Department

POLITICAL, SOCIAL, ATHLETIC, AND OTHER ORGANIZATIONS AND ASSOCIATIONS AND THEIR MEMBERS

Democratic Party   Houston Astros
American Kennel Club   Knights of Columbus
American Medical Association   National Council of Trade Unions

RACES, NATIONALITIES, AND THEIR LANGUAGES

Italian   Swede
Caucasian   Swedish

RELIGIONS AND THEIR FOLLOWERS

Judaism   Jews
Christianity   Christians
Islam   Moslems

cap

26

316

the Almighty	God
the Old Testament	Allah

2 | **Capitalize common nouns used as essential parts of proper nouns.**

Center *Street*	*Mount* Rushmore
Lake Mead	Canadian *Embassy*
Williams *County*	Union *Station*

3 | **Capitalize trade names.**

Coca-Cola	Burger King
Xerox	Ford Mustang

26e | **Capitalize titles when they precede proper names but generally not when they follow proper names or are used alone.**

Foreign Minister Khalil	Khalil, the foreign minister
Professor G. M. Dunning	G. M. Dunning, a professor

26f | **Avoid unnecessary capitalization.**

1 | **Don't capitalize common nouns used in place of proper nouns.**

NOT	The Stadium was closed for repairs.
BUT	Landrum Stadium was closed for repairs.
OR	The stadium was closed for repairs.

2 | **Don't capitalize compass directions unless they refer to specific geographical areas.**

Go *east* to visit, but live in the *West*.

cap

26

3 | **Don't capitalize the names of seasons or the names of academic years or terms.**

fall color	spring semester
winter rains	sophomore year

4 | **Don't capitalize the names of relationships unless they form part of or substitute for proper names.**

my uncle	Uncle John
my grandmother	Grandmother

Note: If you have any doubt about whether a particular word should be capitalized, consult a recent dictionary.

|Using capitals

In the sentences below, draw a line through any letter that should not be capitalized, and draw a line under any letter that should be capitalized. If the capitalization in a sentence is already correct, write *OK* to the left of it.

Example: Steve and <u>s</u>helly got married last ~~S~~ummer.

1. "Helga is part American indian," her Mother said.
2. The freedom of information act has been costly to implement.
3. The Governor gave a radio talk on Christmas.
4. Edith Farrara, president of Grendel corporation, makes monsters for a living.
5. Carol titled her painting *All Alone in The Wheat.*
6. The Riley County Pumpkin-Growing contest was won by Travis and Tyler.
7. John still tells world war II stories on memorial day.
8. The waiter explained, "the soup changes every day."
9. Mike asked grandmother Collins where she was born and heard a fascinating reply.
10. Heffeltooth is a local leader of the republican party.
11. Our family attends the First Methodist Church on Main Street.
12. My Grandfather always forgets to put in his teeth, and Granny then complains.
13. The islamic group distributed literature on friday.
14. His Mother, Martha, plans to give him a new Dodge Station wagon.
15. The U.S. Postal Service becomes less efficient every year.
16. The National Geographic society was founded in 1888.
17. The American consulate would not issue Alphonse a visa.
18. My friend Joe lives on the East side of the Park.
19. The best hunting is in the western part of the state.
20. Ed thinks Wrigley field will have lights by Spring.
21. The book was titled *How to deal with stress.*
22. My friends report that the most enjoyable way to cross the Atlantic ocean is to take a British Ship.

cap

26

23. We pulled into a texaco station to fill the gas tank.
24. Both players are Seniors this year.
25. I had to memorize the dimensions of over 200 paintings for my art course last term; yet I learned almost nothing about their contents.

cap

26

27 | *Italics*

Self-test

In the sentences below, underline any words that should be in italics, and circle any words now in italics that should not be. If a sentence is already correct, write *OK* to the left of it.

Example: The word <u>hoopla</u> comes from French.

1. The selections were from the musical *Godspell.*
2. The Parkersburg Herald wrote a feature on Hull's painting "The Bernasek Porch."
3. Bardiglio is the name for a variety of marble.
4. *"Never* try that again!" she screamed.
5. Common Sense was a pamphlet urging revolution.
6. I often pronounce the t in *often.*
7. The U.S.S. Gompers set sail for the Pacific on April 3.
8. Mr. Tucker read out of *Exodus* from the Bible.
9. Omar lisped when he said isthmus.
10. Her *Newsweek* subscription has run out.

ital

27

     Type that slants upward to the right is known as *italic type.* It is used to distinguish or emphasize words. In handwriting or typing, underline to indicate italics.

27a | **Underline the titles of books, long poems, plays, periodicals, pamphlets, published speeches, long musical works, movies, television and radio programs, and works of visual art.**

BOOK *Ivanhoe*	MUSICAL WORK *Madame Butterfly*
LONG POEM *Lycidas*	MOVIE *On Golden Pond*
PLAY *Hamlet*	TELEVISION OR RADIO PROGRAM
PERIODICAL *The New York Times*	*Hill Street Blues*
SPEECH *Gettysburg Address*	WORK OF ART *Mona Lisa*

Don't underline the Bible or parts of it: Genesis, Matthew.

27b | Underline the names of ships, aircraft, spacecraft, and trains.

the U.S.S. *Turner Joy*   the U.S. *Enterprise*
the *Spirit of St. Louis*   the *Southern Crescent*

27c | Underline foreign words and phrases that are not part of the English language.

Deadly nightshade belongs to the genus *Atropa*.
Osborn's manners were *trés gauche*.

27d | Underline words, letters, numbers, and phrases named as words.

Why does *sour grapes* mean scorning something?
Even small children know there are four *s*'s in *Mississippi*.

27e | Occasionally, underlining may be used for emphasis.

When its trainer held out a chair, the lion *ate* it.

Be careful with this use of underlining, however. Too much underlining for emphasis makes writing sound immature or hysterical.

ital

27

Name _____ Date _____ Score _____

|Using italics

EXERCISE **27-1**

In the sentences below, underline any words that should be in italics, and circle any words now in italics that should not be. If a sentence is already correct, write *OK* to the left of it.

Example: The word emotion pertains to (feelings.)

1. The tankers were blockaded for a week in the *Persian Gulf.*
2. *TNT* was used to demolish the building.
3. The Washington Star usually printed conservative views.
4. The yard became overgrown with *Swedish ivy.*
5. We took a tour of a ship, the North Carolina, for only $2.50.
6. Hamlet contains more violence than does any crime drama on television.
7. The clams were so *gritty* that we could not eat them.
8. Life magazine is a show place for photography.
9. Shaw's *Man and Superman* is more often read than viewed on stage.
10. *The Great Wall of China* was completed in the third century B.C.
11. The strange form was the mem of the Hebrew alphabet.
12. She makes the dots on her i's so large that the page looks like an aerial view of the Charles County Balloon Festival.
13. We read the Bible's first five books and discussed them in class.
14. We had to report on the P. W. Joyce book Old Celtic Romances.
15. *Gree* is an archaic word meaning "satisfaction."
16. A new journal, Fun with Caries, reprinted an article by Brady Hull, D.D.S.
17. 60 Minutes continues to be quite profitable for *CBS.*
18. Miserere is the fiftieth psalm in the *Douay Bible.*
19. Eijkman won the *Nobel Prize* for medicine in 1929.
20. The expression *c'est la vie* never gave me much comfort.
21. The professor published her article in the sociology journal Studies in Poverty.
22. I was surprised to see that Wyeth's Christina's World is not a larger painting.
23. The foxglove belongs to the genus *Digitalis.*

ital

27

24. My husband, for instance, repeatedly mispronounces the word asterisk.
25. My twenty-year subscription to *Boys' Life,* given to me by my uncle, has finally expired.

28 | *Abbreviations*

Self-test

In the sentences below, cross out each abbreviation that is inappropriate and write the correct form above it. If the abbreviation in a sentence is appropriate, write *OK* in the left margin.

Example: He bought 10 ~~gals~~. of gasoline. *(gallons)*

1. The prof. was late only once.

2. Geo. Meany headed the union for many years.

3. She finally got her B.A. in 1982.

4. Browning Corp. interviewed seniors today.

5. Dr. Schmidt recently resigned.

6. She returned to the U.S.A. in March.

7. On Mon. the team visits Ogden.

8. We arrived early on Feb. 16.

9. NATO remains an effective deterrent.

10. Agnes majored in econ. and French.

ab

28

28a | Use standard abbreviations for titles immediately before and after proper names.

BEFORE THE NAME	AFTER THE NAME
Mr. Peter Green	Peter Green, M.D.
Mrs., Ms., Gen., Msgr.	Ph.D., D.D.S., S.J., Sr., Jr.

The abbreviations *Mr., Mrs., Ms., Rev., Hon., Prof., Rep., Sen., Dr.,* and *St.* (for *Saint*) are used only if they appear with a proper name. Spell them out in the absence of a proper name.

NOT	The dr. was late.
BUT	The doctor was late.
OR	Dr. Smith was late.

Abbreviations such as *Jr., Sr., Esq., M.D., D.D., Ph.D.,* and *S.J.,* which generally appear after proper names, are rarely spelled out. Within a sentence they should be preceded and followed by commas. Abbreviations for academic degrees may be used without a proper name.

Arthur Garcia, Sr., sold his business.
Hester Mainz, M.D., practices medicine in Detroit.
He is still trying to earn an M.A.

28b | Familiar abbreviations and acronyms for the names of organizations, corporations, people, and some countries are acceptable in most writing.

An **acronym** is an abbreviation that spells a pronounceable word and is written without periods: NATO, UNESCO. As long as they are well known, acronyms and abbreviations for the names of organizations, corporations, people, and some countries are acceptable in most writing. When the abbreviation consists of three or more letters, it is usually written without periods.

CIA	ABC	JFK	USA (or U.S.A.)
UAW	AFL-CIO	FDR	USSR (or U.S.S.R.)

28c | Use the abbreviations B.C., A.D., A.M., P.M., *no.*, and the symbol $ with specific dates and numbers only.

44 B.C.	A.D. 54	10:15 A.M.	no. 344	$3.60

28d | Generally, reserve common Latin abbreviations such as *i.e., e.g.,* and *etc.* for use in footnotes, bibliographies, and comments in parentheses.

I.e. stands for *id est,* "that is." *E.g.* stands for *exempli gratia,* "for example." *Etc.* stands for *et cetera,* "and so forth." Note that when they are used, they are not italicized.

The council (i.e., the three voting members of the committee) decided against the rule change.
Hardwoods (e.g., maple) make durable furniture.
The hardwoods (maple, oak, etc.) burn well in fireplaces.

ab

28

28e Don't use *Inc.*, *Bros.*, *Co.*, or the ampersand (& for *and*) except when they are part of the official name of a business firm.

NOT   The Brown bros. won the contract.

BUT   The Brown brothers won the contract.

OR   Brown Bros. won the contract.

28f In most writing don't abbreviate units of measurement, geographical names; names of days, months, and holidays; names of people; courses of instruction; and labels for divisions of written works.

NOT   The book, which was a fraction of an *in.* thick and had two *chs.*, was about *Robt.* Ash's struggles every *Tues.* to master *econ.* at the school he attended in *Mo.*

BUT   The book, which was a fraction of an *inch* thick and had two *chapters*, was about *Robert* Ash's struggles every *Tuesday* to master *economics* at the school he attended in *Missouri.*

ab

28

| *Using abbreviations*

In the sentences below, cross out each abbreviation that is inappropriate and write the correct form above it. If the abbreviation in a sentence is appropriate, write *OK* in the left margin.

Example: My gas guzzler has a 350-cubic-~~in.~~ engine.
(inch)

1. The prof. was usually available after class.

2. Television & radio reach a broad audience.

3. Twelve gals. of fuel cost over $15.

4. Mt. Vernon recently raised its admission fee.

5. Greg tried for years to earn a Ph.D.

6. The metric liter equals 1.057 qts.

7. My senator favors greater understanding between the U.S.A. and China.

8. No one remembered when the sgt. had been promoted.

9. The school that I attended was so small that the phys. ed. instructor also taught English.

10. The reunion was held in Hope, Kans., in July.

11. Rep. Tidwell lost in the primary.

12. My fiancé and I have known each other since we were in jr. high.

13. The FBI has lost much of its prestige since J. Edgar Hoover died.

14. The guide was from Sunset Tours, Inc.

ab

28

15. Second St. needs to be repaved.

16. Mr. and Mrs. Key worked hard all their lives.

17. Axel T. Goldfarb, Jr., raised cats for fun.

18. WTOP broadcasts news all P.M.

19. The winning ticket was no. 21-12.

20. All I got was an oz. of shrimp.

21. The juniors, led by Robt. Benz, beat the seniors in intramural basketball.

22. The assignment to read pp. 60 to 190 was unreasonable for a single night's work, and the students objected.

23. Some persons cannot study effectively because of learning problems; e.g., they are unable to concentrate or they read poorly.

24. The rules are meant for freshmen, sophomores, etc.

25. She demanded "compensation" (i.e., cash).

26. The YWCA offers good athletic facilities for a small fee.

27. On Christmas Eve we customarily eat dinner with the Dr. and her family.

28. We invited Dr. Wiona and Msgr. Martignetti to the opening of the Red Cross blood drive.

29. ABC televised all the Olympics until the one in 1980.

30. N.C. State went all the way to the national championship that year.

29 | *Numbers*

Self-test

In the sentences below, cross out any figure that should be spelled out in most writing, and write the spelled-out number above it. Circle any spelled-out number that should be written in figures, and write the figures above it. If numbers are used appropriately in a sentence, write *OK* in the left margin.

Example: ~~1~~ *Two* were lost, but ⟨one hundred and two⟩ *102* were saved.

1. Heath's batting average is .200.

2. The store closed at nine o'clock.

3. Volume three is on reserve at the library.

4. The paint cost six dollars and ten cents.

5. One hundred and ninety pounds is her weight.

6. There were 36 cousins absent from the reunion on May third.

7. The truck broke down 3 days ago.

8. At the meeting, 406 demonstrators were arrested.

9. The tank leaked 100 gallons of fuel.

10. The teacher assigned only two hundred and forty lines of poetry.

num

29

29a | Use figures for numbers that require more than two words to spell out.

Enrollment this term is *9002*.
My smallest class has *127* students in it.

Spell out most numbers of two words or less.

Last year my smallest class had *ninety-seven* students in it.
The administration expects enrollments to climb to *eleven thousand* and then level off.

When you use several numbers together, though, consistently spell them out or consistently express them in figures: *The broker bought 110 shares of mining stock at $10 each, 15 shares of oil stock at $50 each, and 4 municipal bonds at $500 each.*

29b | **Use figures for days and years; numbers of pages, chapters, volumes, acts, scenes, and lines; numbers containing decimals, percentages, and fractions; addresses; scores and statistics; exact amounts of money; and the time of day.**

January 10, 1975 [*January tenth* is also acceptable when it is not followed by a year.]

volume 1, pages 67–68

1.2 quarts, 3½ years

62 percent

327 Avedon Avenue

a score of 18 to 3

$6.28 [Round dollar or cent amounts may be expressed in words: *seven dollars; forty cents.*]

9:27 [Express the time in words when using *o'clock: nine o'clock.*]

29c | **Always spell out numbers that begin sentences.**

NOT   397 people attended the lecture.

BUT   The lecture was attended by 397 people.

OR   Three hundred and ninety-seven people attended the lecture.

Using numbers

In the sentences below, cross out any figure that should be spelled out in most writing, and write the spelled-out number above it. Circle any spelled-out number that should be written in figures and write the figures above it. If numbers are used appropriately in a sentence, write *OK* in the left margin.

Example: ~~Sixty-seven~~ 67 people attended the public meeting, although only (one hundred and fifty) *150* had been expected.

1. The fees rose by 21 percent in 1983.

2. A book of 12 tickets costs $10.

3. Seaver pitched in 35 games last year.

4. They bought a house at Five Cove off Cork Lane.

5. There were 4070 empty seats in the auditorium.

6. My 7-year-old sister can read and comprehend the Bible.

7. My grandmother bought the stock in 1946 at a cost of three dollars and twenty-five cents a share.

8. If you take Route 66 to the Marbury Street turnoff and follow that road east for 2½ miles, you will find the 1492 Restaurant, famous for its Spanish food.

9. One hundred and twelve yards was Jim's rushing total at the end of the game.

10. 2 volumes of poetry remained unsold.

11. The nine o'clock bus came an hour late.

num

29

12. After I dropped out of high school, my parents thought I would never go to college, but 6 years later here I am.

13. August twenty-seventh is her birthday.

14. The confirmation class had 30 members.

15. The Tigers won by the score 7–3.

16. $20 was the cost of the psychology text.

17. In high school I had to memorize over 100 lines from *Romeo and Juliet*.

18. Only eight nations attended the economic summit on June fourth.

19. The most famous eruption of Mt. Vesuvius was in A.D. seventy-nine, when the cities of Pompeii and Herculaneum were destroyed.

20. For 14 gallons of gasoline I paid $24.60 to a station owner who was later arrested for price gouging.

21. The commuter train leaves at 8:15, and the trip takes only twenty minutes.

num
29

22. Volume 5 of the encyclopedia is missing pages 12–506, as well as the last 4 pages.

23. Within 3 miles of the intersection are 12 bars.

24. The package contained 20 cookies and two jars of coffee.

25. Since he is barely 5 feet tall, Uncle Cosmo could not qualify for the police force; so he established his own detective agency and today makes 6 times what he would have made as a police officer.

30 | *Word Division*

Self-test

Many of the following word divisions would be inappropriate in a final manuscript. If a word should not be divided at all, write the word on one blank to the right. If a word should be redivided, write the new division on two blanks to the right. If the word division is appropriate, write *OK* on one blank.

Example: purp-   *pur-*
    ose   *pose*

1. drug-   _____
  ged   _____

2. all-   _____
  ow   _____

3. luck-   _____

4. pan-Ameri-   _____
  can   _____

5. mul-   _____
  tiply   _____

6. compel-   _____
  led   _____

7. self-in-   _____
  dulgent   _____

8. thro-   _____

9. cosig-   _____
  ned   _____

10. obli-   _____
   que   _____

div

30

   When it is necessary to divide words between the end of one line and the beginning of the next, always do so only between syllables. Check your dictionary if you are in doubt about how to break a word into syllables. But not all syllable breaks are appropriate for word division. The following rules will help you decide when and how to divide words.

30a | Don't make a division that leaves a single letter at the end of a line or fewer than three letters at the beginning of a line.

NOT	a- gree	BUT	agree	NOT	e- quip	BUT	equip
NOT	boot- y	BUT	booty	NOT	report- er	BUT	reporter

30b | Don't divide one-syllable words.

NOT	drop- ped	BUT	dropped	NOT	strai- ght	BUT	straight

30c | Divide compound words only between the words that form them or at fixed hyphens.

Compound words are made up of two or more words joined together. If they are joined by a hyphen, the hyphen is called **fixed**.

NOT	for- ty-two	BUT	forty- two	NOT	mid- dle-aged	BUT	middle- aged
NOT	sec- ondhand	BUT	second- hand	NOT	typewrit- ing	BUT	type- writing

30d | Avoid confusing word divisions.

Even when a word is correctly divided into syllables, the first or second half of the word may form a different word or wrongly pronounced syllable that will momentarily confuse the reader.

NOT	cash- ier	BUT	cashier	NOT	an- gel	BUT	angel
NOT	lis- ten	BUT	listen	NOT	ide- alism	BUT	idealism

div

30

|Dividing words correctly

Many of the following word divisions would be inappropriate in a final manuscript. If a word should not be divided at all, write the word on one blank to the right. If a word should be redivided, write the new division on two blanks. If the word division is appropriate, write *OK* on one blank. Consult a dictionary as needed to check syllable breaks.

Example: good-na-   *good-*

tured   *natured*

1. stew-   _____   8. fin-   _____

   ed   _____   ished   _____

2. rel-   _____   9. head-hunt-   _____

   igious   _____   ing   _____

3. control-   _____   10. gui-   _____

   led   _____   ding   _____

4. curr-   _____   11. poe-   _____

   ent   _____   try   _____

5. accomp-   _____   12. car-   _____

   lish   _____   nival   _____

6. Marx-   _____   13. pan-Afri-   _____

   ist-Leninist   _____   can   _____

7. ach-   _____   14. swarth-   _____

   ieve   _____   y   _____

div

30

15. techniq-
ue

16. usa-
ges

17. cover-
ed

18. drag-
ged

19. self-in-
flicted

20. res-
earch

21. lit-
tle

22. sig-
ner

23. nutrit-
ion

24. leng-
th

25. divis-
ion

26. litera-
ture

27. bro-
ught

28. assig-
ned

29. rent-
ed

30. regis-
ter

div

30

VII | Effective Words
31 | *Controlling Diction*

Diction is the choice and use of words. Controlling diction means selecting words that convey your meaning as precisely and concisely as possible.

31a | Choosing the appropriate word

The words you use in any piece of writing depend on who your audience is and on what kind of impression you want to create. For most nonfiction writing in and after college, the appropriate vocabulary is the standard English commonly used and understood by educated writers and readers.

1 | Avoiding slang

Slang, the special conversational vocabulary of a particular group of people, should be avoided in formal writing. It may not be understood by all readers, and it is often imprecise. The slang adjective *straight*, for instance, may mean "honest," "not homosexual," "inclined to wear a vest and tie," or "not on drugs," among other things.

2 | Avoiding colloquial language

Colloquial language is the informal vocabulary of conversation: *He stayed loose; He gave her a hard time.* Like slang, colloquialisms are often imprecise and are generally not appropriate in college, business, or professional writing. In dictionaries colloquialisms are often labeled *colloquial* or *informal.*

3 | Avoiding regional words and expressions

In writing for a general audience, avoid expressions that carry their intended meaning only in certain regions or that vary in meaning from one part of the country to another. Examples of the first type are *redd up* (to tidy or prepare) and *wheel* (a bicycle); an example of the second type is *poke* (sack in some areas, sum of money in others). Dictionaries use labels such as *regional* or *dialect* for such expressions.

d

31

4 | Avoiding nonstandard language

Variant words and expressions that are not usually acceptable in conversation — *ain't got no, hadn't ought to, theirselves* — should be avoided in writing as well. Dictionaries use *nonstandard* or *substandard* to label such usages.

5 | Avoiding obsolete or archaic words and neologisms

Words the dictionary labels *obsolete* or *archaic* should be avoided because they are no longer part of the current American vocabulary. (Examples are *mome* and *dispensator*.) **Neologisms** are recently invented words that are not yet (and may never be) part of the common vocabulary; they too are inappropriate in most writing. (An example is *prioritize.*)

6 | Using technical words with care

In every academic or technical field, practitioners use certain terms, either newly invented or adapted from the general vocabulary, to convey special and highly specific meanings. Botanists speak of an *etiolated* leaf, sociologists of the *ethos* of a culture, psychologists of *reinforcing* a behavior. In writing for a general audience, avoid such terms if possible because not all readers will understand them. Explain any specialized terms that you must use. (See also 31c-4.)

7 | Avoiding euphemisms and pretentious writing

A **euphemism** is an inoffensive substitute for a word deemed potentially offensive or blunt. An example is *the dread disease* as a substitute for *cancer*. Since euphemisms may be vague or misleading, use them only when direct, truthful words would needlessly offend members of your audience. Never use more or longer words than you need to convey what you mean. For example, *She obtruded her presence into my realm of awareness* can be restated simply and unpretentiously as *I noticed her*.

d

31

|Choosing the appropriate word   exercise **31-1**

Circle the word or expression in parentheses most appropriate to standard written English in the given sentence. Eliminate slang, colloquial language, regional words and expressions, nonstandard language, obsolete or archaic words, neologisms, unnecessarily technical words, euphemisms, and pretentious words. Consult a dictionary as needed to verify your choice.

Example: Though the acting was competent, the play itself was (*lousy, no good,* (*bad*)).

1. The committee met to review the (*pres's, president's*) report.
2. Yelling at a referee is not (*wise, cool, kosher*).
3. Sarah, once the best tennis player in town, (*died, passed away*) recently.
4. The book sale will (*surely, sure*) make enough money to repay the club's debts.
5. I was very (*angry, teed off, mad*) when I heard my grade.
6. A (*used, preowned*) Mercedes is quite costly.
7. Lowe's humor is always (*whacko, unconventional*).
8. My paper contained twenty-seven (*errors, typos, goofs*).
9. The dean's expression was (*real, really*) tense.
10. When his sister came to him for help with her chemistry, he felt (*dumb, dopey, inadequate*) at not being able to help her.
11. (*Dough, Money, Bread*) is all the doctor cared about.
12. We studied how New York is doing (*economywise, economically*).
13. I hoped my (*dad, old man, father*) would help me through school, but I was wrong.
14. Though the projector was (*broken, busted, bust*) the audience could still see the slides.
15. The (*cops, bears, police*) knocked on the door.
16. He claims he can (*learn, teach*) anyone to use a personal computer in less than an hour.
17. Even elementary schoolchildren are (*becoming interested in, getting into, digging*) rock music these days.

d

31

18. How can I do well in the course when the teacher will not try to (*deal straight, level, communicate*) with me?
19. The office computer is (*down, busted, not working*).
20. He felt (*beat, bushed, fatigued*).
21. He was (*indisposed, sick*).
22. I had to learn to (*take it easy, relax, be cool*) before I did well in examinations.
23. When children misbehave, parents should *get tough with them, discipline them, crack down on them*).
24. The janitor finally realized he was not going (*anywheres, anywhere*) in his company.
25. The snow (*began, commenced*) on Friday afternoon and continued until Monday morning.

d

31

31b │Choosing the exact word

Because two words in English rarely mean exactly the same thing, a writer's choice of words is crucial to the effectiveness of his or her communication with readers.

1 │ Understanding denotation and connotation

A word's **denotation** is its dictionary meaning. Confusion about denotation can cause a writer to make such mistakes as writing *depreciate* (to lower or underestimate the value of something) in place of *deprecate* (to show mild disapproval). Always check a dictionary when you are uncertain about a word's denotation.

A word's **connotation** is what it implies, the associations it calls up in the reader's mind. Confusion about connotation might lead a writer to express gratefulness for a doctor's "gratuitous" advice. *Gratuitous* does mean "free" or "unasked for," but it also connotes "unwelcome" and "unnecessary." Be sure the connotations of the words you choose contribute to rather than clash with the impression you want to create. There is a great difference, for instance, between *Her skin was as smooth as silk* and *Her skin was as smooth as marble.* Examine the different nuances of synonyms in your dictionary to help you choose the right word.

2 │Balancing the abstract and concrete, the general and specific

Abstract words name qualities or ideas; concrete words name tangible things: objects, places, creatures, institutions, and the like. In writing, use abstract and general words to introduce and sum up the concepts you want to convey, but use specific and concrete words in presenting supporting details.

ABSTRACT	communication, technology, media
CONCRETE	letter from Aunt Paula, Apple computer, *The New York Times*
GENERAL	president, illness, monument
SPECIFIC	Thomas Jefferson, Joe's case of flu, Statue of Liberty

3 │Using idioms

An **idiom** is an expression whose meaning cannot be determined from the words in it. Many idioms include prepositions whose correct use is not always logical. For instance, we say we *search for* something or are *in search of* it. The expression *in search for* is unidiomatic. A list of some common idioms with appropriate prepositions follows.

acquitted *of* a crime
angry *with* someone
charged *for* service
charged *with* a crime
comply *with* an order

correspond *to* the
  architect's plans
correspond *with* a friend
differ *from* someone of
  contrasting appearance
differ *with* someone of
  contrasting views

d

31

343

identical *with* (or *to*)
the original

impatient *with* someone
impatient *for* a result

independent *of* each other

occupied *by* an invading army
occupied *with* a customer

reward *by* giving a present
reward *with* a present

stay *at* my grandmother's
stay *in* town

vary *from* his usual habits
vary *in* length

wait *for* Godot
wait *on* tables

4 | Using figurative language

Figures of speech add richness to writing by comparing the action or thing being described with some other action or thing, using vivid, specific qualities. A **simile** makes the comparison explicitly, using *like* or *as: She's like a rainbow. He's built like a panda.* A **metaphor** implies the comparison, omitting *like* or *as: Life is a carnival. When my soul was in the lost and found, you came along to claim it.* When using a metaphor, be sure to stick with it. A **mixed metaphor** combines incongruous figurative language, destroying the image the writer is trying to create.

MIXED   The Chinese and American ships of state march to different drummers.

REVISED   The Chinese and American ships of state are sailing in different directions.

Personification treats an idea or object as if it were human: *Despair seized her in its merciless grip.* **Hyperbole** is an exaggeration for the sake of emphasis: *She was paralyzed by his stare.*

5 | Avoiding trite expressions

Avoid **clichés,** expressions that have been used so often they have lost their freshness and impact.

TRITE   I had to *work like a dog.*

REVISED   I had to work with all the concentration of a demolition expert.

TRITE   He *ate like a pig.*

REVISED   He ate four large anchovy pizzas.

d

31

| *Understanding denotation* EXERCISE **31-2**

Circle the word in parentheses whose established denotation fits the meaning of the sentence. Consult a dictionary as needed.

Example: Our personalities are (*complimentary*, (*complementary*)).

1. By 9 P.M. we were all hungry and (*eager, anxious*) for the dinner to begin.
2. The old house was the first in Cornwall to have (*dormant, dormer*) windows.
3. Josey became (*historical, hysterical*) when told of her dog's death.
4. The charge is (*presently, currently*) too high.
5. My sister told a (*barefaced, bearfaced*) lie.
6. They lost (*conscience, consciousness*) when the gas leaked from the stove but were fortunate to be saved by a neighbor.
7. Even a weak opponent should not be taken for (*granite, granted*).
8. The (*enormity, vastness*) of the ranch was impressive.
9. The advice is (*patiently, patently*) ridiculous.
10. The lecturer's comments seemed (*irreverent, irrelevant*) to the topic, but I wrote them down anyway.
11. My being late (*irritates, aggravates*) her.
12. By Tuesday the campus decorations reflected that Homecoming was (*immanent, imminent*).
13. The judge listened intently but remained (*disinterested, uninterested*) in the libel case.
14. Most people's casual conversation is too full of (*anecdotes, antidotes*).
15. The (*statute, stature*) that prohibits kissing under water is still on the books.
16. There were (*fewer, less*) pages assigned today than yesterday.
17. We asked him (*respectively, respectfully*) to give us an extra week, but still he said no.
18. Though the governor had (*formally, formerly*) invited them to his dinners, he omitted them from his guest list after they were rude to him.

d

31

19. The seniors are divided into (*clichés, cliques*) and will not talk to new students.
20. Our grandfather (*immigrated, emigrated*) to the United States from Italy when he was a boy.
21. He (*flouted, flaunted*) my authority once too often.
22. Her angry outburst had not been (*expected, suspected*).
23. When he kept harping on the same mistakes days after I had made them, I could see I had a (*hypocritical, hypercritical*) boss.
24. Our supervisor was so (*credulous, credible*) that she believed our story.
25. The lawyer provided sound (*advise, advice*).

Using general and specific words, abstract and concrete words

EXERCISE **31-3**

Each sentence below contains an italicized word that is general or abstract. Write above each italicized word a word or words that are more specific or concrete.

Example: The weather was *beautiful.* *clean and crisp*

1. Mortgage interest rates have been *high*.

2. My roommate is *unsanitary*.

3. Being a *liberal,* she was in favor of the proposed law.

4. The cat's *light* fur reflected sunlight.

5. Children who live in the inner city are *different from* children who live in the suburbs.

6. We won *a lot of* games last fall.

7. A *powerful* wind blew the tower over.

8. The new student union is *more nearly complete* than the old one.

9. All of us have been inspired by her *success* to work harder.

10. The *situation* called for quick action.

11. Though it was hearty, Chuck's *meal* was strange.

12. The fire department needs a new *vehicle*.

13. The commanding officer was *short*.

14. Foreign cars are *better* (or *worse*) than anything made by American manufacturers.

d

31

15. The *animal* started toward us and then changed its mind.

16. All the students clustered around the *car*.

17. On the *chair* sat a tiny man with delicate features.

18. A *tree* fell into the power line.

19. We thought the movie was *awful*.

20. Hoping not to attract anyone's attention, I *walked* across the room.

21. Mary Lin is from *Asia*.

22. *Something* in the air of the room reminded me of my grandmother's house.

23. I am majoring in *science*.

24. A *bug* rested on the sill.

25. The *look* on the lecturer's face told us as effectively as words to stop giggling.

| *Using idioms*

Drawing on the list on pages 343–344 or consulting a dictionary as needed, circle the appropriate preposition in parentheses to complete the idiom in the sentences below.

Example: After much debate, we finally agreed (*with,* ⊙*on*) a new policy.

1. You will never keep up (*to, with*) me.
2. I was impatient (*for, with*) the class to end.
3. Differing (*from, with*) each other only over money, the couple nonetheless decided to divorce.
4. When I returned to class after the break, my seat was occupied (*by, with*) a large, unkempt boy.
5. The room measured six feet (*to, by*) four feet.
6. The request was unreasonable, but she complied (*with, to*) it anyway.
7. Though we were angry (*at, with*) each other, we continued to study together.
8. They corresponded (*to, with*) the same woman for seven years before they learned the truth.
9. The dangers (*in, for*) someone learning to ski are slight.
10. The officer locked the suspect up and charged him (*for, with*) robbery.
11. College is different (*from, than*) high school in unexpected ways.
12. When O'Reilly was acquitted (*for, of*) murder, the townspeople were delighted.
13. During his visit the pope stayed (*in, at*) New York only briefly, but he electrified the city.
14. Although rewarded (*by, with*) increasingly flavorful foods, the pigeon would not learn any new tricks.
15. I waited (*on, for*) his arrival with friends.
16. By the time she was fourteen, Lucy was independent (*of, from*) her parents.
17. My courses vary (*in, from*) difficulty, so I have no trouble setting my priorities when I study.

d

31

18. Some researchers are impatient (*at, with*) the arguments of the theorists.
19. I was preoccupied (*with, by*) my work.
20. The shop charged me (*with, for*) a purchase that I had forgotten.

d

31

Using figurative language EXERCISE **31-5**

Identify the figure or figures of speech in each sentence below. If one or more figures are inappropriate, rewrite the sentence to introduce appropriate ones. If the figures are appropriate, write *OK* to the left of the sentence.

Example: The distinguished-looking man had hair the color of a cement block.

The distinguished-looking man had hair the color of gray flannel.

1. His serve hit the tennis court with all the power of a hand grenade.

2. The test was so difficult it would have made a sailor blush.

3. The opposing team's center charged at me as quickly as a frightened deer.

4. From atop the telephone pole, the kitten eyed my rescue efforts like a trapped rat.

5. The academic rat race comes to a head at exam time.

6. His steel-gray eyes enhance his cold stare.

d

31

7. Taking his position as the basketball team's center, Wilt was as proud as Napoleon.

8. I was deserted by the others, locked high and dry in the basement.

9. The oil slick spread over the blue water like cream poured over peaches.

10. Each year that passes stamps our new college with a nail of respectability.

d

31

|Avoiding trite expressions

EXERCISE **31-6**

Identify the trite expression or expressions in each sentence below, and revise the sentence to eliminate them.

Example: She was meek as a lamb, though she was a superb public speaker.

She was exceedingly shy, though she was a superb public speaker.

1. He writes well, but he is no Shakespeare.

2. The food at Six Chefs restaurant is like Mom's home cooking.

3. A budding genius, my little brother won a mathematics award and two science awards.

4. The student wanted out of the rat race.

d

31

5. The job of moving my grandfather to a nursing home was easier said than done.

6. I did not know for sure, but I had a sneaking suspicion that my friends were planning a surprise party.

7. Our not getting the lease was a crying shame.

8. The sight of my old rival scared me out of my wits.

9. The pregnant woman was as big as a house.

10. I nearly died when I saw the utility bill.

31c | Being concise

Watch out for words and phrases in your writing that are repetitive or simply unnecessary.

1 | Cutting empty words and phrases

Check your writing for padding — expressions that add length without adding substance.

> **PADDED**   Gray is of the opinion that at this point in time, it is no longer acceptable to the American people that their government should lend its support to an agency specializing in activities that are by their very nature covert.

> **REVISED**   Gray believes that Americans no longer want their government to support an agency specializing in covert activities.

2 | Avoiding unnecessary repetition

Another form of padding is saying the same thing two different ways: *my theory that I have come up with; the program's purposes and goals; at the corner where Main Street meets High Street*. Once is enough: *my theory; the program's purposes; at the corner of Main Street and High Street*.

3 | Simplifying word groups and sentences

Don't use a clause if a phrase will do; don't use a phrase if a word will do. Whenever you can, use direct, active verbs; avoid passive verbs and noun constructions substituting for verbs. Also, be wary of indirect sentence beginnings such as *there is* and *it is*.

> **WORDY**   There is a tendency among some writers to have an inflated estimation of the value of sentences which are long, with the result that such sentences can be found with increasing frequency in their writing.

> **REVISED**   Some writers overvalue and overuse long sentences.

4 | Avoiding jargon

Jargon is the special vocabulary of a professional, academic, or technical group. (See 31a-6.) The term also refers to any language that strives to sound professional, academic, or technical rather than clear and direct. The humor of someone's saying *I am not a janitor; I am a sanitary engineering specialist* shows how jargon can hinder effective communication.

d

31

| *Cutting empty words and phrases* | EXERCISE **31-7** |

Revise the sentences below to eliminate empty words and phrases.

Example: The aspects of poetry that I like best are its imagery and its rhythm.

I like the imagery and rhythm of poetry.

1. Due to the fact that they were no longer able to care for him, my parents decided in the final analysis to place my grandfather in a nursing home.

2. There was a call put in by someone for a repairman to come and fix the dishwasher, which was broken and would not work.

3. The problem that arose when the men could not reach an agreement prolonged the meeting an additional hour of time.

d

31

4. The burglar gained access to a crawl space by means of a ladder and then punched a hole in the ceiling in order to enter the apartment.

5. The nature of the changes in the rules makes it difficult to follow them.

6. I was eager to go on the backpacking trip, but two of the others were concerned with the element of risk involved.

7. We asked for laboratory tests, which were for the purpose of giving us a diagnosis of the illness that the pup had.

8. It is important to realize the value of patience, which is always worthwhile.

9. She was excited about having the opportunity for a chance at getting an interview.

10. The reason that the weather was so severe last night was that there was a blizzard.

| Avoiding unnecessary repetition   EXERCISE **31-8**

Revise the sentences below to eliminate redundant phrases and needless or confusing repetition.

Example: The electoral college is involved in the presidential elections in this country because in the United States Constitution it says that the president is to be elected by the electoral college.

The United States Constitution specifies that the president be elected by the electoral college.

1. He decided to retire and not work at his job beyond the age of sixty.

2. The cost of the $300 dehumidifier was worth it, because it took the moisture out of the air.

3. The blue ribbon, which signified first place in the 100-yard dash, was awarded to Susan for winning the race.

d

31

4. Engaged in agriculture, the farmer is governed by a wide variety of government regulations put out by the Department of Agriculture.

5. The subway system is an important form of urban mass transit to move large numbers of people throughout the city.

6. We were assigned a Hardy novel as required reading for our homework outside class.

7. The commercial I find most interesting is the new one I just finished watching, which is the one that is on television these days for an abrasive soap.

8. Picking up trash yourself is a way that you should contribute to helping to keep the city park in a state of cleanliness.

d

31

9. The editorial claimed in its argument that capital punishment should not be used to put murderers to death.

10. Just after sunset in the evening is the time when other people's houses look most inviting.

Simplifying word groups and sentences

Revise the sentences below to simplify word groups and to introduce strong, active verbs.

Example: A red sky and thin, horizontal clouds at sunset are signals that the winds to come will be blustery.

A red sky and thin, horizontal clouds at sunset signal blustery winds to come.

1. He was feeling angry because the game was delayed.

2. Owners who applied for tax relief were given it, and all of them applied.

3. She has the ability to be able to fall asleep anywhere she chooses to do so.

d

31

4. Federal laws prohibit the buying and selling of handbags made out of alligator skin.

5. The essays and writing assignments were required to be turned in on Monday.

6. He had the idea that the pay raise would make his check bigger in the month of November.

7. Both the two of us had a fear of going on the mountain road.

8. The drink, made from ice, water, sugar, and lemon juice, really made us cooler, and the heat did not bother us as much as it had before we had the drink.

9. We have a suspicion that the administration has a plan to cut the faculty by a third.

d

31

10. The Museum of Modern Art in New York had on exhibit a sports car that is red and low-slung and that was built in the 1930s.

32 *Using the Dictionary*

A dictionary can tell you how to spell and pronounce a word, give you the forms of irregular nouns and verbs, tell you the meaning of an unfamiliar word, and introduce you to new words. Besides containing an alphabetical list of words with their meanings, many dictionaries include synonyms, word origins, biographical and geographical listings, material on the history and grammar of English, and other useful supplements. In addition, most dictionaries indicate whether words are slang, colloquial, regional, or otherwise restricted in their use.

32a | Choosing a dictionary

There are many different types of dictionaries, including abridged, unabridged, and special dictionaries.

1 | Abridged dictionaries

Abridged dictionaries, while not exhaustive, contain most commonly used words and brief descriptions of their meaning and usage. The following abridged dictionaries (listed alphabetically) are recommended:

> *The American Heritage Dictionary of the English Language.* 2nd coll. ed. Boston: Houghton Mifflin, 1982.
> *Oxford American Dictionary.* New York: Oxford Univ. Press, 1980.
> *The Random House Dictionary of the English Language.* Coll. ed. New York: Random House, 1982.
> *Webster's New Collegiate Dictionary.* 8th ed. Springfield, Mass.: Merriam, 1981.
> *Webster's New World Dictionary of the American Language.* 2nd coll. ed. New York: Simon & Schuster, 1978.

2 | Unabridged dictionaries

The most scholarly and comprehensive of dictionaries, unabridged dictionaries emphasize the history of words and the range of their uses. When you need detailed information about a word or want to find an obscure word, consult one of the following:

> *The Oxford English Dictionary.* 13 volumes plus 4 supplements (in progress). New York: Oxford Univ. Press, 1933, 1972, 1976. Also available in a photographically reduced, two-volume edition, 1971.
> *The Random House Dictionary of the English Language.* New York: Random House, 1980.
> *Webster's Third New International Dictionary of the English Language.* Springfield, Mass.: Merriam, 1981.

32

3 | Special dictionaries

Special dictionaries limit attention to a particular type of word, problem, or field. Especially helpful for writing are dictionaries of usage, which discuss common problematic words and constructions, and dictionaries of synonyms, which list together words that are similar in meaning. The following are recommended:

> Bernstein, Theodore M. *The Careful Writer.* New York: Atheneum, 1965.
>
> *Webster's New Dictionary of Synonyms.* Springfield, Mass.: Merriam, 1973.

32b | Working with a dictionary's contents
1 | Finding general information

Dictionaries contain a wide range of information — for instance, famous people's birth and death dates and major achievements; facts about plants, animals, chemicals, and events; pictures of architectural elements and musical instruments; interpretations of concepts; names and locations of colleges and universities. Every dictionary's table of contents lists the special sections that supplement the word listings.

2 | Answering specific questions

A dictionary's function is to provide information about words. The main entry first shows spelling and word division — where to break the word if you have to divide it at the end of a line. Next comes the pronunciation, usually including all major variations. (Most dictionaries explain their pronunciation symbols in their opening pages and at the foot of every page or every other page.) The word is then identified by part of speech, and its principal parts are given. Its **etymology** — its origin — may follow; in some dictionaries, though, etymology is given last. Meanings are given next, grouped by part of speech if the word can function as more than one. Sometimes major differences in meaning and usage are listed under separate entries. Various definitions may be labeled as obsolete, slang, foreign, and the like. Often a word's main **synonyms** (words with similar meaning) and **antonyms** (words with opposite meaning) are also given.

32

| *Using the dictionary* EXERCISE **32-1**

Use a college-level desk dictionary to answer the questions below.

Name of dictionary _____

Publisher _____

Date of publication _____

A. Abbreviations and symbols

1. On what pages does your dictionary explain the abbreviations and symbols used in its entries? (The guide to abbreviations and symbols may be listed separately in the table of contents, or it may be included in an overall guide to the dictionary.)

   _____

   _____

2. Write out the meaning of the following abbreviations or symbols. If any of them are not used in your dictionary, leave the spaces blank.

   Example: n. pl. *or* pl. n. __*plural noun*__

   a. syn. _____   f. [ ] (bracketed matter) _____

   b. dial. _____   g. Icel. _____

   c. LL. _____   h. obs. _____

   d. lit. _____   i. mil. _____

   e. var. _____   j. intr. v. _____

B. Spelling

On the blanks below, reproduce the way your dictionary lists the words given. Provide capitalization, syllable breaks, word spaces, and hyphens as well as spelling. Note that the form provided here is not necessarily the only correct option.

Example: dessertspoon _*des·sert·spoon*_

1. riverbed _____

2. speakeasy _____

3. backwater _____

4. living room _____

5. catlike _____

6. hayloft _____

7. freeze-dry _____

8. Italy _____

9. self-government _____

10. suckerfish _____

C. Pronunciation

1. On what pages does your dictionary explain the symbols used in its guides to the pronunciations of words? (The symbols are probably listed in a separate pronunciation key. They may also be included in full or abridged form at the bottom of the dictionary's pages.)

_____

_____

2. Copy out exactly the pronunciation given by your dictionary for the following words. If the dictionary gives more than one pronunciation for a word, provide both. Consulting the pronunciation key, sound out the word until you can pronounce it accurately and smoothly.

Example: beguile _*bĭ-gīl′*_

32

a. pastoral _____

b. err _____

c. invalid _____

d. schism _____

e. often _____

f. statistics _____

g. Caribbean _____

h. kiln _____

i. irrelevant _____

j. puberty _____

3. In what order does your dictionary list two or more pronunciations of

the same word? (The principle will be described in the guide to the dictionary.)

_____

_____

D. Grammatical functions and forms

1. List and label the past-tense and past-participle forms of the following verbs exactly as provided in your dictionary. Note that most dictionaries provide both forms only if they are different. Check the guide to your dictionary to determine its practice. If it provides only one form, list only one.

Example: have *had (past tense and past participle)*

a. prefer _____

b. work _____

c. break _____

d. echo _____

e. wring _____

2. List and label the comparative and superlative forms of the following adjectives and adverbs exactly as given in your dictionary. Note that some dictionaries provide the comparative and superlative forms only when they are formed by a means other than the simple addition of -er and -est; and most dictionaries do not provide comparative and superlative forms when they can be made only by adding *more* and *most*. Check the guide to your dictionary to determine its practice. Write below only what the dictionary actually includes in the entry.

Examples: small *smaller (comparative), smallest (superlative)*

beautiful *(no forms given)*

a. inner _____

b. lovely _____

32

c. cross (*adj.*) _____

d. ill _____

e. median _____

E. Etymology

1. Trace the origins of the words listed below as they are given in your dictionary. List (1) the initial language and word from which our word is derived (ignore Indo-European roots if these are given); (2) the meaning of the initial word (sometimes not listed separately if it is the same as the given word); and (3) the other languages through which the word has passed on its way to us. Use the full names of languages, not abbreviations (consult the key to the dictionary's abbreviations if necessary). The guide to the dictionary will tell you how to read the etymology of a word if you need help.

Example: logic (1) *Greek logos*

(2) *speech, reason*

(3) *Late Latin, Old French, Middle English*

a. induce (1) _____

(2) _____

(3) _____

b. lieutenant (1) _____

(2) _____

(3) _____

32

c. quake (1) _____

(2) _____

(3) _____

d. shirt (1) _____

(2) _____

(3) _____

Name _____

e. rhythm (1) _____

(2) _____

(3) _____

2. Provide the origins of the following words as they are given in your dictionary.

Example: ohm _After Georg Simon Ohm (1787–1854), German physicist_

a. zipper _____

b. jargon _____

c. astronaut _____

d. jerk _____

e. quisling _____

F. Meanings

1. How does your dictionary arrange the different meanings of the same words: chronologically, as they developed, or in order of current common use? Consult the guide to the dictionary.

_____

_____

2. List two different meanings for each of the following words as they appear in your dictionary.

a. specie (n.) (1) _____

(2) _____

b. gall (n.) (1) _____

(2) _____

32

c. hound (v.) (1) _____

(2) _____

d. go (v.) (1) _____

(2) _____

e. card (v.) (1) _____

(2) _____

G. Synonyms

The synonyms listed below for the noun *pay* differ slightly from each other in meaning. Consult your dictionary for the precise meaning of each word, and use the word in a sentence. (Your dictionary may provide under one of the words a paragraph that explains the distinctions among them.)

1. *pay:* meaning _____

sentence _____

_____

2. *wage:* meaning _____

sentence _____

_____

3. *salary:* meaning _____

sentence _____

_____

4. *stipend:* meaning _____

sentence _____

_____

32

H. Labels

1. Consult the guide to your dictionary for the labels it uses to designate words or meanings of words with restricted usage. (The description of labels is usually under a heading like "Usage" or "Labels.") List below the specific labels mentioned in the guide.

_____

_____

2. Provide the label applied by your dictionary to each of the following words or meanings of words. If your dictionary does not apply a label to a given word, write "no label" in the space. From the description of labels in the guide to the dictionary, what does each label indicate about the word's usage?

Example: ain't *nonstandard (not appropriate for standard written English*

a. critter (noun meaning "animal") _____

_____

b. enthuse (verb meaning "to show enthusiasm") _____

_____

c. knock (verb meaning "to criticize") _____

_____

d. rod (noun meaning "revolver") _____

_____

32

e. humdinger (noun meaning "something remarkable") _____

_____

I. Other information

1. Where does your dictionary provide biographical information on important persons: in the main alphabetical listing or in a separate section (give the page numbers if a separate section)? _____

   _____

2. Where does your dictionary provide geographical information on countries, cities, rivers, mountains, and so on: in the main alphabetical listing or in a separate section (give the page numbers if a separate

   section)? _____

   _____

3. Does your dictionary contain a history of the English language?

   _____

4. Does your dictionary contain a guide to punctuation and mechanics?

   _____

5. Does your dictionary contain a list of colleges and universities?

   _____

6. List below the other special features of your dictionary.

   _____

   _____

   _____

32

33|*Improving Your Vocabulary*

Effective communication depends not only on knowing how to use words but also on knowing a variety of words to use.

33a |Understanding the sources of English

English is part of the Indo-European language family, whose origins go back perhaps seven thousand years. The earliest known language in England was Celtic. But the English we speak is descended from the language of Germanic tribes that conquered the Celts in the fifth and sixth centuries, leaving us with such common words as *heaven, earth, our, three,* and *day.* The vocabulary of Old English, as this early form of English is called, was later enriched by Danish invaders in the ninth and tenth centuries and by the French-speaking Normans who conquered England in 1066 and reigned for nearly two hundred years. The resulting Middle English included large numbers of words derived from French, such as *catch, cattle,* and *cavalry.* In the fifteenth and sixteenth centuries, the Renaissance and the introduction of the printing press caused further changes in our language and vocabulary, introducing many Latin and Greek words and leading to Modern English. English continues to change today as we drop old words, coin new ones, and adopt others from languages throughout the world.

33b |Learning the composition of words

Breaking up a word into its component parts is often a good way to see where it came from and to figure out what it means.

1 |Learning roots

At least half the words in English have Latin or Greek roots. Some Greek words that commonly serve as roots in English words are *theos,* "god" (*theology, atheist*); *philia,* "loving" (*Philadelphia, bibliophile*); *demos,* "people" (*democracy, epidemic*); and *sophia,* "skill" or "wisdom" (*sophisticated, philosophy*). Some common Latin roots are *pater,* "father" (*paternal*); *mater,* "mother" (*matron*); *bellum,* "war" (*bellicose, antebellum*); and *dictum,* "something said" (*dictate, indict*).

2 |Learning prefixes

A **prefix** is one or more syllables that can be added to the front of a word or root to change its meaning. Many standard prefixes come from Latin or Greek. A list of common prefixes follows.

33

a-, an-	without, not, away from (*atheist*)
ad-	toward, next to (*adjacent*)
ante-	before (*antecedent*)
anti-	opposite, against (*antipathy*)
arch-	chief (*archduke*)
auto-	self (*automobile*)
col-, com-, con-	with (*concur*)
demi-	half (*demitasse*)
dis-	not (*dissatisfied*)
ex-	from, out of (*exhaust*)
extra-	beyond (*extrasensory*)
hyper-	excessively (*hypertension*)
il-, im-, in-, ir-	not (*immobile*)
inter-	between, among (*international*)
intra-	within (*intramural*)
mal-	wrong, bad (*malcontent*)
pan-	all (*pan-American*)
poly-	many (*polyglot*)
post-	after (*postwar*)
pre-	before (*premeditate*)
pro-	before, forward, in favor of (*propose*)
semi-	half (*semisweet*)
sub-	under (*submarine*)
super-	above (*supervisor*)
sym-, syn-	together (*sympathy*)
trans-	across (*transport*)
un-	not (*unhealthy*)

3 | Learning suffixes

A **suffix** is one or more syllables that can be added to the end of a word or root to change its meaning or function. Common noun suffixes include the following:

-ity	*-er* or *-or*	*-ship*
-ence or *-ance*	*-ist*	*-hood*
-sion or *-tion*	*-ism*	

Common verb suffixes include the following:

-en	*-ify*
-ize	*-ate*

Common adjective suffixes include the following:

-ful	*-able* or *-ible*	*-ous*
-ish	*-al* or *-ial*	*-ive*
-ble	*-ic*	*-ant* or *-ent*

33c | Learning to use new words

Examining a word's components is one way to understand its meaning. Other ways are examining its context and looking it up in the dictionary.

33

1 | Examining context

The way a word is used in a sentence or paragraph often gives clues to its meaning. Take the sentence *Most aficionados of musical comedy admire Lerner and Loewe's My Fair Lady.* If you did not know the word *aficionado*, you could guess from its relation to *musical comedy, admire,* and *My Fair Lady* that it means something like "fan" or "enthusiast."

Sometimes you can infer the meaning of an unfamiliar word if it is used in parallel structure with a more familiar word: *Casual theatergoers think of My Fair Lady as a pleasant musical comedy; but the true aficionado of musical comedy knows that it is based on George Bernard Shaw's biting play Pygmalion.* Since the sentence contrasts the *true aficionado* and the *casual theatergoer,* you know that the aficionado is not casual but the opposite, perhaps enthusiastic.

Expressions like *also known as, sometimes called,* and even *is* can point to a definition of an unfamiliar word. Or a definition may be set off by dashes, parentheses, or commas: *To the aficionado — the devoted follower of musical comedy — My Fair Lady is a gem.* Examples also can help you figure out what a word means: *Such aficionados as Walter Kerr of The New York Times and Brendan Gill of The New Yorker — both long-time theater critics — have applauded this new production of My Fair Lady.*

2 | Using the dictionary

The dictionary can give you the precise meaning of a word whose general sense you have guessed from its context. The dictionary may also help you fix the word in your memory by showing its spelling, pronunciation, grammatical functions and forms, etymology, and synonyms and antonyms.

33

Using roots, prefixes, suffixes   EXERCISE **33-1**

By referring to the lists of roots, prefixes, and suffixes given on pages 373–74, identify each word below as a noun (n.), verb (v.), or adjective (adj.) and guess at its meaning. If you are unable to guess, look the word up in your dictionary.

Example: antebellum *before a war (adj.)* _____

1. belligerent _____

2. demigod _____

3. anterior _____

4. quadrennial _____

5. prorate _____

6. retroactive _____

7. advocate _____

8. Francophile _____

9. interdict _____

10. theosophy _____

11. polymer _____

12. synchronize _____

13. subvert _____

14. preposterous _____

15. transceiver _____

16. atheism _____

33

17. kilocycle _____

18. intersperse _____

19. demimonde _____

20. maladjusted _____

21. demagogue _____

22. archdeacon _____

23. amoral _____

24. illaudable _____

25. transcend _____

33

| Learning new words
| through context   EXERCISE **33-2**

Use contextual clues to guess at the meanings of the italicized words in the passages below. Write out the meanings. Then check your definitions in your dictionary.

Example: From a lance among the lead band of warriors fluttered a *pennon* bearing the symbol of Armingild.

pennon *narrow banner or streamer; flag*

1. The *impresario* who developed the oil field considered the private jet as one of his *perquisites.*

   impresario _____

   perquisite _____

2. His sole aim in *augmenting* his income was to buy a swimming pool, a luxury car, and other trappings of *hedonism.*

   augment _____

   hedonism _____

3. The newspaper's *spurious* argument was based on forged statistics and a *paucity* of real evidence.

   spurious _____

   paucity _____

4. A *genealogist* may spend hours looking through birth records, baptismal certificates, marriage licenses, death warrants, and ship passenger lists and still not find any *substantive* information on your family.

   genealogist _____

   substantive _____

33

5. The *diminutive* lady peered up at the cans of soup on the grocery shelf and then stood on tiptoe to grasp one.

   diminutive _____

6. His *caustic* reply to my request for help stung me.

   caustic _____

7. The *philanthropist* set up a trust fund for homeless cats, and that act left his heirs *bemused* but not angry.

   philanthropist _____

   bemused _____

8. His *gaffe* of calling the teacher by the wrong name went unnoticed, for the teacher was *immersed* in a calculus problem.

   gaffe _____

   immersed _____

9. She took *umbrage* at the boss's comments, but he had not meant to criticize her.

   umbrage _____

10. Sue seemed to be *ubiquitous*. When I went to the post office, she was there. When I went to the bank, she was there. When I came home, she was in front of the house, walking her dog.

    ubiquitous _____

33

34 *Spelling*

English spelling is not always logical. Learning to spell words correctly takes effort, but the investment is repaid by readers' respect.

34a Avoiding typical spelling problems

Most spelling difficulties relate to differences between how a word sounds and how it is spelled. The same spelling may be pronounced more than one way, and the same pronunciation may have different spellings.

1 Avoiding excessive reliance on pronunciation

George Bernard Shaw is said to have observed that the word *fish* could be spelled *ghoti: gh* as in *tough, o* as in *women,* and *ti* as in *action.* When in doubt about how to spell a word, look it up in your dictionary; and if you don't find it, try to think of other ways the word's sound might be spelled.

Frequent sources of confusion are *homonyms,* words that are pronounced the same but spelled differently, and near homonyms, which are pronounced similarly but not identically. Here are some examples of both types:

accept, except	hole, whole
affect, effect	its, it's
allusion, illusion	no, know
board, bored	peace, piece
brake, break	right, rite, write
capital, capitol	their, there, they're
desert, dessert	to, too, two
fair, fare	which, witch
formally, formerly	who's, whose
hear, here	your, you're

2 Distinguishing between different forms of the same word

Often the root of a word changes slightly in spelling when the word's form and function change.

VERB	NOUN		ADJECTIVE	NOUN
breathe	breath		brief	brevity
choose	choice		curious	curiosity
devise	device		deep	depth
envelop	envelope		long	length
proceed	procedure		wide	width
succeed	success		wise	wisdom

sp

34

Many verbs form their principal parts irregularly: *drive, drove, driven; throw, threw, thrown; swim, swam, swum.* Some nouns also change their root spelling from singular to plural: *foot, feet; leaf, leaves; mouse, mice.*

3 | Using preferred spellings

Some words can be spelled more than one way. Often variants of the preferred spelling are British: *our* instead of *or* (*colour, color*); *ae* instead of *e* (*anaemic, anemic*); *ise* instead of *ize* (*realise, realize*); *ll* instead of *l* (*travelled, traveled*). Use the form in your writing that the dictionary designates as preferred, usually the first form listed.

34b | Following spelling rules

Learning a few basic rules of English spelling can help you avoid misspelled words.

1 | Distinguishing between *ie* and *ei*

The rule for *ie* and *ei* is "*I* before *e* except after *c*, or when pronounced 'ay' as in *neighbor* and *weigh*": thus, *believe* (*i* before *e*) but *receive* (except after *c*). There are some exceptions: common ones are *either, foreign, forfeit, height, leisure, neither, seize, seizure,* and *weird.*

2 | Keeping or dropping a final *e*

When adding an ending such as *-ing* or *-ly* to a word that ends in a silent *e*, drop the *e* if the ending begins with a vowel (*change + ing = changing*), but keep the *e* if the ending begins with a consonant (*brave + ly = bravely*). There are a few exceptions to this rule. Words that could be confusing if the *e* were dropped keep the *e* (*dye + ing* does *not* become *dying*). Words ending in a soft *c* or *g* keep the *e* when an ending is added that begins with *a, o,* or *u* (*notice + able = noticeable*). Sometimes when the *e* is preceded by another vowel, it is dropped before an ending that begins with a consonant (*due + ly = duly*).

3 | Keeping or dropping a final *y*

When a final *y* is preceded by a consonant, the *y* changes to *i* when an ending is added (*baby + s = babies*), except if the ending is *-ing* (*babying*). When a final *y* is preceded by a vowel, or when it ends a proper name, the *y* stays as is (*say + s = says; Kelly + s = Kellys*).

4 | Doubling consonants

In adding an ending to a one-syllable word, double the final consonant if it is preceded by a single vowel (*sit + ing = sitting*). Do not double the final consonant if it is preceded by two vowels (*fail + ing = failing*) or by another consonant (*suck + ing = sucking*). In adding an ending to a word of more than one syllable, double the final consonant if it is preceded by a single vowel and the stress falls on the last syllable of the stem once the ending is added (*prefer* + *ing* = *preferring*). Do not double the final consonant if it is preceded by two vowels (*remain* + *ing* = *remaining*) or by another consonant (*remark* + *able* = *remarkable*), or if the stress falls on a syllable other than the stem's last syllable once the ending is added (*prefer* + *ence* = *preference*).

5 | Attaching prefixes

The addition of a prefix does not change the spelling of the word it is attached to: *un* + *necessary* = *unnecessary*; *un* + *able* = *unable*; *mis* + *spell* = *misspell*; *mis* + *adventure* = *misadventure*.

6 | Forming plurals

For most nouns, form the plural by adding *-s* to the singular form (*horse* + *s* = *horses*; *pea* + *s* = *peas*). For some nouns ending in *f* or *fe*, change the ending to *ve* before adding *-s* (*life* + *s* = *lives*). For singular nouns ending in *-s*, *-sh*, *-ch*, or *-x*, add *-es* (*mess* + *es* = *messes*; *bash* + *es* = *bashes*; *itch* + *es* = *itches*; *box* + *es* = *boxes*). For nouns ending in *o* preceded by a vowel, add *-s* (*scenario* + *s* = *scenarios*); but if the *o* is preceded by a consonant, add *es* (*potato* + *es* = *potatoes*). A few nouns that were originally Italian, Greek, Latin, or French form the plural as in their original language (*solo* becomes *solos*, not *soloes*; *datum* becomes *data*, not *datums*).

Compound nouns form plurals in two ways. When two or more main words (usually nouns, verbs, or adjectives) form the compound, make only the last word plural (*streetwalker* = *streetwalkers*; *superman* = *supermen*; *strongbox* = *strongboxes*). When the parts of the compound are not equal — when a noun is followed by one or more other parts of speech — make only the noun plural (*sister-in-law* = *sisters-in-law*).

sp

34

|*Spelling and pronunciation*   EXERCISE **34-1**

Choose the correct spelling from the pairs given in parentheses. On the blank to the right, divide the correct word into syllables, with the help of your dictionary if necessary, and indicate which syllable has the primary accent.

Example: Our school has spent nearly $50,000 making   *ath·lét·ics*
the girls' (*atheletics, athletics*) program equal
to the boys' program.

1. The community (*accepted, excepted*) the compa-   ————————————
ny's (*preference, prefrence*) for (*nucular, nuclear*)
power.   ————————————

————————————

2. Barry Maison cross-examined the witness for   ————————————
more than an (*hour, our*) in an attempt to (*il-
licit, elicit*) evidence of Miss Fallana's allegedly   ————————————
(*illicit, elicit*) activities.
————————————

3. The (*government, goverment*) provided a good   ————————————
(*enviorment, environment*) for the (*immagrants,
immigrants*).   ————————————

————————————   *sp*

34
4. Later Miss Fallana herself refused to (*brake,*   ————————————
break) under his (*ineffective, inaffective*) questioning. She remained (*discretely, discreetly*)   ————————————
(*bored, board*).
————————————

5. Finally, Judge Krater's (*patience, patients*) failed, and with a (*mischievous, mischievious*) (*allusion, illusion*) to Miss Fallana's (*guerrilla, gorilla*) (*past, passed*), he ruled Maison's line of questioning (*irrevelant, irrelevant*).

_____

_____

_____

_____

_____

sp

34

| Distinguishing between
different forms of the same word;
using preferred spellings   EXERCISE **34-2**

A. Write on the blanks to the right the appropriate forms of the words in parentheses. If necessary, check your spellings in a dictionary.

Example: The candidate declined to enter into a (dis-   *discussion*
cuss) about (omit) from his disclosure of cam-
paign fund sources.   *omissions*

1. We (swim) at the pool last week for the (nine)   _____
   time.
                                                    _____

2. The drama was termed a great (tragic), and it   _____
   (whole) met our expectations.
                                                    _____

3. Her (Britain) (pronounce) drew smiles.   _____

                                                    _____

4. He (ordinary) (omit) the roll call during all of _____
   last term.
                                                    _____

5. Last night she (mean) to frighten both (thief)   _____
   by screaming.
                                                    _____

6. He thought it (desire) to be in charge of build- _____
   ing (maintain).
                                                    _____

7. All the (woman) thought (persevere) would pay   _____
   off.
                                                    _____

sp

34

8. His act was the (high) of (hypocrite).   _____

_____

9. Do not seek to (deception) her with a false (ar-   _____
gue).

_____

10. After the (occur) of the accident, both drivers   _____
lost their (license).

_____

B. The following paragraph was written by an English exchange student. Underline the British spellings and write the American spellings below. The first one is done for you.

There are differences between the American sense of <u>humour</u> and the British. One British comedian told an American audience of a kidnapper who sought a licence for his criminal activity so that he would not have to go to gaol. It was a real labour for the audience to laugh, especially since many had travelled several miles to get to the theatre in which the comic performed. The comedian took the next aeroplane out of the country, having done little to honour his profession in America.

_____*humor*_____   _____

_____   _____

_____   _____

_____   _____

Distinguishing between
ie *and* ei

Insert *ie* or *ei* in the blanks below. Remember: *"I* before *e* except after *c* or when sounded 'ay' as in *neighbor* or *weigh."* Also keep the exceptions in mind, and check the dictionary as needed.

Example: for_*ei*_gners

1. ach_____ve

2. w_____ght

3. fr_____nd

4. ch_____f

5. sl_____gh

6. h_____ght

7. rec_____ve

8. gr_____ve

9. n_____ther

10. conc_____ve

11. f_____nd

12. b_____ge

13. c_____ling

14. bel_____ve

15. hyg_____ne

16. p_____rce

17. _____ghth

18. forf_____t

19. conc_____t

20. perc_____ve

21. l_____sure

22. fr_____ght

23. s_____ze

24. w_____rd

25. dec_____t

sp

34

Keeping or dropping
a final e or y

Keep or drop the final vowels as necessary when adding endings to the following words. Consult your dictionary freely.

Example: supply + -er *supplier* _____

1. suspense + -ful _____

   suspense + -ion _____

2. desire + -able _____

   desire + -ous _____

3. gay + -ly _____

   gay + -ity _____

4. beauty + -ful _____

   beauty + -ous _____

5. apply + -ed _____

   apply + -s _____

6. die + -ing _____

   die + -d _____

7. defy + -ing _____

   defy + -ance _____

8. service + -er _____

   service + -able _____

sp

34

9. true + -est _____

   true + -ly _____

10. gratify + -ed _____

    gratify + -ing _____

11. practice + -ing _____

    practice + -able _____

12. lone + -ly _____

    lone + -some _____

13. duty + -ful _____

    duty + -s _____

14. love + -ly _____

    love + -able _____

15. solve + -ing _____

    solve + -able _____

16. notice + -ing _____

    notice + -able _____

17. glory + -ous _____

    glorify + -ed _____

18. hate + -ing _____

    hate + -ful _____

19. sure + -ly _____

    sure + -est _____

20. agree + -ing _____

    agree + -able _____

Doubling consonants;
attaching prefixes;
forming plurals

EXERCISE **34-5**

I. Write on the blanks to the right the appropriate forms of the words in parentheses. Check your dictionary as needed.

Example: There is a kangaroo (hop) across the plain.   *hopping*

1. There is no (differ) in the approaches.   _____

2. Have you (ride) a horse before?   _____

3. Has he (travel) far?   _____

4. She was my (advise).   _____

5. He (submit) his resignation yesterday.   _____

6. Have you been (refer) to a doctor?   _____

7. When will an eclipse (re + occur)?   _____

8. The reservation was (cancel).   _____

9. Your concern is (un + necessary).   _____

10. We were not (permit) to enter.   _____

11. The car needed (anti + freeze).   _____

12. Ten words were (mis + spell).   _____

13. The shuttle (re + enter) the atmosphere.   _____

14. They were (co + conspirators).   _____

15. He (dis + approved) of the movie.   _____

16. Your (remit) was due last week.   _____

17. Her position is (pre + eminent).   _____

sp

34

18. She (transfer) last fall. _____

19. He was heard (admit) guilt. _____

20. They were innocent of (mis + spending) the _____ funds.

B. Write the plurals of the following words and compounds, checking your dictionary as needed.

Example: chief _*chiefs*_

1. buffalo _____

2. tomato _____

3. mother-in-law _____

4. sheep _____

5. amoeba _____

6. fox _____

7. series _____

8. shelf _____

9. index _____

10. bureau _____

11. handful _____

12. passerby _____

13. analysis _____

14. economy _____

15. ox _____

34c | Developing spelling skills

The best ways to improve your spelling are to pronounce words carefully, to use memory tricks, and to study words you are likely to misspell.

1 | Pronouncing carefully

Many common inaccurate spellings come from inaccurate pronunciation. Be careful with words like *library, February, recognize, nuclear, mischievous,* and *height* not to add or omit letters in either pronouncing or spelling them.

2 | Using mnemonics

Mnemonics are tricks for memorizing. Some are standard: sta-la*c*tites grow down from the *c*eiling, but stala*g*mites grow up from the *g*round; *stationery* has an *er* like **letter paper.** But you can also make up your own. For instance, remember that *embarrass* has two *r*'s and two *s*'s to match the double letters in *stutter* and *stammer,* an embarrassed person's actions. *Inoculate* has no double letters — one shot is enough.

3 | Studying spelling lists

Learning to spell the words in the following list will reduce your spelling errors. Study them a few at a time.

absence	certain	illiterate	recommend
abundance	column	indefinite	reference
academic	conceit	independent	referring
accommodate	condemn	infinite	reminisce
achieve	definite	license	renown
acknowledge	descendant	luxury	rhythm
acquaintance	describe	marriage	roommate
across	develop	mathematics	safety
address	dictionary	medicine	seize
aggravate	dining	necessary	separate
aggressive	embarrass	neither	sergeant
all right	emphasize	occasion	several
all together	entirely	occur	similar
a lot	entrance	occurrence	sincerely
already	environment	omission	sophomore
altogether	etc.	parallel	sponsor
appearance	exaggerate	perform	succeed
argument	existence	perhaps	supersede
athlete	fascinate	possess	than
attendance	February	precede	then
audience	foreign	prejudice	tragedy
basically	forty	prevalent	truly
believe	fourth	primitive	until
benefited	friend	privilege	usually
Britain	government	procedure	vacuum
calendar	grammar	proceed	villain
category	harass	quizzes	weird
cemetery	height	receive	writing

34d | Using the hyphen to form compound words
1 | Forming compound adjectives

When two or more words function as a single adjective before a noun, hyphenate the words: *well-heeled benefactor,* a *decision-making problem.* When the same word group stands alone or follows the noun, hyphens are not needed: *We need a benefactor who is well heeled; Decision making is her main problem.*

2 | Writing fractions and compound numbers

Fractions and numbers from twenty-one to ninety-nine are always hyphenated: *one-half; thirty-six.*

3 | Forming coined compounds

When you are linking a group of words to serve as a temporary (coined) adjective, hyphenate them: *Carly let out her there's-a-squirrel-in-that-tree bark.*

4 | Attaching some prefixes and suffixes

Most prefixes do not take a hyphen: *prewar, semiannual.* When a prefix consists of or precedes a capital letter, however, use a hyphen: *anti-British.* Prefixes that are complete words by themselves usually take hyphens: *self-indulgent, all-around.* Also hyphenate *ex-* meaning "former": *ex-president.*

Suffixes normally do not take hyphens, except for *-elect: senator-elect.*

5 | Avoiding confusion

Use a hyphen after any prefix or in any compound when the resulting word, without the hyphen, might be misread (*re-echo, anti-intellectual*) or confused with another word (*re-create, un-ionized*). Also hyphenate adjective groups that could be misread: *new-gas prices* (meaning the prices for newly discovered gas).

*Using the hyphen
in compound words, fractions,
and compound numbers*   EXERCISE **34-6**

A. Write out the following numbers, using hyphens when appropriate.

Example: 4500 *forty-five hundred* _____

1. 10¹/₄ _____

2. ²¹/₂₂ _____

3. 39 _____

4. 102 _____

5. 3,000,152 _____

6. 92 _____

7. 25 _____

8. 25,095 _____

9. ³/₁₀ _____

10. 260 _____

sp

34

B. As appropriate for correct spelling, leave each of the following pairs of words as two words or make each pair one word by inserting a hyphen or closing up the space. Check your dictionary as needed.

Example: anti Soviet *anti-Soviet* _____

1. ante bellum _____

2. pro American _____

3. self serving _____

4. car port ——————————

5. porch light ——————————

6. news stand ——————————

7. hot dog ——————————

8. non partisan ——————————

9. ninth century (adj.) ——————————

10. co author ——————————

11. post Victorian ——————————

12. red eyed ——————————

13. re shuffle ——————————

14. long handled ——————————

15. red handed ——————————

16. soft hearted ——————————

17. pre fabricated ——————————

18. life boat ——————————

19. life like ——————————

20. anti imperialist ——————————

sp

34

Answers to Self-tests

Numbers in parentheses refer to sections applying to the answers.

Chapter 6 | Case of Nouns and Pronouns

1. I (6a) 2. them; us (6b) 3. us (6c)
4. me (6b) 5. we (6a) 6. whom (6g-2)
7. he; I (6a) 8. me (6b) 9. she; I (6a)
10. he; she (6a)

Chapter 7 | Verb Forms, Tense, Mood, and Voice

1. swam (7a) 2. broken (7a) 3. were (7f-1)
4. showed (7e-2) 5. sat (7b, 7d) 6. were
(7f-1) 7. lying (7b) 8. rung (7a, 7d) 9.
lasted (7d) 10. mistaken (7a)

Chapter 8 | Agreement

1. is (8a-4) 2. his (8b-3) 3. its (8b-4)
4. his (8b-3) 5. are (8a-3) 6. his (8b-3)
7. is (8a-4) 8. were (8a-2) 9. asks (8a-1)
10. was (8a-10)

Chapter 9 | Adjectives and Adverbs

1. most (9e-4) 2. really (9a) 3. bad (9b)
4. good (9b) 5. worse (9e-2, 9e-4) 6. nicer
(9e-4) 7. slowly (9a) 8. naturally (9a)
9. worst (9e-2) 10. carefully (9a)

Chapter 10 | Sentence Fragments

Incomplete sentences: 2 (10d) 4 (10a)
6 (10b) 8 (10c) 10 (10b)

Chapter 11 | Comma Splices and Run-on Sentences

1. c (11a) 2. b (11b) 3. c (11a) 4. a
5. b (11a) 6. b (11a) 7. b (11a) 8. b (11b)
9. b (11a) 10. c (11b)

Chapter 12 | Pronoun Reference

1. When I saw my teachers greeting my
   friends, I said hello to them. (12a)
2. The man's shadow loomed against the
   wall, which alarmed John. (12c-1)
3. After Hilda's snake escaped, Martha
   would not go into her room. (12a)

4. As long as the council members refused
   to meet the developers, there would be
   no end to their frustration. (12a)
5. When he saw how much the parts cost
   for the repairs, he decided to obtain
   them elsewhere. (12a)
6. OK
7. It says on the bottle not to drink its contents. (12d, 12c-2, 12e)
8. In Agnes's glove compartment, she kept
   a revolver. (12c-2)
9. After my roommate insulted my father,
   he refused to speak to him. (12a)
10. Alice told Karen that Esther found her
    purse. (12a)

Chapter 13 | Shifts

1. We entered the museum not knowing
   you were supposed to pay. (13a)
2. She wanted to know whether to take the
   job and did it pay well. (13d)
3. We planned to commute by car, but bus
   was found to be cheaper. (13c)
4. Oliver had no way of knowing we were
   there until he walks through the door.
   (13b)
5. The intensity of a person's feelings can
   cause you to act foolishly. (13a)
6. OK
7. A person should always have professional playing experience before they
   coach. (13a)
8. To revise a paper, read it through for errors, and then you should examine its
   structure. (13b)
9. OK
10. I had to decide whether to go on the trip
    and could I afford it? (13d)

Chapter 14 | Misplaced and Dangling Modifiers

1. Art only walked to the campus once last
   month. (14c)

2. Looking in the mirror, the new suit was very becoming. (14g)
3. She kept the dog in the closet that was housebroken. (14b)
4. After calling the repairman, the furnace started working. (14g)
5. He kept the marble cups that he bought in Taiwan during his tour last spring in the closet. (14a)
6. Having hired an attorney, the lawsuit was under way. (14g)
7. OK
8. Two teams were in the play-offs that were undefeated. (14b)
9. To gain entry, a special pass is necessary. (14g)
10. Six of us ordered drinks at the bar that tasted like after-shave lotion. (14b)

Chapter 15 | Mixed and Incomplete Sentences

1. M (15a) 2. M (15b) 3. I (15d-1) 4. OK
5. I (15d-3) 6. I (15d-4) 7. M (15a) 8. I (15c) 9. M (15b) 10. M (15a)

Chapter 16 | Using Coordination and Subordination

1. a (16b) 2. b (16b) 3. a (16b) 4. b (16b) 5. b (16b) 6. b (16c-1) 7. a (16b)
8. b (16b) 9. a (16b) 10. b (16b-2)

Chapter 17 | Using Parallelism

1. Going to a professional football game is better than to watch one. (17a-3)
2. The Episcopalians and those who are Catholics have more ritual in their services than Methodism has. (17a-1, 17a-3)
3. OK
4. Men's clothing styles and the clothes that women wear have grown similar in recent years. (17a-1)
5. In both the campus and in the town, sentiment for drug control was strong. (17a-2)
6. OK
7. The seniors, juniors, and the sophomores all helped raise money. (17a-4)
8. To coach professional baseball and coaching professional football were both career possibilities for him. (17a-1)
9. Listening to records and attendance at live concerts are both enjoyable. (17a-1)
10. In many aspects of technology, the Japanese excel over England. (17a-3)

Chapter 18 | Emphasizing Main Ideas

1. a (18a-2) 2. b (18a-1, 18a-2) 3. a (18d)
4. b (18e) 5. a (18a-1) 6. b (18e) 7. b (18a-2) 8. a (18a-1, 18a-2) 9. a (18a-1)
10. b (18a-1)

Chapter 19 | Achieving Variety

1. a 2. b

Chapter 20 | End Punctuation

1. The sign on the mailbox read, "William Morris, Esq." (20b)
2. He asked whether I had played varsity. (20a)
3. OK (20a, 20b)
4. "Did you return the package?" she asked. (20c)
5. OK (20a)
6. Hiram P. Luce, B.A., edited the anthology. (20b)
7. Her former home is Washington, D.C. (20b)
8. "Ready!" he shouted. (20f)
9. The talk was titled "When Will We Have Rights?" (20c)
10. The report will be available at noon. (20a)

Chapter 21 | The Comma

1. Some walls in the old house were painted yellow, and others were covered with dark paneling. (21a)
2. Before the mail arrived this morning, we were waiting impatiently for word. (21b)
3. Tuition, of course, is high this year. (21c-3)
4. OK
5. The vandalized, dilapidated building was the gym. (21f)
6. At sixty, workers are eligible for retirement. (21i)
7. "I can't," she said, looking apologetic. (21h-1)
8. OK
9. The time to act is now. (21j-1)
10. The rally ended with the familiar song "We Shall Overcome." (21c-2)

Chapter 22 | The Semicolon

1. A foreign coin jammed the vending machine; however, the coin was soon dislodged. (22b)
2. OK (22e-1)
3. She called to say she would arrive at

noon; therefore, we ran out for groceries. (22b)

4. His face tightened with tension; he clenched his fists. (22a)
5. OK (22e-1)
6. They had met twice before; nevertheless, he did not remember her. (22b)
7. OK (22c)
8. OK (22b)
9. The following gave generously: E. E. Edwards, a broker; R. Zikowicz, a contractor; and L. Peters, a banker. (22d)
10. OK (22e-1)

Chapter 23 | The Apostrophe

1. The princes' reputations have been impugned. (23a-3)
2. At today's prices, we can't afford to eat out. (23a-1; 23c)
3. The women's coats were left in the pew. (23a-1)
4. The child asked how many *s*'s are in *Mississippi*. (23d)
5. Karen will graduate in the spring of '86. (23c)
6. OK (23b)
7. OK (23b)
8. Students' privileges are limited. (23a-3)
9. Children's art will be featured. (23a-1)
10. "It's a big job," she said. (23c)

Chapter 24 | Quotation Marks

1. "Were the books damaged?" he asked. (24a; 24g-3)
2. "Jeff said 'Okay' when I asked him," Peg remarked. (24a; 24b; 24g-1)
3. "Moon Drool" is the title of her latest song. (24d)
4. "Asia," Burke wrote, "will remain a puzzle eternally." (24a; 24g-1)
5. Blake's poem "The Tiger" was not assigned. (24d)
6. "The audience shouted 'Bravo!' each time she came on stage," her agent reported. (24a; 24b; 24g-1; 24g-3)
7. Did the waitress say, "As soon as I can"? (24a; 24g-3)
8. He asked, "Why are you home?" (24a; 24g-3)
9. "A pile of ashes," he said, "is all that's left." (24a; 24g-1)
10. There are two reasons the poet wrote "O Eager Bleat": to celebrate the sheep industry and to earn money. (24d; 24g-2)

Chapter 25 | Other Punctuation Marks

1. J. S. Mill (1806–1873) was considered the brightest man of his time. (25c-1)
2. A good student, he still lacks an important quality: patience. (25a-1)
3. First editions — especially rare ones — can be costly. (25b-2)
4. The pool will be closed on the following days: July 4 and September 2. (25a-1)
5. OK (25e)
6. "The lessor and/or the agent is responsible," the attorney stated. (25f)
7. The rebate ($250) prompted her to buy the car. (25c-1) (Or ". . . rebate — $250 — prompted"; 25b-2)
8. OK (25d)
9. We were given a choice of (1) a term paper, (2) five book reports, or (3) a lab project. (25c-2)
10. Of the cities we investigated, three cities — Rockville, Monroe Heights, and West Greenway — had a surplus of rental housing. (25b-2)

Chapter 26 | Capitals

1. He has a fondness for Asian art. (26d-1)
2. Woodworth's lyric entitled "The Old Oaken Bucket" gives me chills. (26b)
3. My mother sent Grandfather a box of Cuban cigars. (26f-4)
4. OK (26e, 26d-1)
5. "The worst season here is summer," Doctor Ellis said. (26f-3; 26e)
6. Joan, a professor of music, owns many classical music tapes. (26e; 26d-1)
7. The east side of the woods borders Claytor Lake. (26f-2; 26d-2)
8. His latest book is *The Era of the Frog: A Study in Green*. (26b)
9. She has thirty copies of "Ode to My Bunny." (26b)
10. Elmo majored in physics at Greenburg State College. (26d-1)

Chapter 27 | Italics

1. OK (27a)
2. *The Parkersburg Herald* wrote a feature on Hull's painting *The Bernasek Porch*. (27a)
3. *Bardiglio* is the name for a variety of marble. (27c)
4. OK (27e)
5. *Common Sense* was a pamphlet urging revolution. (27a)

6. I often pronounce the *t* in *often*. (27d)
7. The U.S.S. *Gompers* set sail for the Pacific on April 3. (27b)
8. Mr. Tucker read out of Exodus from the Bible. (27a)
9. Omar lisped when he said *isthmus*. (27d)
10. OK (27a)

Chapter 28 | Abbreviations

1. The professor was late only once. (28a)
2. George Meany headed the union for many years. (28f)
3. OK (28a)
4. Xerox Corporation interviewed seniors today. (28e)
5. OK (28a)
6. OK (*or* USA) (28b)
7. On Monday the team visits Ogden. (28f)
8. We arrived early on February 16. (28f)
9. OK (28b)
10. Agnes majored in economics and French. (28f)

Chapter 29 | Numbers

1. OK (29b)
2. OK (29b)
3. Volume 3 is on reserve at the library. (29b)
4. The paint cost $6.10. (29b)

5. OK (29c)
6. There were thirty-six cousins absent from the reunion on May third (or 3). (29a; 29b)
7. The truck broke down three days ago. (29a)
8. OK (29a)
9. The tank leaked one hundred gallons of fuel. (29a)
10. The teacher assigned only 240 lines of poetry. (29a)

Chapter 30 | Word Division

1. drugged (30b)
2. al-
   low (30a)
3. lucky (30a)
4. pan-
   American (30c)
5. OK
6. com-
   pelled
7. self-
   indulgent (30c)
8. through (30b)
9. co-
   signed (30d)
10. oblique (30d)

Index

Plurals
    formation of, 383, **393–394**
    of nouns, 143, 145
    possessive case of, 295–296
    of verbs, 144
Poetry, quoting from, 302, **305–306**
Poetry, titles of
    capitalization of, 315
    italics for, 321
    quotation marks for, 302–303, **305–306**
Positive degree, 83, 156–157
Possessive case, 111–113, **115–119**
    apostrophes to indicate, 71, 112, 295–296,
        297–300
Post hoc fallacies, 67, **70**
Predicates
    agreement of, with subjects, in meaning,
        217–218, **221–222, 225**
    agreement of, with subjects, in number,
        143–145, **147–148, 153**
    compound, 103, **105–106**
    identifying, 71, **75**
    omission of, in elliptical clauses, 95
    separation of, from subjects, 206, **211–212**
    simple, 72
Prefixes
    attaching, spelling and, 383, **393–394**
    hyphenation of, 396
    as vocabulary aid, 373–374, **377–378**
Prejudice, in argumentation, 65, **69**
Prepositional phrases
    dangling, 207
    defined, 87
    identifying, 87, **91–92**
    misplaced, 205
    as sentence fragments, 164
Prepositions
    accidental omission of, 219
    defined, 87
    list of, 87
Present infinitives, 130
Present participles
    defined, 122
    use of, 130
    in verbal phrases, 88, 164
Present perfect participles, 130
Present perfect tense, 129
Present tense
    formation of, 72, 124, **127–128**
    identifying, 129, **131–134**
    infinitives in, 121
    special uses of, 129
Pretentious words, 340, **341–342**
Process analysis, in paragraph development,
    51, **59–60**
Progressive tense, 129

Pronouns. *See also* Indefinite pronouns; Per-
    sonal pronouns; Relative pronouns
    agreement of, with antecedents, 149, **151–
        152, 153**
    cases of, 111–113, **115–119**
    coherence and, 36–37, **46**
    consistency in person and number of, 37,
        43, 199–200, **201–204**
    implied or indefinite antecedents to, 190–
        192, **195–197**
    types of, 72
    unclear or remote antecedents to, 189–190,
        193–194, 197
Pronunciation
    dictionaries for, **366–367**
    spelling and, 381, **385–386,** 395
Proper adjectives, 316–317
Proper nouns, 71
    capitalization of, 316–317
Punctuation. *See individual marks*

Question marks, 262, **263–264**
    with quotation marks, 303
Questions
    direct, 262
    forming, 107, 130
    incomplete sentences in, 165
    indirect, 261
    tag, 269
Quotation marks
    avoiding unnecessary, 303
    commas with, 274, **275–276,** 303, **305–306**
    for definitions, 303, **305–306**
    for dialogue, 302, **305–306**
    with direct quotation, 301, **305–306**
    other punctuation with, 303, **305–306**
    for poetry, 302, **305–306**
    for prose, 302, **305–306**
    with quotations within quotations, 302,
        305–306
    for titles, 302–303, **305–306**
Quotations. *See* Direct quotation; Indirect
    quotation

Races of peoples, capitalization of, 316
Reasoning
    deductive, 67
    faulty, 67, **70**
    inductive, 66–67
Reflexive pronouns, defined, 72
Regionalisms, 339, **341–342**
Regular verbs, 71–72, 121
Relative pronouns
    defined, 72
    list of, 95
    in subordinate clauses, 95, **101–102,** 164

411